Environmental Health Law

Environmental Health Law

An Introduction

Russellyn S. Carruth and Bernard D. Goldstein

JB JOSSEY-BASS™

A Wiley Brand

Published by Jossey-Bass
A Wiley Brand
One Montgomery Street, Suite 1200, San Francisco, CA 94104-4594—www.josseybass.com

Chapter opening images Chapter 1, page 1, © Bonnie Jacobs/iStockphoto.com. Chapter 2, page 23, © DHuss/iStockphoto.com. Chapter 3, page 41, © U.S. National Archives and Records Administration. Chapter 4, page 77, © PhilAugustavo/iStockphoto.com. Chapter 5, page 107, © Bettmann/Corbis. Chapter 6, page 131, © David Sailors/Corbis. Chapter 7, page 157, © endopack/iStockphoto.com. Chapter 8, page 179, © Jack Smith/AP/Corbis. Chapter 9, page 193, © Tony Gutierrez/ /AP/Corbis. Chapter 10, page 203, © Tyler Olson/Dreamstime.com. Chapter 11, page 225, © Wavebreakmedia Ltd /Dreamstime.com. Chapter 12, page 241, © Mike Boyatt/AgStock Images/Corbis. Chapter 13, page 261, © 97/iStockphoto.com. Chapter 14, page 285, © Moodboard_Images/iStockphoto.com

Jossey-Bass books and products are available through most bookstores. To contact Jossey-Bass directly call our Customer Care Department within the US at 800-956-7739, outside the US at 317-572-3986, or fax 317-572-4002.

Wiley publishes in a variety of print and electronic formats and by print-on-demand. Some material included with standard print versions of this book may not be included in e-books or in print-on-demand. If this book refers to media such as a CD or DVD that is not included in the version you purchased, you may download this material at http://booksupport.wiley.com. For more information about Wiley products, visit www.wiley.com.

Library of Congress Cataloging-in-Publication Data
Carruth, Russellyn S., 1945-
 Environmental health law : an introduction / Russellyn S. Carruth and Bernard D. Goldstein.
  pages cm
 Includes bibliographical references and index.
 ISBN 978-1-118-16234-7 (pbk.)—ISBN 978-1-118-41944-1 (pdf)—ISBN 978-1-118-42087-4 (epub)
 1. Environmental law—United States. 2. Public health laws—United States. 3. Environmental health—Government policy—United States. I. Goldstein, Bernard D. II. Title.
 KF3775.C39 2014
 344.7304′6—dc23
                                                        2013027748

Printed in the United States of America
FIRST EDITION

PB Printing   10 9 8 7 6 5 4 3 2 1

Contents

List of Text Boxes, Figures, and Tables

Boxes

Figures

Tables

This book is dedicated to the environmental and public health practitioners who do their jobs every day for our protection—be it in federal, state, or local environmental agencies, health departments, nonprofit organizations, or industry.

Preface

This book is based on a course taught to graduate-level public health students, but of interest beyond the public health profession. It introduces nonlawyers to American law as it relates to the protection of environmental and occupational health. Most of the book covers major federal statutes designed to protect the environment, defined broadly to include worker protection laws as well as food and drug laws. We also discuss executive regulations and judge-made law relevant to environmental protection.

With a topic this broad, our coverage here cannot be comprehensive. Our study of these laws will focus not so much on the specific content of each law as on the various approaches, strategies, standards, and enforcement mechanisms that are utilized. You will learn mainstream rules and concepts, but please keep in mind that there are always exceptions, limitations, and variations. These are usually not spelled out, partly in order to avoid confusion and distraction, and partly to keep the book to a manageable length.

There is another good reason to focus here on general concepts and tools of environmental protection: laws change. Usually they evolve slowly, but sometimes they change abruptly. Understanding general concepts—rather than memorizing specific details—will better prepare you to grasp future changes.

There are several specific objectives of this book:

- To introduce you to the American legal system: what law consists of, who makes it, how it is made, and how it is enforced.

- To demystify the law and equip you to better interact with lawyers and the legal system.

- To familiarize you with major environmental laws. This includes laws governing pollution of air and water; laws regulating the manufacture, distribution, use, and disposal of hazardous substances; laws protecting workers and the workplace; and laws protecting the safety of our drugs, food, and drinking water.

- To ground you in the common issues and building blocks of these laws so that you will have a foundation for understanding and evaluating future changes and developments in environmental law.

- To introduce you to issues, controversies, and developments in environmental law.

Most federal environmental statutes were initially enacted in the 1970s, which is often referred to as the environmental decade. In the preceding years, public awareness of the environment and its vulnerability had slowly developed, fueled by events such as killer smogs and by writings, notably Rachel Carson's *Silent Spring*, published in 1962. Public demand for environmental protection grew. At first, the federal government stood back and let state governments take the lead. What resulted was great disparity in environmental standards from state to state. Unfortunately, states that were more protective of the environment suffered economically. Why? Because compliance with protective laws is costly for industry. Accordingly, companies took their factories and jobs to states with laxer standards, where it was cheaper to operate. As states competed for industry and jobs, the tendency was toward a downward spiral in environmental standards—a trend sometimes called the "race to the bottom." The only way to combat this problem was the adoption of uniform national standards—something that only the federal government could do.

Federal environmental statutes form a patchwork quilt rather than a tidy, perfectly logical body of law. This is hardly surprising when you realize that all legislation is the product of politics, lobbying, and negotiating. The common law, too, is a sprawling patchwork. Like all law, environmental law is a web, rather than a linear subject with a clear starting point for study. Our goal for you is to explore the subject, not master it.

A NOTE ON REFERENCES

We reference both the scientific literature and the legal literature in this book. To the mutual dismay of the coauthors, science and the law have two very different canons of referencing. In the scientific literature, despite many different formats in different publications, the common approach is reasonably informative, as it lists authors, title of paper or chapter, title of journal or book chapter, volume, pages, and year. References to articles in law journals are generally analogous to those in scientific journals. Citations to statutes, regulations, and court opinions are more abbreviated but not hard to understand.

Federal Statutes: 42 USC § 7408(a)

USC refers to the many-volume United States Code. (If you see a reference to USCA, that just means US Code with annotations.) The first number indicates the citation is to **Title 42**, Public Health and Welfare. Titles are the major divisions of the Code. Others important to us are Titles 21 Food and Drugs; 29 Labor, and 33 Navigation and Navigable Waters. Titles are divided into Chapters, Subchapters, and Sections. **§ 7408(a)** identifies the individual section. You'll find the hard-copy US Code in any law library, where the librarian will probably be glad to help you. Statutes can be accessed for free on a number of online sites. One which the authors find user-friendly is www.law.cornell.edu/uscode/text, maintained by Cornell University. You can add the title and section for more direct access: www.law.cornell.edu/uscode/text/42/7408.

Federal Regulations: 40 CFR § 261.4(b)

CFR refers to the Code of Federal Regulations, which is divided into Titles, Chapters, Parts, and Sections. The first number indicates the citation is to Title 40 Protection of the Environment. The second number above refers to Section 261.4(b) within Title 40. You may see a citation to a Part instead of an individual section. Cornell maintains a good site for online access at www.law.cornell.edu/cfr/text. There are a number of others.

Court Opinions: *Massachusetts v. EPA*, 127 S.Ct. 1438 (USSC 2007)

The case name is given in italics. "127 S.Ct. 1438" means volume 127 of the Supreme Court Reporter, starting at page 1438. "(USSC 2007)" indicates this is a decision of the US Supreme Court entered in 2007. Proper format for a Supreme Court case cites to three different sets of volumes; we have not been so formal. But you will see citations to "US" (for United States Reporter) instead of "S.Ct."

The sequence of the citation is the same for lower federal courts and for state courts. There is a separate set of volumes for the US Courts of Appeal, and another for the US District Courts, and there is a shorthand designation for each court. For example the US Court of Appeal for the Fifth Circuit is referred to as "5th Cir." or sometimes "C.A. 5." State court decisions are published in their own sets of volumes. Court opinions, if they are not too old, can often be found online by a general search using the case name. You can also access decisions of many courts at the individual court website.

FOR INSTRUCTORS AND STUDENTS

An instructor's supplement is available at www.josseybass.com/go/carruthgold stein. Additional materials such as videos, podcasts, and readings can be found at www.josseybasspublichealth.com. Comments about this book are invited and can be sent to publichealth@wiley.com.

ACKNOWLEDGMENTS

We would like to thank the following people for their contributions to this book: John Applegate, Sherry Broder, Tom Buchele, Peter Jutro, Jayne Michaud, Joe Osborne, and John Rohe. None of them are responsible for any of our remaining mistakes. Mark Robson cajoled one of us (RSC) to begin the course on which this book is based, and has been an inspiring guide ever since.

We would like to thank proposal reviewers Lynn Burgess, Michael Kennedy, Tricia A. Metts, Babette J. Neuberger, and Mark Robson, who provided valuable feedback on the original book proposal. Lynn Burgess, Babette J. Neuberger, and Chuck Treser provided thoughtful and constructive comments on the complete draft manuscript.

We gratefully acknowledge the encouragement and guidance of Andrew Pasternak, Senior Editor at Jossey-Bass. His recent death is a great loss to all of us in the field of public health.

We also wish to thank all of the staff members at Jossey-Bass, including Seth Schwartz, Justin Frahm, and Brian Grimm.

A special thanks to our literary agent, Joan Parker, for her highly professional expertise in scientific publishing.

The Authors

Russellyn S. Carruth, JD, is a graduate of University of California-Berkeley and of the University of California-Davis School of Law. She practiced law for over two decades in Anchorage, Alaska, with the law firm of Burr, Pease and Kurtz. Her practice was in general civil litigation, including toxic torts and involvement in the *Exxon Valdez* oil spill litigation. Soon after moving to New Jersey she was invited by the newly formed New Jersey Graduate Program in Public Health to develop and teach a course in environmental health law for public health students. This course was refined and expanded on when Ms. Carruth moved to the University of Pittsburgh Graduate School of Public Health. At the University of Pittsburgh School of Law, she has taught environmental science for lawyers and toxic torts, in addition participating in the Environmental Law Clinic.

Bernard D. Goldstein, MD, is a graduate of New York University Medical School. After residency training in internal medicine and in hematology, his interest in the environment led to his serving in the US Public Health Service Division of Air Pollution in 1966–1968. He has enjoyed a long career in environmental health sciences and in public health, which has included serving as assistant administrator for Research and Development of the US Environmental Protection Agency and as the founding director of the Environmental and Occupational Health Sciences Institute in New Jersey. Dr. Goldstein's research on the health effects of environmental agents has led to his election to the National Academies of Science Institute of Medicine. He has chaired over a dozen National Academy committees, most recently the Committee on Sustainability at the US EPA. He has also chaired working groups for the World Health Organization and the United Nations Environmental Program, and served as president of the Society for Risk Analysis and chair of the National Board of Public Health Examiners. Dr. Goldstein is currently emeritus professor of environmental and occupational health, and emeritus dean of the University of Pittsburgh Graduate School of Public Health. He serves as chair of the Gulf Region Health Outreach Program Coordinating Committee and is active in issues related to shale gas development.

Environmental
Health Law

Chapter 1

Overview of the US Legal System

Key Concepts

- *Checks and balances*: Governmental power is divided between the national government and the states, and between the executive, legislative, and judicial branches, to avoid any one group wielding excessive power.

- *Enumerated powers*: The federal government is a government of limited powers, having only those powers explicitly granted it by the Constitution.

- *Law*: There are various kinds of "law" that come from multiple sources.

The purpose of this chapter is to provide an introduction to the American legal system, governmental structures, and sources of law. The concepts discussed here are fundamental to all American law; they are not unique to environmental law. But these fundamentals provide a context for understanding environmental law.

THE STRUCTURE OF AMERICAN GOVERNMENT

The United States was created—or "constituted"—in 1789 by a document called the Constitution. The document was drafted by chosen representatives and then approved by the original thirteen states. At the time, this was a unique new phenomenon—a government created by, rather than imposed on, the governed.

balance of powers
The balance achieved by separating governmental powers among multiple entities, to avoid abuse of power by any single entity

The people of America had very recently won their independence from England, and they were eager to protect their independence. Above all, they shied away from power concentrated in too few hands, which they saw as a recipe for tyranny.

The founders—the drafters of the Constitution—sought to establish a government strong enough to govern and defend the country while at the same time protecting the rights of the states and the people. They invented a system of government based on a new idea: separation and **balance of powers**.

checks and balances
A strategy of dividing power among separate segments of government to avoid abuse of power by any one segment; this is a hallmark of the American system

Power is divided among separate segments of government, as a check against abuse of power by any one segment. This idea, often called **checks and balances**, is a hallmark of American government.

SEPARATION OF POWERS: FEDERAL AND STATE

The Constitution created a unique federal system, consisting of a central—federal—government existing alongside sovereign individual states. The Constitution lists—or "enumerates"—specific powers allocated to the federal government, for example, the powers to declare war and print money. All other powers are reserved to the states and the people. Thus, the federal government is often called a government of **enumerated powers** or "limited powers." The federal government exists in parallel to the state governments, now grown to fifty in number. Their structures and laws are largely similar, but not identical, to the federal government's structure described below. This separation of powers between the federal government and the states—often referred to as a vertical separation of powers—is one of the checks and balances introduced by the Constitution to protect against tyranny (see table 1.1).

enumerated powers
Powers explicitly given to the federal government by the Constitution

In practice, the division between federal and state power is not quite as neat as in concept. The enumerated powers are explicit, but subject to interpretation. As a result, disputes are not infrequent as to whether a particular federal law crosses the line and encroaches on the powers reserved to the states. This is the theoretical question in debates over **states' rights**. The ultimate arbiter is the US Supreme Court. Because the Court is a part of the federal government, you might think that states would always lose the dispute. But that is not so. At times in

states' rights
A sobriquet for powers constitutionally reserved to the states rather than conferred on the federal government

TABLE 1.1   Separation of Powers between National Government and States

National Government	States
Enumerated Powers	**Reserved Powers**
Delegated by Constitution	**Any Powers Not Delegated to National Government**
Includes:	Includes:
<ul><li>Regulate interstate and foreign commerce (*authority for federal environmental laws*)</li><li>Establish foreign policy</li><li>Print money</li><li>Etc.</li></ul>	<ul><li>Environmental protection</li><li>Protection of public safety and welfare</li><li>Regulate *intra*state commerce</li><li>Create local governments</li><li>Etc.</li></ul>

Note: The authority of national and state governments overlaps in many areas, including environmental protection.

our history, the Court has interpreted enumerated powers broadly—stretching the language like elastic—but at other times it has interpreted federal powers narrowly, ruling in support of states' rights.

Separation of Powers: Branches of Government

In addition to the vertical **separation of powers** between the federal and state governments, the Constitution created what is often called a horizontal separation of powers within the federal government. There are three fundamental powers or functions of government: legislative, executive, and judicial. Historically, in other nations, all of these powers were exercised by one sovereign individual or group. By contrast, the US Constitution divided these functions in the federal government among three separate and independent branches: Congress, the executive branch, and the judiciary (the courts). This horizontal separation of powers is another of the checks and balances introduced by the Constitution to protect against the risk of tyranny that comes with concentration of power in too few hands (see table 1.2).

separation of powers
The division of governmental powers among multiple entities, intended to avoid abuses by any single entity

Legislative Branch   Legislation is the adoption of **statutory law**—what most people think of when they hear the word "law." Congress is the federal branch vested with legislative power. It consists of two elected houses—the Senate and the House of Representatives. The Senate consists of two senators elected from each state. Thus, all states have equal weight in the Senate, regardless of population. By contrast, the number of representatives elected to the House from each state is proportionate to its population. America's *bicameral* (two-house) legislature provides a layer of

statutory law
Laws enacted by Congress or a state legislature

TABLE 1.2   Branches of Government

Legislative Branch	Executive Branch	Judicial Branch
Congress	**President**	**Federal Courts**
Consisting of:	Assisted by:	Consisting of:
• Senate	• Vice president	• US Supreme Court
• House of Representatives	• Heads of agencies	• Circuit Courts of Appeal
		• District Courts

Note: This table is intended to emphasize that the branches of government are independent and equal. Although the table specifically depicts the federal branches, it could equally serve to illustrate the branches of a state government.

power-balancing. A bill (proposal) cannot become law unless approved by a majority of both houses.

Executive Branch   The federal executive branch consists of the president, vice president, and various departments and agencies. The head of each department (usually called the secretary) and the heads of some of the agencies (called administrators), along with a few other officials, comprise the president's cabinet. The president and vice president are elected. The heads of departments and agencies are appointed by the president, but must be approved by the Senate (another example of balancing powers).

Judicial Branch   The federal judiciary forms a pyramid with three tiers. The large bottom tier is the trial court level, called the US District Courts. The term "District" here refers to state-based geographic areas, for example, the Western District of Pennsylvania. The narrower middle tier is the appellate level, called the US Courts of Appeal, often referred to as "Circuit Courts." The term "circuit" refers to a geographic area covering several states (see figure 1.1). For example, the Third Circuit encompasses Pennsylvania, New Jersey, and Delaware, so the US Court of Appeals for the Third Circuit presides over all the District Courts in those three states. The peak of the pyramid is the United States Supreme Court. A decision of an appellate court, such as the Third Circuit Court of Appeals, is binding only on the courts within its own circuit—that is, its own "jurisdiction." But, if persuasive, its decision might be followed by courts in other circuits. Decisions of the Supreme Court are binding on all federal courts in all circuits. The Supreme Court agrees to hear relatively few cases each year. One major reason the Supreme Court might agree to accept an appeal is if there is a conflict among the decisions of two or more Circuit Courts of Appeal.

Federal judges are not elected. When there is a vacancy on a court, a new judge is appointed by the president, subject to confirmation by the Senate. The requirement of Senate approval, as with executive department heads, is another example of that hallmark American concept, the separation and balance of powers. The concept is carried even further with the federal judiciary. New executive department heads are appointed by each new president, and they can be removed by the president. By contrast, federal judges are appointed for life. They may not be involuntarily removed from office unless impeached by Congress. The reason is to protect the independence of the judiciary from the political branches—the legislature and executive. Courts often have to decide cases whose outcome could

FIGURE 1.1 Geographic Boundaries of United States Courts of Appeal and United States District Courts

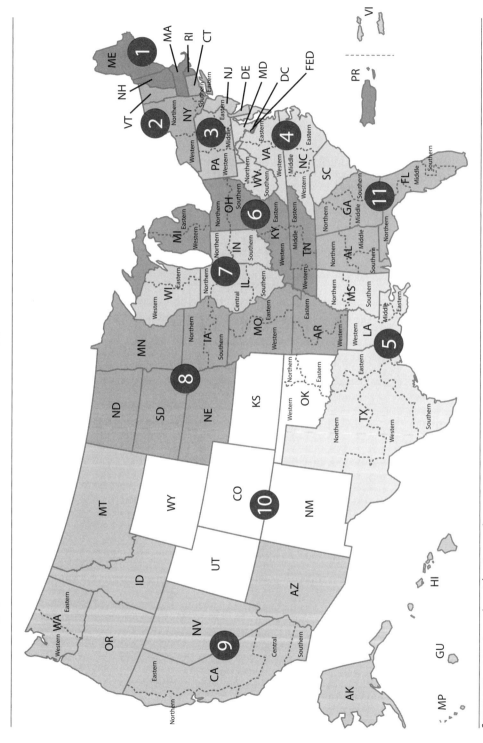

Source: www.uscourts.gov/court_locator.aspxAy

be adverse to the wishes of those other branches. Judges could not be expected to rule impartially if they risked being fired every time their decisions displeased the other branches.

State Governments   States do not derive their power from the federal government; each state is a sovereign government. Yet each state government is very similar in structure to the federal government. This structure is not imposed on the states by federal law. Rather, everybody does it because it works. Each state has its own constitution establishing the branches of government and how they are constituted and selected.

State legislatures almost all have two houses, just like Congress. (The sole exception is Louisiana, which has just one house.) Each state's constitution provides how many legislators serve in each house and how they are chosen. The names vary; for example, a state might call its legislative houses the Senate and Assembly.

The governor of each state is its chief executive officer, corresponding to the office of president in the federal government. There may also be an officer called lieutenant governor, or something similar, corresponding to the vice president. Each state has executive entities called departments or agencies or commissions that do the daily work of government, similar to the departments and agencies at the federal level. Typically, a state has a Department of Environmental Protection—or similarly named entity—corresponding to the federal Environmental Protection Agency.

States commonly have a three-tiered judicial structure—trial courts, intermediate appellate courts, and a supreme court—just like the federal judiciary. States vary considerably, however, in the methods of selecting judges—for example, whether they are appointed or elected, and how that is accomplished. The term of office served by judges also varies from state to state.

Local Governments   Local governments are not sovereign; they are created by and derive their authority from the state. They have varying degrees of authority and autonomy, delegated by the state. Local governments come in various shapes and sizes, and they have various names—for example city, county, borough, and township. Local governments often play an important role in environmental protection—through zoning, planning, issuance of permits, enforcement, and in many other ways.

Who Takes Care of Health and the Environment?

Attention in this book will focus mainly on the **Environmental Protection Agency (EPA)**. The EPA is responsible for administering most federal environmental

Environmental Protection Agency (EPA)
The federal agency that implements and enforces most federal environmental acts

legislation, and its sole mission is environmental. But other executive entities also play an important role in environmental protection, and many programs involve the work of multiple agencies in cooperation. For example, the Department of Energy's (DOE) mission includes extensive environmental aspects, such as current energy production issues and dealing with the contamination of former atomic bomb production sites. The DOE and the EPA both are designated to participate in a Nuclear Response Team under the leadership of the Department of Homeland Security (DHS), in case of a nuclear or radiological incident. The Federal Emergency Management Agency (FEMA), an agency within the Department of Homeland Security, plays a leadership role in disaster planning and response, often working closely with the EPA. Later chapters of this book discuss the roles of the Occupational Safety and Health Administration and the Food and Drug Administration in environmental health protection. The Department of Justice provides legal counsel to the EPA (and other agencies), as well as representing it in litigation.

In addition to EPA, FDA, and OSHA, other federal, state, and local agencies have statutory roles in responding to human health threats related to the environment, to food safety, and to the workplace. Sorting this out can be bewildering in any given instance, but recognizing the roles of these public health agencies is essential to understanding the response. A number of federal organizations focusing specifically on environmental health issues are part of the Department of Health and Human Services. The National Institute of Environmental Health

National Toxicology Program
An interagency program, led by NIEHS, that scientifically evaluates chemicals and other agents of concern to public health

Sciences (NIEHS) is part of the National Institutes of Health. NIEHS funds research on environmental health issues; is the lead federal agency for the **National Toxicology Program**; publishes the leading journal in the field, *Environmental Health Perspectives*; and, under CERCLA, runs Superfund research centers and hazardous waste worker programs. The Centers for Disease Control and Prevention (CDC) of the US Public Health Service includes the Center for Environmental Health (CEH). CEH is the primary federal response agency for environmental public health issues, working closely with the EPA. CEH also performs public health surveillance related to environmental issues, including a long-term survey of blood levels of over a hundred environmental agents. Another CDC component, the **Agency for Toxic Substances and Disease Registry (ATSDR)**, overlaps organizationally with CEH. As described in the chapter on CERCLA, ATSDR provides the health component to the Superfund program. It is also the source of easily read as well as comprehensive "toxicological profiles" which are excellent sources of information about individual chemicals.[1] The National Institute of Occupational Safety and Health, which works with OSHA, is also a CDC component.

Agency for Toxic Substances and Disease Registry (ATSDR)
A part of the federal Centers for Disease Control, whose research and evaluation of public health risks is relied on in many contexts

Although this book talks mainly about federal agencies, a large proportion of the people who take care of health and the environment work for state agencies. These agencies play a big role in carrying out federal law, as well as implementing their own state laws. Congress has also given the EPA the authority to provide funding to state programs that innovate better approaches to environmental control. One example is the Pollution Prevention Act of 1990, which focuses on ways to reduce pollution at the source, such as green chemistry initiatives.[2] As with the environment, there is no specific constitutional delegation of public health functions to the federal government. Thus, states have the primary responsibility for public health. When the EPA was formed in 1970, the Division of Water Pollution and the Division of Air Pollution, along with their legal mandates, were moved from the US Public Health Service into the EPA. Similarly, in response to the awakening of the environmental movement, most but not all states developed a separate environmental agency which to a variable degree subsumed functions previously held by their health departments. States also differ in the extent to which their public health functions are delegated to municipal and county health departments, and this may vary even within a state. For example, in Pennsylvania the Allegheny County Health Department, which includes Pittsburgh in its jurisdiction, retains air pollution control functions that for other Pennsylvania counties are run by the state Department of Environmental Protection.

SOURCES OF AMERICAN LAW

There are multiple sources or types of American law, including environmental law. The most fundamental type of law is constitutional law, the source of which is the constituents—that is, the people. The types of law that will receive most attention in this book are legislation, executive regulations, and judge-made law.

Constitutions

There is a constitution of the United States and, in addition, every state has its own constitution. A constitution is a document that creates a government, designates and allocates fundamental governmental powers, identifies and protects fundamental rights. The US Constitution was originally drafted at a constitutional convention, convened specifically for the purpose, and composed of representatives from the original thirteen states. Each of the original states ratified the US Constitution, as did all the states that later joined the Union. Each state also has its own state constitution, generally drafted at a special constitutional convention. Constitutions generally deal in broad, important principles reflecting values that are deeply held and not to be changed lightly. By design, therefore, it is difficult to amend a constitution. Amendment generally requires a new constitutional convention or other intentionally laborious process.

Commerce Clause
The constitutional provision giving the federal government power to regulate interstate commerce, it has become the source of authority for most federal environmental legislation; also called the *Interstate Commerce Clause*

Authority to protect and regulate the environment is not explicitly included in the federal powers enumerated in the US Constitution. Most federal environmental acts rely for their constitutional justification on the **Commerce Clause**, which gives Congress the authority to regulate interstate and foreign commerce: "The Congress shall have Power . . . To regulate Commerce with foreign Nations, and among the several States. . . ."[3] As with many constitutional provisions, this language has proven elastic, its interpretation gradually evolving to support a large role for the federal government in environmental protection.

Unlike the US Constitution, several state constitutions contain explicit environmental provisions. As an example, the Pennsylvania Constitution provides:

> The people have a right to clean air, pure water, and to the preservation of the natural, scenic, historic and esthetic values of the environment. Pennsylvania's public natural resources are the common property of all the people, including generations yet to come. As trustee of these resources, the Commonwealth shall conserve and maintain them for the benefit of all the people.[4]

Because states have broad retained powers, a special constitutional provision is not needed to establish a state's authority in the environmental sphere.

Nonetheless, such a provision can be important as a declaration of state policy, which can be called upon in support of legal or political action to protect the environment.

One other provision of the US Constitution is important to introduce here, namely the **Supremacy Clause**:

Supremacy Clause
The constitutional provision that, within its enumerated powers, federal law takes precedence over state law

> This Constitution, and the Laws of the United States which shall be made in Pursuance thereof . . . shall be the supreme Law of the Land; and the Judges in every State shall be bound thereby, any Thing in the Constitution or Laws of any State to the Contrary notwithstanding.[5]

This means that, within its enumerated powers, federal law is supreme; it cannot be countermanded or undermined by the states. Federal law is said to **preempt** (essentially trump) state law within those borders. Congress may explicitly bar states from lawmaking in some areas, making federal *preemption* complete. Or a court may infer from circumstances that Congress intended its legislation to be the only law on a particular matter. But for the most part, the enumerated powers are not off-limits to states. A state can enact laws, so long as they do not conflict with federal law. In the environmental context, this means that a state may impose a stricter environmental standard, but it may not allow a laxer standard than that set by federal law.

preempt
The superseding of state law when it conflicts with or otherwise is disallowed by federal law

Legislation

Laws enacted by a legislature are called statutes. When most people think of environmental law, they think of federal statutes such as the Clean Air Act and Clean Water Act, enacted by the US Congress. Statutory law is formal written and codified law; it applies to everyone or to broad categories, not to specific individuals; and it is prospective—that is, it sets rules for the future. The term "act," as in the Clean Water Act, generally connotes a coherent compilation of statutory law addressing a unified topic.

Federal Environmental Legislation

Congress sets the national environmental agenda, its authority limited only by the Constitution. Congress decides what problems to address and how to address them. The president or others may propose new laws, but the decision whether to enact them lies with Congress. For example, when Congress determined that smog had become a serious problem, it enacted the Clean Air Act with the intention of regulating ambient air pollution and protecting public health.

Most of the major federal environmental acts were enacted between 1969 and 1980. Accordingly, the 1970s are often referred to as the "environmental decade." Congress has made various amendments to these acts over the years. Sometimes Congress has discarded old approaches if experience has proved them ineffective. Sometimes it has tightened controls if new technology makes it possible or new science makes it appear necessary for safety and health. One important message here is that statutory law, like all law, is not static. Lawmaking can be seen as a governmental effort at problem solving. It can and does change over time.

Environmental acts can be confusing, and not just because they deal with complex matters. To be enacted, a bill (the proposed act) must be approved by a majority vote of both houses of Congress. Often, the final version is the product of negotiation. The give-and-take needed to get enough votes can result in final language that may be garbled or internally inconsistent.

Balance of Power at Work Congress's lawmaking power is subject to checks and balances by the other two branches. The president has the power to veto a bill enacted by Congress. Congress, in turn, has the power to override the president's veto. But that requires a two-thirds vote by each house, rather than a simple majority. As a further rein on Congress's power, the courts have the power to declare a law unconstitutional—essentially nullifying it. The president does not need a particular reason to justify a veto. But a court can strike down legislation only if it exceeds Congress's enumerated powers or otherwise conflicts with the Constitution. Ultimately, of course, voters provide another check on legislative powers. If senators or representatives perform unsatisfactorily, they can be voted out at the next election.

State Legislation Each state of the United States also has its own state statutes enacted by its own legislature. Within its own borders, a state's legislature has broad lawmaking powers, but there are certain limits. Most of those limits are analogous to the federal system. The state governor typically has power to veto legislation. The state legislature can typically override a veto by a super-majority, commonly two-thirds of each house. In further analogy to the federal system,

ANATOMY OF A FEDERAL ENVIRONMENTAL ACT

Most environmental acts consist of broad goals and standards, with authority delegated to a specified agency—usually the Environmental Protection Agency—to implement and enforce the act. Although each act is different, certain common features are written into most federal environmental acts:

Articulation of *national policy*, for example, the protection of human health and the environment.

The *problem* to be addressed, for example, air pollution from increased population, urbanization, and industrialization.

Constitutional authority for the act—that is, which of its constitutionally enumerated powers Congress is relying on to enact the statute. For environmental acts, this is usually the Commerce Clause, which gives Congress the power to regulate foreign and interstate commerce.

The *goal*, for example, controlling pollution in order to protect health and the environment.

A *mandate* to a designated executive agency to implement the goal. A legislative "mandate" refers to both meanings of the word. It is both a *mandatory directive* and a *delegation of authority* to the agency, which would otherwise have no power to act.

The *standard* the agency is to meet. This is frequently stated in broad, general terms, for example, directing the agency to regulate air emissions so as to "protect public health" with "an adequate margin of safety."

The *target* community or entities subject to regulation, such as industrial sources emitting more than a specified number of tons per year of pollutants into the ambient air.

Methods of *enforcement*, for example, mandatory monitoring and reporting.

Penalties for violations.

Definitions: Anyone working with an act needs to pay attention to the Definitions sections, because many ordinary-sounding words are given specialized, and even counterintuitive, meanings in statutes.

courts can strike down a state statute that conflicts with either the state or federal constitution. There is one additional ground for a court to strike down a state statute—if it is preempted by federal law under the Supremacy Clause.

Subject to those limits, states can and do enact legislation pertaining to all aspects of our lives, particularly concerning protection of public health, safety, and welfare. State legislatures are an important source of environmental law. Some state laws provide more protective standards; some cover contaminants or other things not reached by federal law. Sometimes states develop new programs or approaches that work well and serve as a model for new federal legislation. Even when state environmental laws are carbon copies of federal law, they provide another layer of enforcement and protection.

The federal government encourages state participation in enforcement of environmental law. For example, if a state enacts laws adequate to meet federal requirements under the Clean Air Act, the EPA can authorize the state to essentially take over implementation of the federal act. The same is true of most major environmental statutes.

Executive Lawmaking

The executive branch makes law in the form of agency (or departmental) regulations and executive orders.

Regulations   In each federal environmental act, Congress delegates to a designated agency—usually the EPA—the task of implementing the act. The agency must translate the act's broad goals and directives into concrete rules and standards, which are codified in enforceable regulations. To accomplish this task, the agency engages in policymaking, scientific analysis, and risk assessment. For example, if an act says to control a pollutant so as to protect public health, the agency must interpret those words. Does "protect" mean the goal is zero excess cases of a disease—so that exposure to the pollutant will not add even one asthma attack to the background level of asthma from other causes? Or perhaps no more than one excess illness per million population? Or something else? This is one example of a policy decision. Once it decides the act's intended goal, the agency must determine how much of the pollutant can be allowed and still meet that goal. Most statutes also require the EPA to weigh potential benefits against costs. Ultimately, the agency must develop clear, detailed rules, including numeric limits—for example, how much of a specific pollutant a factory may discharge into a river. Unless the requirements are clear, even a willing factory won't know how to comply, and the act will be unenforceable.

Regulations are a form of lawmaking by executive agencies. Whereas Congress's authority to enact laws is limited only by the Constitution, there are two additional major limitations on an executive agency's rulemaking power—one substantive and one procedural.[6]

Substantively, an agency cannot exceed the authority delegated by Congress in the statute. This means an agency may promulgate only those regulations reasonably necessary to carry out the intent of the act. This legislative delegation is the sole source of the agency's power. The scope of the agency's authority may be gray around the edges—that is, there may be debate about the act's intent and about what is "reasonably necessary" to accomplish it. But it is unquestionably the act that sets the boundaries, and the agency has no authority to act outside those boundaries.

The other limitation is procedural. In order to issue valid regulations, the agency must follow certain procedural steps, often referred to as **notice and comment process**. These procedural requirements are intended to promote **transparency** and responsiveness to the public—another hallmark of the American system of government. The basic requirements, which may vary slightly depending on the context, are as follows:

- *Notice of proposed regulation*: The agency must publish the text of proposed regulations and related material in the **Federal Register**. For environmental regulations the related material includes, for example, the scientific data and analysis on which a pollution standard is based. The Federal Register is not everyday reading for most people. But enough organizations read it—including industry, environmental groups, and the media—to get the word out to interested **stakeholders**.

- *Opportunity for comment*: The agency must allow a reasonable time for interested persons to submit written objections and comments. In matters of substantial

notice and comment process
Short name for the procedural requirements executive agencies must follow in issuing regulations or taking other formal actions

transparency
The concept that officials should conduct the business of the public in full public view—not in secret

Federal Register
The official federal organ for publication of any notices or other material that must be published

stakeholders
People and entities with an interest in a particular matter; commonly connotes those who should be included at the table when issues are discussed and decided

importance, public hearings may be held at which interested persons may present their arguments. For proposed environmental regulations, comments often contain detailed scientific data and analysis. The agency is supposed to consider all comments. Sometimes the agency revises a proposed regulation in response to comments. If the revision is significant, the agency must give notice of the new draft and allow opportunity for further comments; thus, the process can be an iterative one.

- *Notice of final regulation*: Once the agency approves a regulation in final form, it must give public notice, again by publication in the Federal Register.

- *Record*: The agency must compile and maintain a record of the rulemaking process. Much of this record must be published with the final regulation, including the scientific data and analysis justifying the regulation, the comments received, and the agency's response to those comments.

Administrative Procedures Act
The federal act that prescribes procedural requirements for executive agency rulemaking and other formal actions; it applies except where more specific requirements are established in a specific act, such as the Clean Air Act

Requirements for agency rulemaking are specified in most federal environmental acts. Absent specified requirements, a federal law called the **Administrative Procedures Act** establishes the default procedural requirements. States have similar procedural acts. All of these procedural statutes are intended to ensure that the government's work be done in plain view of the public, with opportunity for public participation.

Agency regulations are subject to judicial review, meaning that someone opposed to the final regulation may challenge it in court. The basic grounds for challenging a regulation are threefold: that it is unconstitutional; that it is not within the scope of authority delegated by the statute; or that the agency did not follow required procedure. (Judicial review will be discussed further later in this chapter and in chapter 2.)

Executive Orders   In addition to agency regulations, the executive branch makes law in the form of executive orders. These are orders issued by the president essentially in his role as chief executive officer of that very large organization, the federal government. The orders apply directly to the federal executive branch, but indirectly they can have a much larger effect. In the environmental context, for example, the president could issue an order requiring that all federal offices use recycled paper, or that the federal government purchase only vehicles with hybrid engines. With even broader effect, the president can issue orders affecting federal contractors—for example, that alternative energy use by bidders be included in the criteria for awarding government contracts.

States similarly have state regulations issued by state agencies and executive orders issued by their governors.

PRESIDENTIAL DIRECTIVES

Although their authority comes from legislative delegation, the manner in which agencies use that authority is guided by presidential policy. Agency and departmental heads are appointed by the president, and they have a political imperative to follow his lead. Before agency regulations and other actions are undertaken, they must have White House approval. For example, proposed regulations are routinely subject to review by the White House Office of Management and Budget (OMB). The OMB also issues OMB Circulars which give agencies guidance on subjects as diverse as the rules and regulations allowing federal agencies to give technical support to states, and the appropriate methods for federal agencies to perform economic cost-benefit analyses justifying a regulation.[7]

Presidential directives are one instrument for guiding agency action. The concept of these directives arose after World War II for intelligence and defense matters, and they have been used ever since. Each president gives them a different name, such as Presidential Decision Directive (PPD), Homeland Security Presidential Directive (HSPD), or National Security Presidential Directive (NSPD). After the terrorist attacks of September 11, 2001, these directives have been heavily utilized to direct agency action in areas affecting national security—including environmental matters.

Presidential Decision Directive 63 issued by President Clinton in 1998 (as well as the successor Homeland Security Presidential Directive 7 issued December 17, 2003, by President Bush) deals with the protection of critical infrastructure.[8] It divides federal responsibility for various sectors or functions (roads, hospitals, communications, banking, and so forth) among agencies. The EPA was assigned lead responsibility for the drinking water sector. Several other PPDs assign specific responsibilities to EPA, such as directives concerning preparedness, chemical threats, and biological threats.

The September 11, 2001, attacks were the catalyst for the EPA to be given new authority and responsibilities, but these are not uniquely related to terrorist incidents. National security is affected by accidents and extreme weather events, for example, not just by terrorist events.

Judge-Made Law

Courts play an important role in making law, including environmental law. Unlike Congress, the judiciary cannot set its own agenda. A court's function is to decide issues raised by the parties to a lawsuit. Absent a lawsuit, an American court cannot make decisions or issue orders about the environment or any other subject. The idea is that when there is a genuine "case and controversy," the opposing sides will present all the relevant issues and arguments so that the court can make an informed decision.

Stare Decisis　It is through decisions in individual lawsuits that courts make law. Judge-made law differs from statutes and regulations in that it is not codified; it is not intended as an organized and sweeping treatment of a broad issue such as air pollution; and it is not directly applicable to broad segments of society such as industrial polluters. Rather, a court's judgment applies only to the parties before it and addresses only the specific questions those parties raised in their lawsuit. So how do such judgments have any real impact? Because of their precedential value. The court's decision in one case sets a precedent to be followed in future cases. This is the doctrine of **stare decisis**, which is Latin for "stand by the decision," and which reflects the value placed on fairness and predictability in law. In future cases, courts apply the precedent—tweaking as needed to fit different facts—and their decisions in turn become precedents. Decisions in individual cases gradually accumulate into a body of law. *Stare decisis* is not an absolute rule. But a court will not depart from precedent without strong reasons. Usually, the tendency is toward slow evolution rather than abrupt changes in judge-made law. This situation is similar at both the federal and state levels.

stare decisis
"Stand by the decision"—the concept of following precedent in deciding cases in order to promote consistency and fairness

Common Law　Most Americans have some familiarity at least with the concept of constitutions, statutes, and regulations. But there is another body of law—a very large body of law—entirely independent of any constitution, statute, or regulation. This is called **common law**. The common law is an accumulation of judicial precedents with roots dating back centuries, which came to us originally from England. Common law largely predated statutory law. In America, each state has its own common law which has evolved and

common law
A body of common legal principles that has developed from years of accumulated precedents, and which courts use to decide new cases

continues to evolve. Common law (like statutory law) is not identical from state to state, but generally there are more similarities than differences. Common law is primarily state law. Federal common law is limited to subjects of national concern, which includes some major environmental issues.

Common law is particularly well developed in the areas of property law, contract law, and tort law, because there was no statutory law governing these matters until fairly recent times. Common law is still in effect today except where expressly preempted by statutory law. A later chapter will discuss common law and its important role in the environmental context (see chapter 14).

Judicial Review Courts are the ultimate authority in interpreting and applying the Constitution and all other law. When disputes come before it, a court exercises this authority to decide the validity of laws adopted by the other branches. This function is called **judicial review**. The criteria for reviewing—and potentially invalidating—a law depend on whether it is a statute or an agency regulation. A statute can be invalidated only if the court determines it is unconstitutional.

judicial review
Review by a court of a contested action or decision of a lower authority; the context could be a challenge to an executive regulation or an appeal from the judgment of a lower court

We can assume Congress considered the statute to be constitutional, or it would not have been enacted. But with respect to the meaning of the Constitution and the extent of the enumerated powers, Congress's opinion is trumped by the courts. Where possible, though, courts will try to mitigate the disruption that can result from striking down a major piece of legislation. Where feasible, a court will carve out the particular portion that violates the Constitution, thus preserving the rest of a legislative act. If a statute is ambiguous, a court will choose the interpretation consistent with the Constitution. As with common law, judicial decisions interpreting statutes and constitutional provisions are accorded precedential value under the doctrine of *stare decisis*.

A regulation can be invalidated not only if it is unconstitutional, but also if it exceeds the authority delegated by statute or if procedural requirements were not met. As with statutes, courts will preserve regulatory programs where possible, by carving out a severable portion or by attributing a meaning that can be upheld.

It is customary for a court to give substantial weight to the views of an agency, both in the interpretation of statutes the agency is responsible to implement and in factual issues involving the agency's expertise. This is commonly referred to as

judicial deference
The custom of courts to respect and defer to the expertise of an executive agency on certain issues

binding precedent
A principle of law already decided by a higher court; it *must* be followed by any lower court under the higher court's jurisdiction

influential (or persuasive) authority
A principle of law decided by one court that *may* be adopted by another court because of its persuasive reasoning; it doesn't matter if the original court is in a different jurisdiction or is a lower level court, as long as its decision is convincing

judicial deference to agency expertise. While customary, judicial deference is not absolute. The court has ultimate authority to decide the validity and meaning of the law. (Judicial review of agency regulations and other actions will be covered further in chapter 2.)

Binding versus Persuasive Authority   How much precedential value does a court's decision actually have? That depends on what court we're talking about. A court's ruling is **binding precedent** (or *binding authority*) only for the courts below it. But a well-reasoned judicial decision may persuade courts in other jurisdictions as well. Although nonbinding, such decisions may be cited as **influential (or persuasive) authority**. A ruling by the US Supreme Court on federal law is binding in all federal circuits. Similarly, a ruling by a state appellate court is binding on the state courts below it, but can also be persuasive to courts in other states. State court rulings can also influence federal courts and vice versa, depending on how persuasively they are reasoned.

CONCLUSION

The American governmental system was an experiment, designed by a people who were unwilling to entrust anyone with unchecked power. They therefore divided power among multiple entities, each balanced by and subject to checks from the others. On the one hand, the result can sometimes be sloppy, inefficient, and frustrating. But on the other hand, this system has evolved and adapted reasonably well to changing needs and values over the years. So far, nobody has devised a better plan.

KEY TERMS

Administrative Procedures Act

Agency for Toxic Substances and Disease Registry (ATSDR)

Balance of powers

Binding precedent

Checks and balances

Commerce Clause (or Interstate Commerce Clause)

Common law

Enumerated powers

Environmental Protection Agency (EPA)

Federal Register

Influential (or persuasive) authority

Judicial deference

Judicial review

National Toxicology Program

Notice and comment process

Preempt

Separation of powers

Stakeholders

Stare decisis

States' rights

Statutory law

Supremacy Clause

Transparency

DISCUSSION QUESTIONS

1. If you were founding a new government, how would you organize it? Who would have what rights and powers?

2. Do federal agencies have to jump through too many procedural hoops in order to issue regulations? Why are there more procedural requirements for agency regulations than for Congress to enact legislation?

3. A nonelected branch of government (the Supreme Court) has the power to overturn laws enacted by Congress, an elected branch. Is this good or bad? Why?

4. The size and composition of our population has changed dramatically since the country was founded. How well has the governmental structure created by the Constitution accommodated those changes? Are there more adaptable approaches?

NOTES

1. www.atsdr.cdc.gov/toxprofiles/index.asp.

2. www.epa.gov/greenchemistry/pubs/epa_gc.html.

3. Constitution of the United States, Article I, Section 8.

4. Constitution of the Commonwealth of Pennsylvania, Art I, Sec 27.

5. Constitution of the United States, Article VI, Section 2.

6. The EPA, as well as state agencies, often publishes policies that do not have the force of law. They may describe the form in which a permit applicant should provide necessary reporting or the preferred measurement techniques. Although using alternative approaches may be legal, if the applicant wishes a rapid and sympathetic response it is usually preferable to follow agency policy.

7. www.whitehouse.gov/omb/circulars_default.

8. Available at www.fas.org/irp/offdocs/pdd/pdd-63.htm; www.dhs.gov/homeland-security-presidential-directive-7.

Chapter 2

Transparency and Accountability in the Executive Branch

Judicial Review and the National Environmental Policy Act (NEPA)

Key Concepts

- Exposing executive agencies to scrutiny—both public and judicial—makes them accountable for their actions and promotes good government.

- NEPA requires federal agencies to consider environmental consequences of their actions, beginning with the initial proposal and continuing throughout the decision-making process. NEPA does not compel a particular outcome, but it makes the agency publicly accountable.

- Judicial scrutiny holds agencies accountable if their actions exceed their legitimate authority or if they fail to take actions mandated by statute. A court will review final agency actions, not proposals or other interim steps.

transparency
The concept that officials should conduct the business of the public in full public view—not in secret

Americans historically do not trust anyone with too much power; hence our system of checks and balances. Transparency is one check on the exercise of government power. **Transparency** refers to the custom or requirement that a governmental body's decision-making and other actions occur in public view. This enables the public to scrutinize, criticize, and hold the government accountable.

Transparency is especially important in the executive branch. Most of us have far more contact with executive agencies than with the other branches of government, and transparency helps assure they exercise their power appropriately. Two major means of promoting transparency of agency actions are judicial review and the National Environmental Policy Act (NEPA). NEPA provides a check specifically on executive actions affecting the environment. Judicial review is much broader, applying to executive actions regardless of subject matter.

judicial review
Review by a court of a contested action or decision of a lower authority; the context could be a challenge to an executive regulation or an appeal from the judgment of a lower court

JUDICIAL REVIEW

If an aggrieved party files suit, a court can review an executive agency's rule making or other actions to determine whether the agency exceeded its authority, or failed to follow required procedures, or otherwise violated law. This is called **judicial review**. If the court concludes the agency acted inappropriately, it can overturn the agency's action.

Judicial review is available for various significant agency actions, such as the granting or denial of a permit or the imposition of administrative sanctions. But this chapter will focus on the agency function of issuing regulations.

STANDING TO SUE

To file any legal action, including a suit for judicial review, the plaintiff must have standing. Essentially this means the plaintiff must have an interest—a personal stake—in the subject of the suit. One very simple reason for this is that only the person whose interest is injured is entitled to the remedy. For example, if you carelessly hit John Doe with your car, only John can sue you for the cost of his medical bills. John's neighbor can't file the suit, because he's not the person injured, and he's not entitled to the compensation.

Moreover, having a stake in the matter is important to ensure that the plaintiff will thoroughly litigate the issues, so that the court can make an informed decision. At the extreme, the standing requirement avoids sham lawsuits where parties with like interests collude to reach a certain result, which would be unfairly binding on others. For example, assume John Doe's neighbor also happens to be your sister. If she were allowed to assert John's claim against you, she might conspire with you to soft-pedal the evidence so that a lower verdict would be entered against you. Even in less extreme circumstances than an actual sham, justice is served when parties are motivated to make the best case possible. That requires having some threshold level of stake in the outcome.

In John Doe's case, there is only one person with standing. In some cases, including a challenge to agency regulations, there are many people (or entities) who could potentially have standing. For example, assume the EPA issues a regulation that affects how much sulfur dioxide (SO_2) can be emitted from industrial smokestacks. Companies that emit SO_2 have a legitimate interest, because they incur costs when they have to reduce emissions. People with asthma have a legitimate interest, because SO_2 in the air can harm their health. Public officials in affected areas have authority to represent the interests of their citizens. Any of these interested parties could file an action for judicial review, so long as they made their objections to the agency first, during the comment period.

Review of Agency Regulations

In chapter 1, we saw that an agency must meet procedural requirements in the adoption of regulations, commonly called the *notice and comment* process. To recap, the agency must publish a notice of proposed regulations, allow time for public comment, and then publish final regulations with a formal record. The record must include objections and other comments from the public, as well as an explanation of why any suggestions were or were not accepted into the final version. Although there are variations, such as the length of the comment period, these are the basic statutory requirements designed to ensure agency transparency.

The right to make objections during the comment period does not mean everyone will be satisfied with the final regulations. On the contrary, there are often people unhappy with final regulations. Opponents have one more recourse: they can sue the agency, seeking judicial review. At this point we can appreciate the importance of that formal record. The reviewing court does not take new evidence; what it reviews is the agency record. Hence, it is critical that all relevant factual evidence be submitted to the agency during the comment period, so that it will be included in the record. For environmental regulations, that factual evidence commonly includes scientific data and analysis.

The Requirement of Finality

exhaustion of administrative remedies
Using all available means at the administrative level to obtain the desired relief from the agency itself — a prerequisite to challenging the agency in court

Courts place great value on *judicial economy*, meaning they don't want to waste time. One important illustration is that courts require the **exhaustion of administrative remedies** before they will hear a challenge to agency action. A court will not second-guess an agency if there is still opportunity to get your desired relief from the agency itself. Only **final actions** are subject to review.

final actions
A completed significant act by an agency, such as promulgation of a regulation or the issuance or denial of a permit, as distinguished from proposals, analyses, or other or interim steps leading up to the final action

Consistent with this policy, courts will grant judicial review of final regulations, but not of proposed regulations. To allow challenges to mere proposals or other interim steps would disrupt orderly government action. A challenger must raise objections during the comment period, to give the agency the opportunity to correct its own mistakes. The court will not waste its time on issues and evidence that the challenger didn't bother to raise during the agency process.

Standard of Review

Courts apply different standards of review in different situations. The **standard of review** refers to the level of scrutiny the court will apply—in other words, the degree to which the court will second-guess the agency. Two standards you will frequently see applied are *arbitrary and capricious* and *substantial evidence*.

- If the standard of review is **arbitrary and capricious**, the court will uphold the agency action unless the agency had no reasonable basis for its decision.

- The **substantial evidence standard** is slightly more demanding. It doesn't require that all or even most of the evidence support the agency's decision. But it must be supported by more than a scintilla (tiny bit) of evidence. There must be evidence that a reasonable person might find sufficient to support the decision.

Judicial Deference

There is a tradition of **judicial deference** to agencies with respect to policy decisions, as well as factual decisions within the agency's expertise.

One major type of policy decision consists of interpreting a statute that the agency is charged with implementing. An example would be the Clean Air Act's mandate to "protect public health." Other interpretations are conceivable, but the EPA interprets these words to require setting air quality standards that will prevent air pollutants from causing *any* increase in the incidence of disease. Courts are the ultimate authority on interpreting law, but there are good reasons for a court to defer to the EPA. First, environmental protection is a highly technical area, in which the EPA has far more expertise than any court. Further, Congress gave the mandate to the EPA rather than to the courts; so when a statute is subject to multiple interpretations, the EPA's interpretation should be given great weight. Moreover, judicial deference promotes stability in society and the economy. If every statutory interpretation by the EPA had to be litigated all

standard of review
The degree of strictness or deference a court applies in evaluating a challenged decision of a lower court or agency; the standard varies, depending on the circumstances

arbitrary and capricious
A very deferential standard of review, under which the court will uphold a challenged decision unless there is no reasonable basis for it

substantial evidence standard
A fairly deferential standard of review, under which the court will uphold a decision as long as there is some evidence a reasonable person might find sufficient to support the decision

judicial deference
The custom of courts to respect and defer to the expertise of an executive agency on certain issues

the way to the Supreme Court, nobody could rely on regulations until the final ruling years later.

Courts are even more deferential on factual issues, which commonly involve complex scientific questions within the EPA's special expertise, and for good reason. The EPA often deals with questions on the cutting edge of science, where there is no definite "right" answer. The court will not upset the EPA's judgment just because the scientific evidence could support other possible conclusions. Otherwise, the agency's regulatory efforts would be hamstrung in unending litigation. Therefore, the inquiry on review is whether the agency reached a scientifically reasonable conclusion, not whether it reached the best or only conclusion.

Remedies

Judicial deference does not mean the court always upholds an agency regulation. If the court decides the regulation is defective, what happens then? It varies depending on the circumstances. One thing the court won't do is write the regulation itself.

One fault the court might find is that the agency failed to follow the required procedures. In that case, a court typically sends the regulation back for the agency to start over.

If the court finds the agency exceeded its statutory authority, the court can invalidate the regulation or some discrete portion of it. Alternatively, a court may limit the regulation's applicability, if that would cure the problem. Or the court may send the regulation back to the agency to try again.

Judicial Review of Agency Inaction

The EPA can be taken to court not only to challenge its actions, but also to challenge its failure to act. If the EPA fails to issue regulations, or to perform some other nondiscretionary action mandated by statute, an appropriate party can file suit asking the court to compel the agency to act. Most federal environmental acts allow citizen suits for this purpose, which can be filed by a private individual or group that has **standing** (see text box). State and local governments have standing to file suit for the protection of their constituents.

standing

Having a sufficient stake in, or connection to, a matter to be eligible to sue

For a remedy, the court can issue an order compelling the agency to perform the mandated action. Courts often set deadlines for agency compliance. This is sometimes a frustrating exercise for the court and plaintiffs. If the agency chooses to drag its feet, or is hampered by circumstances, courts have limited leverage.

SUIT TO COMPEL AGENCY ACTION: *MASSACHUSETTS V. EPA*

After exhausting their administrative remedies, several states, local governments, and environmental groups sought judicial review to compel the EPA to regulate carbon dioxide (CO_2) and other greenhouse gases under the Clean Air Act. The act mandates adoption of emission standards for pollutants which, in the EPA administrator's judgment, "cause or contribute to air pollution which may reasonably be anticipated to endanger public health or welfare"[1] (commonly referred to as the **endangerment finding**). One of the numerous arguments raised in defense of the EPA was that greenhouse gases are not "air pollutants" because the administrator had not determined that they endanger the public health and welfare. The EPA did not deny such danger. Rather, the EPA had not undertaken a review of greenhouse gases that might lead to an endangerment finding.

endangerment finding
Formal determination by the EPA administrator that a pollutant's emissions may reasonably be anticipated to endanger public health or welfare

In 2007, the US Supreme Court ruled that the Clean Air Act required the EPA to undertake the scientific review that would enable the administrator to determine whether greenhouse gases pose a danger.[2] The EPA did not immediately comply with that ruling. The endangerment finding was ultimately made after the next presidential election, when the executive branch, including the EPA, changed hands. This is a reminder that politics plays a role in environmental regulation—a good reason to insist on transparency in government.

NATIONAL ENVIRONMENTAL POLICY ACT (NEPA)

Whereas most environmental laws regulate industry and other polluters, the National Environmental Policy Act (NEPA)[3] regulates federal officials. In enacting NEPA, Congress recognized that nearly all federal activities affect the environment in some way. NEPA mandates that, before federal agencies make decisions, they must consider the effects of their actions on the quality of the human environment. Moreover, the agency's decision-making process must be documented and open to public view.

Because the EPA's entire mission and mandate is environmental protection it is largely exempt from NEPA's requirements. NEPA applies to agencies that might not otherwise think to put environmental impact on their agenda.

NEPA is intended to ensure that federal officials make informed decisions that are based on an understanding of environmental consequences. Before undertaking any major action with significant environmental consequences, a federal agency must ask itself—and answer—two threshold questions in order. First, what is the purpose of the proposed project? Second, what are the reasonable alternatives to the project? The agency must then follow NEPA procedures to evaluate the potential environmental impacts not only of the proposal, but also the alternatives. The way an agency shows it has complied with NEPA is by publishing a document called an **environmental impact statement (EIS)**. The EIS is the most visible product of NEPA.

environmental impact statement (EIS)
Formal documentation that a federal agency has identified and considered potential environmental impacts before undertaking a major action

NEPA created the Council on Environmental Quality (CEQ), which implements the act and is responsible to ensure the compliance of federal agencies. In addition, CEQ serves as principle environmental advisor to the president, advising on the development of environmental policies and initiatives.

NEPA Doesn't Compel a Specific Action

Once it considers the environment and demonstrates that it has followed procedural requirements, a federal agency has fulfilled its obligations under the act. NEPA does not require an agency to choose the course of action that causes least harm to the environment. At first blush this may sound ridiculous. But remember, federal agencies have to consider competing factors as well, such as the economy, national defense, and public safety.

When Is an EIS Required?

The requirement of an EIS is triggered by any *major federal action significantly affecting the quality of the human environment.*[4] This statutory "triggering" language is not self-explanatory, and it has given rise to extensive litigation. As evolved in the courts, here is an explanation of what those terms mean.

Federal Action   Under NEPA, an action is deemed a federal action if there is some degree of federal control. Obviously, this includes a project actually undertaken by a federal agency, as when the Army Corps of Engineers builds a dam. Less obviously, it includes projects funded with federal money, such as a state airport receiving funds from the Federal Aviation Administration. Similarly, a project requiring a federal permit is deemed a federal action—for example, if a private developer needs a dredge and fill permit from the Corps of Engineers in connection with building a shopping mall.

Major   An activity is deemed a major federal action if it involves a substantial commitment of federal money or other resources.

Environmental Impact   There must be a reasonably close causal relationship between the action and the impact. The impact can be to the physical environment or to public health.

Significant   This means the environment is impacted in a significant *way* or to a significant *extent*. The agency is required to take a hard look at this issue, meaning that it must scrutinize closely to see if the proposed action would have a significant impact. Each agency must define the term *significant* in relation to its overall actions.

EIS Process

The environmental impact statement is what you hear the most about, but it is merely the product and the documentation of a process. That process is the real meat of NEPA. The Council on Environmental Quality has emphasized that development of the EIS should serve as an important contribution to the decision-making process, not simply rationalize or justify decisions already made.

NEPA sets out a number of steps required for the decision-making process.[5] The EIS essentially serves as a checklist to ensure the steps were taken and show if they were done right. The required steps, which are also the required contents of the EIS, are detailed in the following sections.

Project Proposal   In formulating the proposed action, the agency must first articulate the *purpose* of the project. As bland as it sounds, this is critically important. The purpose of a project is a slippery concept. The goal of the act would be frustrated if an agency were allowed to define the purpose so narrowly as to eliminate competing "reasonable alternatives" (see text box on Sugar Creek Lake).

SUGAR CREEK LAKE—DEFINING PURPOSE

In the 1980s, the City of Marion, Illinois, needed more water. So did the nearby Lake of Egypt Water District. The City of Marion devised a plan to build a dam and reservoir on a stream called Sugar Creek. The envisioned Sugar Creek Lake could supply Marion's own water needs, plus enable it to sell water to the Lake of Egypt Water District. Under the Clean Water Act, Marion needed a permit from the US Army Corps of Engineers (the Corps) before it could build such a project. The need for Corps approval made the proposed dam a federal action within the meaning of NEPA.

Based on Marion's plan, the Corps defined the purpose of the project as supplying two users (Marion and the Lake of Egypt Water District) from a single source. The Corps declined to consider alternatives that would have supplied the two users from separate sources, even though the Corps never justified why there had to be a single source. After going through the NEPA steps, the Corps issued a final EIS favorable to the Sugar Lake Creek project and approved the permit.

Several stakeholders sued. The plaintiffs contended that specifying single-source in the definition of purpose essentially rigged the outcome. The plaintiffs lost at the District Court level, but won on appeal. The appellate court held that the Corps failed to meet NEPA's requirement of considering reasonable alternatives. The court stressed that federal officials cannot be allowed to execute an end run around NEPA's core requirement by limiting an inquiry without justification.[6]

The project proposal must also describe any connected actions that are closely related to the project, whether current or contemplated for the future.

This requirement is designed to deter what's called **segmentation (piece-mealing)**. Looking at a project (or segment of a project) in isolation tends to understate its potential adverse impacts, as weighed against its benefits. Environmental and public health advocates prefer that related projects be analyzed as a whole, so that cumulative impacts are clearly reflected in the balancing of costs and benefits. (See text box on Piece-Mealing: Shipping Coal to Asia.)

segmentation (piece-mealing)
Looking at parts of a project in isolation, which tends to understate the potential adverse impacts of the whole

---

PIECE-MEALING: SHIPPING COAL TO ASIA

A permit from the Army Corps of Engineers would be required to build the proposed Port of Morrow coal terminal project in Oregon. This is one of at least six proposals for exporting coal (from Wyoming and Montana) to Asia through Oregon and Washington. There are numerous local and global environmental concerns related to these projects, including coal dust and diesel emissions from loading and transport; impacts on the Columbia River and endangered species; increased greenhouse gas emissions; rail traffic; increased mining activity on public lands; and increases in the transport of particulate matter and mercury from Asia back to the United States. Environmentalists have called for the Corps to analyze the total impact of these proposed coal export projects under NEPA rather than looking at the piecemeal effects of each one in isolation. During the 2012 comment period on the Port of Morrow project, the EPA expressed a similar view, urging a cumulative impacts analysis of coal exports. The first of several projects was under review at the time of this writing.[7]

Environmental Assessment (EA) The environmental assessment is an initial screening to decide whether a full-blown EIS is required. The issues addressed, which are to be documented in the written environmental assessment report, are

- Why is the project needed—that is, what purpose will it serve?

- What are the reasonable alternatives to the proposed project (including the "no project" alternative)?

- What are the environmental impacts of the proposed project and the various alternatives?

- Who has the agency consulted so far, such as the EPA, the host state, and residents of the neighborhood where the proposed project will be? Public involvement and interagency consultation are not required at this stage, but they are strongly encouraged by the Council on Environmental Quality.

finding of no significant impact
An agency's formal conclusion, after an environmental assessment, that a proposed project will not have a significant environmental impact, thus obviating the requirement for an environmental impact statement

If the agency decides from this screening that there is sufficient environmental impact to warrant an EIS, then the environmental assessment serves as an initial outline. But if the agency decides *not* to do an EIS, the process doesn't quite end there. In that case, the agency must make a formal **finding of no significant impact**, with the wonderful acronym *FONSI*. The most important thing to understand about a FONSI is that it constitutes a *final agency action* and is therefore subject to judicial review. An agency cannot simply sweep its negative decision under the carpet.

SUGAR CREEK LAKE — THE FONSI

The City of Marion proposed to build a dam on Sugar Creek, to create a reservoir (see earlier text box on Sugar Creek Lake in this chapter). The new Sugar Creek Lake would flood hundreds and hundreds of acres of wetlands, woods, fields, and farms. Habitats of bald eagles and two federally protected bats would be destroyed. Two aquatic creatures in Sugar Creek would be (in the Corps' phrase) "extirpated." Moreover, the proposed dam would block one of the last free-flowing streams in southern Illinois. Every state and federal agency with environmental competence called for an environmental impact statement, at a minimum.

The Corps apparently was not impressed — it issued a formal finding of no significant impact (FONSI). The FONSI eliminated the obligation for an environmental impact statement, and the Corps proceeded to issue a permit to Marion for its dam project. Several affected landowners and the Sierra Club challenged the FONSI in court. Not surprisingly, the court vacated the permit and forbade the Corps to issue another until it completed an environmental impact statement.

The Seventh Circuit Court of Appeals later said the Sugar Creek Lake case provides a textbook vindication of the wisdom of Congress in insisting that agencies follow NEPA procedures. The case certainly alerts us to the risk that some agencies might just pay lip service to NEPA's requirements. Further, it shows how vital it is that a FONSI is a final agency action and therefore subject to judicial review.[8]

Scoping Process   If the agency decides after environmental assessment that an EIS is needed, its next step is referred to as scoping. As the name hints, this step establishes the scope and boundaries of the EIS. Scoping includes identifying significant issues for in-depth analysis and adopting a schedule and plan for the EIS process. It also raises the segmentation issue. The agency is required to identify related actions and consider whether multiple small actions need to be comprehensively addressed in a single EIS. (See text box on Piece-Mealing: Shipping Coal to Asia.)

Most important, the scoping process invites public participation. Whereas public involvement is encouraged earlier, it becomes mandatory at this stage. The agency must disseminate information to, and solicit input from, a wide variety of **stakeholders**—that is, people and entities with an interest in the proposal. These include:

stakeholders
People and entities with an interest in a particular matter; commonly connotes those who should be included at the table when issues are discussed and decided

- Federal, state, and local agencies that have jurisdiction or special expertise.

- The proponents of the proposed project.

- Anyone who has asked for such information, which generally includes opponents of the project.

- Other interested persons. This will vary with the type of project, but might, for example, include neighborhood residents and local businesses.

Draft Environmental Impact Statement   The next step in the EIS process is to prepare and publish a draft EIS. NEPA and CEQ regulations specify the required contents, which ideally reflect careful and impartial analysis by the agency. In practice, the proponent of the federal action—such as the applicant for a federal permit—commonly prepares the initial draft. This is not quite as bad as it sounds. Much of the material in a draft EIS consists of scientific data and analysis, which the proponent has to provide to the agency anyway in support of its application. Although we can't look inside the decision maker's head, the Council on Environmental Quality stresses that the agency must not simply rubber-stamp the proponent's work.

The first time you see a draft (or final) EIS, you might be surprised to realize it looks like several large telephone books. The draft EIS must address all of the following issues, and the supporting material can be voluminous.

- What are the environmental impacts of the proposed action? This includes both positive and negative impacts. It includes both direct and indirect impacts, as well as cumulative impacts if there are related projects. The draft EIS must show the scientific data and analytic process from which the agency determined what those impacts would be.

- If the proposal goes forward, what are the unavoidable adverse environmental impacts? If there is not adequate scientific knowledge to provide an answer, that does not excuse the agency from addressing the question. The agency must provide whatever credible scientific evidence exists, and extrapolate from that using generally accepted theoretical or research methods.

- What are the alternatives to the proposed action, and how do their environmental impacts compare with the proposal? The agency must consider all reasonable alternatives, not just alternatives the agency itself has the power to accomplish. The alternative of "no action"—that is, keeping the status quo—must always be considered. This is important so that inertia doesn't keep a poorly conceived project moving forward. Notice that the identification of alternatives relates closely to the *purpose* articulated for the project. In the Sugar Creek Lake example, the Army Corps of Engineers considered only single-source alternatives because of its artificially narrow definition of purpose.

- What measures might be taken to mitigate adverse environmental impacts? The agency is only required to discuss this issue. It is not required to make any commitment to mitigation measures.

- Are there any irreversible and irretrievable commitments of resources involved if the project is implemented? This is somewhat related to the segmentation issue. Narrowly focusing on a proposal can sometimes obscure peripheral costs or risks. This provision requires the agency to look at the big picture.

- Are there any **environmental justice** issues? The agency must consider whether the proposed project would have disproportionate impacts on minority and low-income communities. If so, the agency must further consider possible mitigation measures.

environmental justice
The concept that minority and poor communities should not be burdened with a disproportionate share of adverse environmental impacts

Solicit Comments   The agency must disseminate the draft EIS to, and solicit comments from, affected federal, state, and local agencies; the proponent of the project; and other interested parties including opponents. Ideally, at this stage, if not earlier, the process fosters interdisciplinary cooperation with other agencies to deal optimally with environmental impact.

Comments on the draft EIS often include objections or suggestions supported by scientific and technical data. The agency is expected to give serious consideration to the comments it receives; the agency may be persuaded by comments to modify the proposed action. If the modifications are substantial, a revised draft EIS is needed, to give stakeholders the opportunity to comment on the revised plan.

Develop and Publish Final EIS   The final EIS must incorporate the same contents as the draft EIS, with some additions:

- The comments received, including any scientific and technical supporting evidence

- The agency's assessment of comments received, including why the agency was or was not persuaded to revise its action based on those comments

- If the agency rejected any environmentally preferable alternative, it must explain why

Judicial Review

An agency may be challenged in court on grounds that the agency did not comply with NEPA requirements.

When Is Review Available?   As discussed earlier in this chapter, only a final action of an agency is subject to judicial review. There are two alternative final actions in the EIS process. The first is a FONSI—a finding of no significant impact. A FONSI concludes the agency's EIS process, and it is therefore reviewable. In the alternative, the agency's compliance with NEPA is reviewable when the final EIS is published.

Who Can Seek Review? In practice, a challenge at either point is filed by a party that opposes the proposed project. This may be a state or local agency. NEPA also allows citizen challenges by private parties interested in the matter, provided they have raised their objections at the comment stage.

Standard of Review A hybrid sort of rule has developed, reflecting judicial deference combined perhaps with frustration that some agencies have simply gone through the motions to justify a desired result. The court conducts a "substantial inquiry" to determine whether the agency has taken a "hard look" at the requisite issues and if the agency has given fair and adequate consideration to the relevant

hard look doctrine
An extra aspect of the standard of review applicable in certain situations, under which the court is to scrutinize a challenged matter very closely

evidence. This is called the **hard look doctrine**. Provided the court is satisfied with the agency's process, the court will not disturb the agency's decision unless the court finds the decision was arbitrary and capricious. This is a lenient standard of review, which respects the agency's right to select among competing policies, so long as there is some reasonable basis for its decision. As stated in one Supreme Court decision:

> If the adverse environmental effects of the proposed action are adequately identified and evaluated, the agency is not constrained by NEPA from deciding that other values outweigh the environmental costs. . . . Other statutes may impose substantive environmental obligations on federal agencies, but NEPA merely prohibits uninformed—rather than unwise—agency actions.[9]

Does NEPA Do Any Good?

Some developers and agencies criticize NEPA for imposing burdensome and time-consuming requirements. Some environmentalists criticize NEPA's lack of substantive teeth.

Does making agencies go through the EIS process help protect the environment? It's probably impossible to say for certain, but it's certainly plausible.

NEPA forces officials to go through a science-based analytical process. Awareness of potential environmental harm could influence officials' attitudes. It's certainly plausible that officials will think twice before proposing actions that involve excessive environmental harm, because they know the public will be looking over their collective shoulder. NEPA does have teeth, in that it allows others—notably courts, Congress, environmental activists, and voters—to examine the evidence and the agency's reasoning, and to draw their own conclusions.

CONCLUSION

The National Environmental Policy Act and the process of judicial review are not directly related, and they are not generally paired together in books. They are combined here to emphasize their common goal—holding federal agencies accountable for their actions. In other times and places, the powerful have conducted the business of government in the proverbial smoke-filled back room. A major accomplishment of our system of government is to bring the exercise of power out into the open.

KEY TERMS

Arbitrary and capricious	Judicial deference
Endangerment finding	Judicial review
Environmental impact statement (EIS)	Segmentation (piece-mealing)
Environmental justice	Stakeholders
Exhaustion of administrative remedies	Standard of review
Final action	Standing
Finding of no significant impact (FONSI)	Substantial evidence standard
Hard look doctrine	Transparency

DISCUSSION QUESTIONS

1. Would federal agencies function more efficiently and effectively with less transparency? Would we be better off without it? What would be the best balance?

2. Regulations are sometimes delayed for years due to litigation. By what criteria would you assess whether the benefits of judicial review are worth it?

3. We first see the Sugar Creek Lake case in 1997, when the court sent the Army Corps of Engineers back to the drawing board for the second time. That was nine years after the City of Marion applied for a permit, and it still didn't have a new water supply. Could you think of a way to better balance the value of a timely response with the time needed for a thorough review?

NOTES

1. 42 USC § 7521(a)(1).

2. *Massachusetts v EPA*, 549 US 497 (USSC 2007).

3. 42 USC §§ 4321–4370h.

4. 42 USC § 4332(2)(C).

5. 42 USC § 4332(2)(C).

6. *Simmons v. US Army Corps of Engineers*, 120 F.3d 664 (7th Cir. 1997).

7. William Yardley, "Oregon Town Weighs a Future with an Old Energy Source: Coal," *New York Times*, April 18, 2012.

8. *Simmons v. US Army Corps of Engineers*, supra, citing and quoting from an unpublished decision of the US District Court for the Southern District of Illinois, issued earlier in the same case.

9. *Robertson v. Methow Valley Citizens Council*, 490 US 332 (USSC 1989).

Chapter 3

Clean Air Act (CAA)

Key Concepts

- Different types of pollutants are regulated differently by the Clean Air Act,[1] depending primarily on their health effects.

- Different polluters are regulated differently, depending on several factors. Most notably, newly constructed sources are subject to stricter controls, as are sources located in high-pollution areas.

- Some regulatory standards are based on the desired health outcome, whereas others are based on what is technologically feasible. Standards under the Clean Air Act may be "technology-forcing."

BACKGROUND

In 1948, a temperature inversion trapped steel mill emissions and created a killer smog in the small town of Donora, Pennsylvania. Over the course of four days, twenty people died and at least a third of the population of 14,000 was sickened. Four years later in London, a killer fog imbued with coal smoke killed thousands of residents in less than a week. These catastrophes were wake-up calls. Until then, most people reacted to rising levels of air pollution with complacency—or even welcomed it as a hallmark of industrial productivity. In 1962, Rachel Carson published *Silent Spring*, which documented the environmental harm from DDT and other pesticides and criticized the performance of chemical companies and public officials. Increased public concern in the 1960s led to a grassroots demand for environmental protection, which prodded governmental action. Congress enacted the original Clean Air Act (CAA) in 1963.

Initially the federal government played a relatively passive role, providing funding and research, but deferring to the states to regulate pollution. This did not work well. Some states were conscientious about environmental protection, but many were not. The reason is not hard to understand. It is expensive for industry to comply with antipollution laws, which gives companies an incentive to build new factories where regulation is less strict. States with lax regulations were therefore perceived to have a competitive edge in attracting new industry and new jobs. This potential advantage of looser environmental regulation resulted in what is often called the **race to the bottom**.

race to the bottom
The tendency of some states to be lax in environmental protection, in the absence of national standards, in order to attract new industry and jobs

Congress responded to the lack of state action in 1970—the same year the Environmental Protection Agency was formed—by significantly revamping the Clean Air Act. A major feature of the revised act is **uniform national standards** that states are required to meet and maintain. Several other federal environmental laws were enacted by Congress over the next ten years, which is sometimes called the "environmental decade."

uniform national standards
Federal standards that apply uniformly across the country

INTRODUCTION TO THE CLEAN AIR ACT

In typical fashion, Congress begins the Clean Air Act with findings and a declaration of purpose. In its findings, Congress defines the problem thus: "[T]he growth in the amount and complexity of air pollution brought about by urbanization, industrial development, and the increasing use of motor vehicles, has resulted in mounting dangers to the public health and welfare."[2]

The explicit purpose of the act is "to protect and enhance the quality of the Nation's air resources so as to promote the public health and welfare."[3] The meaning of "public health" is clear enough. The term "welfare" is used broadly here, encompassing such things as effects on soils, water, wildlife, visibility, and climate as well as property damage, transportation hazards, and effects on economic values and personal well-being.[4]

The Environmental Protection Agency (EPA), in conjunction with the states, implements the Clean Air Act. (For convenience, we will usually refer in this chapter and elsewhere just to the EPA, but many of the actions—such as issuance of permits—are often done by state authorities.) The act is composed of multiple programs attacking various aspects of air pollution. Several of the most important programs will be discussed here. Congress made additional major revisions to the act in 1977 and 1990 to strengthen and improve its protection of our air.

Sometimes new regulations issued by the EPA to implement the act cannot be achieved with existing technology. This forces industry to develop new pollution-reducing techniques and technologies, which otherwise it would have no incentive to do. Although these "technology-forcing" regulations are often decried by industry, they have helped protect our air quality.

NATIONAL AMBIENT AIR QUALITY STANDARDS (NAAQS)

National Ambient Air Quality Standards (NAAQS)
A program of the CAA that sets allowable concentrations of criteria pollutants in the ambient air

The **National Ambient Air Quality Standards (NAAQS)** Program is the centerpiece of the Clean Air Act. The NAAQS program focuses on outdoor air pollutants that endanger public health, welfare, or both. Principle targets are ozone and airborne particles such as soot that create what we commonly call smog. This part of the CAA mandates that the EPA identify the relevant pollutants and determine what levels are safe in the air we breathe. Later sections of this chapter deal with regulatory efforts to achieve those safe levels.

Criteria Pollutants

criteria pollutants
A short list of pollutants that are pervasive in the ambient air and harmful at ambient levels

The EPA's first task in the NAAQS program is to identify pollutants that (1) come from many sources and are pervasive in our outdoor air, and (2) pose a danger to public health or welfare at ambient (outdoor) levels.[5] The pollutants meeting this definition are called **criteria pollutants**. It's not a very descriptive term, but everyone uses it. The list of the EPA-designated criteria pollutants is short:

- Sulfur dioxide (SO_2)

- Nitrogen oxides (NO_x)

- Particulate matter (PM_{10} and $PM_{2.5}$)

- Carbon monoxide (CO)

- Ozone

- Lead

These are not the only dangerous air pollutants, but they are the only ones that the EPA recognizes as pervasive and for which there is clear evidence of adverse effects at ambient levels—such as the sulfur dioxide and particulates responsible for the Donora and London killer smog episodes. Many noncriteria pollutants pose the risk of serious hazards, including cancer. But the evidence is not derived from observations of people at ambient exposure levels; rather, it is extrapolated from effects observed in people exposed to much higher levels (usually in workplaces) or from laboratory animal studies. Such pollutants, called hazardous air pollutants, are discussed later in this chapter.

There is intense controversy at present about how to regulate carbon dioxide (CO_2) and other greenhouse gases, including controversy over whether the EPA should designate them as criteria pollutants and add them to this list.

Ambient Air Standards

The EPA's second task under the NAAQS program is to set ambient air standards, specifying how much of each criteria pollutant is allowed in the air we breathe. These must be uniform national standards. This innovation in 1970 was a significant change from the previous piece-meal state control, and it effectively counteracted the harmful "race to the bottom" referred to earlier. The EPA may make distinctions for certain sensitive areas, such as national parks. But distinctions are not allowed among the states.

The act requires two types of standards: **primary standards** related to public health and **secondary standards** related to the public welfare. Congress's instructions here are quite cryptic. The EPA is told to adopt primary standards "requisite to protect the public health" allowing an "adequate margin of safety" and secondary standards "requisite to protect the public welfare."[6] It is the EPA's job to interpret what Congress means by these cryptic phrases and then to translate Congress's intent into standards—mostly numeric standards—based on the best science available. We will focus on primary standards in discussing how the EPA proceeds.

primary standards
Standards intended to protect human health

secondary standards
Standards intended to protect the public welfare

Interpreting the Legislative Goal   What did Congress mean when it told the EPA to adopt standards "requisite to protect the public health"? Interpreting the intent of these words, the EPA had to make some important policy decisions:

- *Who* is to be protected? The EPA decided that protecting "*public* health" means standards adequate to protect the general population, including sensitive subpopulations such as children, pregnant women, the elderly, and people with chronic illnesses, such as asthma. This interpretation of the act's language is not inevitable. The EPA could conceivably have interpreted *public* to refer, for example, to the average healthy individual or to the most vulnerable individual.

background level
The incidence of a disease (or other measurable condition) in the absence of a particular factor of concern

- *How much* protection? For every primary standard it sets, the EPA conducts an extensive and detailed study, intended to estimate, based on the best scientific evidence available, what impacts would be sustained by what sensitive groups of people from various ambient levels.[7] Estimates are generally based on conservative assumptions, so as to err on the side of safety. The EPA does not interpret the act as demanding zero risk. As a goal, the EPA seeks to identify ambient levels that will not cause any excess incidence of disease (that is, over and above the occurrences of disease from other causes, called the **background level**).

In practice, what constitutes *protection of public health with an adequate margin of safety* cannot be objectively pinpointed. The EPA must exercise discretion, and it is usually upheld by the courts. In general, the courts pay great deference to an agency's interpretation of a statute it is charged with implementing, as well as factual determinations within the agency's expertise. Even if there are other conclusions the EPA could reasonably have reached, and even if the court thinks a different decision would have been better, the court will uphold the EPA's discretion in setting a standard so long as there is some reasonable basis for it.[8]

Setting Numerical Standards   Having interpreted the congressional intent, the EPA's next task is to translate it into numeric ambient standards sufficient to protect public health with an adequate margin of safety. The act directs the EPA to use the best available science. In contrast to many standards it sets, the EPA does not consider cost at this point (although it is considered at a later stage when control options are developed). The CAA does not explicitly bar the EPA from taking cost into account in setting ambient standards, but both the EPA and the courts have interpreted it that way.[9]

Primary standards for criteria pollutants are stated in terms of allowable concentration in the ambient air. Ambient concentrations vary over time, so standards are stated as a maximum concentration averaged over a specified period. The EPA sets each standard based upon the toxicology of the individual pollutant and on the likely scenarios of exposure. With respect to four of the criteria pollutants (CO, NO_2, $PM_{2.5}$, and SO_2), the EPA has established two primary standards averaged over different time periods. For example, carbon monoxide (CO) has a dual standard: a maximum of 9 ppm (parts per million) averaged over an eight-hour period, and 35 ppm averaged over a one-hour period. Why? Because CO attaches to blood hemoglobin (red blood molecule), displacing the oxygen it should be carrying. Scientific studies have determined the CO blood level that impairs oxygen-carrying capacity enough to increase the risk of angina attack among people with preexisting heart disease (a sensitive subpopulation). That level is reached when people breathe an average of 9 ppm for eight hours, or 35 ppm for one hour.

The CAA requires the EPA to review national ambient air quality standards every five years.[10] While the EPA has often missed deadlines, it has made several revisions to the standards over the years based on advances in scientific knowledge and understanding of exposure. For example, the ozone standard was originally set as a one-hour average, but was later changed to an eight-hour average. That decision illustrates the importance of science in the EPA's standard-setting. Ozone results when hydrocarbons and nitrogen oxides from vehicle exhaust bake for a few hours in sunlight. Not surprisingly, ozone levels in Los Angeles peaked a few hours after the morning rush hour—back when the one-hour standard was first set. But by the 1990s, rush hour in Los Angeles lasted virtually all day, keeping ozone levels high throughout daylight hours. That change in exposure scenario, plus toxicological evidence that the lung damage caused by ozone accumulates over this multihour period, meant that the one-hour standard was not adequate protection, especially for children. Children are a sensitive subpopulation, because their size and immature development make them more vulnerable to toxic effects, such as that of ozone. Children tend to play outdoors all day during summer, so an eight-hour exposure is a realistic scenario for them. Moreover, running and playing means they breathe more heavily, thus taking in even more ozone. Based on consideration of all these factors, the EPA revised the ozone standard to set a maximum concentration averaged over an eight-hour period.

SCIENTIFIC ADVISORY COMMITTEES

The EPA has in-house scientists, but it has also established several committees of independent scientific experts to assist in setting science-based standards. One of the earliest advisory bodies was created not by the EPA itself, but by congressional mandate in the Clean Air Act. This is the Clean Air Science Advisory Committee (CASAC). Its mission is to advise the EPA on air pollution issues, based on the best science available. In particular, CASAC advises on how much of the criteria pollutants can be allowed in the ambient air and still meet Congress's goal—in essence, the no-excess-effects threshold.

It isn't possible to pinpoint this important threshold exactly. The committee reviews and discusses all the relevant scientific data, and each member forms his or her own judgment of the most likely threshold. These individual judgments vary, but they are usually clustered fairly closely together. In essence, that cluster reflects the range of reasonable scientific opinion as to where the actual (but unknowable) threshold lies. CASAC recommends to the EPA—as its consensus opinion—that the standard for the relevant pollutant be set within that range, usually pointing out that the upper end of the range does not provide any margin of safety.

The EPA administrator is the individual authorized to set the numerical standard (and to make other determinations under the act). He or she is a political appointee, whose decisions are based on both scientific and policy considerations. Traditionally, the administrator sets the standard somewhere within the range recommended by CASAC, although this is not mandatory. Setting the standard toward the lower end of CASAC's recommended range is one way the EPA often provides a margin of safety.

Although other scientific advisory boards are created by the EPA itself rather than by statute, they tend to operate in similar fashion, using a consensus approach to establish a reasonable range of estimates for some number that is impossible to pinpoint exactly. On particularly contentious issues, the EPA—either on its own initiative or at the direction of Congress—often seeks advice from the National Academy of Sciences.

REGULATING EMISSIONS

To have clean air, you need to worry not only about pollutant levels in the ambient air, but also about what is coming out of industrial smokestacks (stationary sources) and vehicle tailpipes (mobile sources). You can't achieve NAAQS unless you control pollutant *emissions*—that is, pollution measured at the point of discharge. The following sections relate to stationary sources. Mobile sources will be discussed later in the chapter.

The Clean Air Act distinguishes between stationary sources based on several factors. The way polluters are regulated depends in large part on whether they are new or existing sources, and whether they are located in an attainment or nonattainment area. Other distinctions that affect regulation include the amount of pollution a source is capable of emitting (major versus minor source) and **industrial category**. What we have is a framework of intersecting regulations for stationary sources, not a single one-size-fits-all. Each **emission standard** is commonly referred to by an acronym, adding even more confusion (see table 3.1).

Defining New Sources

As is often true with legislation, ordinary-sounding words don't mean quite what they seem to mean. A **new source** under the Clean Air Act means a facility that was constructed *or modified*

industrial category
The *Standard Industrial Classification Manual* published by the federal Bureau of the Budget identifies and assigns code numbers to different industries and subindustries

emission standard
A restriction on how much of a pollutant an industrial source may emit into the air; the particular standard that applies depends on the type of pollutant and other circumstances

TABLE 3.1 Alphabet Soup: Emission Standards for Stationary Sources

Standard	Pollutants	Sources	Comment
NSPS New Source Performance Standards	Criteria	New sources in both attainment and nonattainment areas	Uniform national standards based on best adequately demonstrated technology (BADT).
BACT Best Available Control Technology	Criteria	New major sources in attainment areas	Ad hoc standard for any pollutant a proposed facility will emit in significant amounts. At least as strict as NSPS.
RACT Reasonable Available Control Technology	Criteria	Existing major sources in nonattainment areas	The EPA issues guidance, but standards are set by individual states.
LAER Lowest Achievable Emission Rate	Criteria	New major sources in nonattainment areas	Ad hoc standard, based on strictest state standard, or best achieved in practice, or NSPS, whichever is most stringent.
MACT Maximum Achievable Control Technology	HAPs	New and existing major and area sources, in attainment or nonattainment areas	Uniform national standard based on "maximum" emission reduction achievable. Maximum is defined differently for new and existing sources.

new source

A new or modified source—generally one that was constructed or modified after an applicable standard was first proposed or announced

after an applicable standard was first announced. A source is deemed modified if physical or operational changes result in emitting either more of a pollutant or a new pollutant. Stricter regulation of new sources makes sense, because a newly constructed facility can be designed to include the latest pollution-prevention techniques. Treating a modified source like a new source also makes sense. If you remodel a facility enough to increase pollution, good planning should enable you to build in antipollution improvements.

New Source Performance Standards (NSPS)

The Clean Air Act distinguishes between new and existing stationary sources, imposing stricter standards on new sources. For *new sources*, the Clean Air Act directs the EPA to establish **New Source Performance Standards (NSPS)**.

New Source Performance Standards (NSPS)

Uniform emission standards for emissions of criteria pollutants by new sources under the CAA

The act requires uniform national NSPS emission standards which reflect the degree of emission limitation achievable through the best "adequately demonstrated" technology, taking into consideration cost, energy requirements, and other (non-air) environmental impacts.[11] For *existing sources*, the job of regulating criteria pollutants is left to the individual states (so long as the area is in compliance with NAAQS, which is addressed later). The EPA offers guidance, and it must approve a state's implementation plan, but the EPA does not directly set emission limits.

Although NSPS rules apply nationwide, actual emission limits based on those rules are not the same for everyone. Industries differ in the types and amounts of pollutants they emit and how much they can feasibly reduce emissions. Therefore, for each designated industry category, the EPA develops NSPS standards with respect to the pollutants it emits. For example, standards for oil refineries are different than standards for cement manufacturers.

New Source Review (NSR)

New Source Review (NSR)

A CAA program requiring review and issuance of a permit before construction of a new emission source is begun

New Source Review (NSR) is a program that helps with implementation and enforcement of regulations pertaining to new and modified sources, by requiring that projects be reviewed and a permit issued before construction can begin. The requirement of a permit enables the EPA or state environmental authorities to monitor, control, and, if circumstances warrant, bar development of a pollution-producing facility. These NSR permits are also commonly referred to as construction permits or preconstruction permits.[12]

SETTING *TECHNOLOGY-BASED STANDARDS*

To set emission standards, the EPA has to interpret Congress's intent and translate it into enforceable—commonly numeric—standards. The term **best adequately demonstrated technology (BADT)** implies technology that is successfully in use by industry, as opposed to technology that is cutting edge or on the drawing board. The EPA's general approach is to review the emission reduction systems in existence in the industry and their effectiveness, compare their respective cost, energy use, and non–air side effects, as required by the act. Examples of "nonair quality health and environmental impacts" that could occur when pollutants are removed from air emissions include increased water pollution or increased production of hazardous waste. With regard to cost, the EPA does not look at whether an emission standard would be too expensive for an individual company, but rather whether it would significantly harm the industry as a whole.

technology-based standards
Standards based on technological feasibility as opposed to desired health outcome

best adequately demonstrated technology (BADT)
A uniform technology-based emission standard; the standard applicable to emissions of criteria pollutants by new major sources

The EPA does not prescribe the technology or process that an industrial emitter must use to control emissions. Rather, the EPA determines the level of emissions from the best performers in the industry that use adequately demonstrated technology and extrapolates reasonable emission limits from these role models. Essentially the EPA says, "If they can keep emissions down to this level, you can too." Companies then have flexibility to decide how to meet the required standards—for example, through pollutant reduction equipment, cleaner energy sources, alternative raw materials, or some combination of factors.

Notice the difference between NSPS and NAAQS. NAAQS is a **risk-based standard**. NSPS is a technology-based standard, so called because the EPA primarily assesses technology (as well as other factors) to determine what degree of pollution control is feasible.

risk-based standard
A standard based on the desired outcome, as opposed to a technology-based standard that is based on feasibility

major sources
Under the CAA, a source whose emissions meet a threshold volume that varies depending on various factors but most commonly are set at either 100 or 250 tons per year

The NSR program is aimed at **major sources**. It is common for regulatory programs to focus on large stationary sources that produce the most pollution. Whether a source is major depends on the quantity of a regulated NSR pollutant it emits, or has the potential to emit. The threshold for a new or modified source to be deemed a major source may vary, depending on the pollutant, the type of source, and whether located in an attainment or nonattainment area. Generally, though, thresholds are set at either 100 or 250 tons per year (TPY) of emissions.

Congress originally anticipated that existing sources would gradually disappear through attrition. But compliance with standards for new sources is costly, and thus industry has gone to great lengths to preserve existing sources. Industry has nursed along old facilities, aggressively fought new source rules in court, and designed modifications to fall just short of triggering new source rules. As a result, many old facilities are still in existence, operating under the laxer existing source rules. Determination of whether changes in a facility rise to the level of a modification, thus triggering stricter standards applicable to new sources, is one of the most frequently disputed issues under the Clean Air Act.

An NSR permit specifies what construction is allowed and what emission limits and other requirements must be met. The emission limits and other requirements will depend, to a large extent, on where the facility is located—specifically whether the area is or is not in compliance with the National Ambient Air Quality Standards. An area *not in compliance*—called a

nonattainment area
An area not in compliance with national ambient air quality standards for one or more criteria pollutant

nonattainment area—is subject to much stricter **Nonattainment New Source Review (NNSR)** environmental controls (see below), and these are reflected in the preconstruction permit. In particular, NNSR requires the proposed facility to employ emission reduction measures adequate to satisfy the tough Lowest Achievable Emission Rate (LAER) standard, as well as securing emission reductions from another area source as offsets. An area *in compliance* with NAAQS is subject to less stringent requirements set forth in the Prevention of Significant Deterioration (PSD) program (discussed later in this chapter), and which are reflected in preconstruction permits. Less stringent does not mean lax. To get the permit, a facility must employ emission reduction measures sufficient to satisfy the best available control technology (BACT) standard.

Nonattainment New Source Review (NNSR)
A stricter version of New Source Review applicable to a proposed new source that will emit a pollutant for which the area is not in attainment

All preconstruction permits include requirements for monitoring, recording, and reporting emissions to assure the source complies with its permit.

PERMIT PROGRAMS

Permits are a useful tool for implementation and enforcement of environmental laws. When a law, such as the Clean Air Act, requires a construction permit, it gives the authorities an effective mechanism for deciding whether to allow construction of new pollution sources, and what conditions to attach. This tool helps curb the proliferation of new pollution sources in areas where there is already too much pollution. Further, it helps ensure that when new construction is allowed, harm will be minimized.

Another type of permit is the operating permit, which is provided for in the Clean Air Act and some other laws. Many industrial polluters are subject to multiple standards and requirements. The operating permit brings all requirements together into one document tailored to the individual facility. This facilitates compliance by the facility and enforcement by the authorities. Key provisions of any operating permit include emission limits and requirements for monitoring, record keeping, and reporting.

Who is required to have a permit depends on the statute involved. Under the Clean Air Act for example, operating permits are required for major sources and certain specific categories of nonmajor sources (for example, waste incinerators, Portland cement plants). Who is authorized to issue permits also depends on the statute involved. Under the Clean Air Act, for example, the states generally issue operating permits, and each state must have a federally approved program for that purpose.

The issuance of any permit is a public process, requiring public notice and opportunity for the public to voice comments or objections. Supporters or opponents of a permit can seek intervention by the EPA and can ultimately challenge a permit decision in court.

Nonattainment New Source Review

Almost the entire nation has met the outdoor standards for carbon monoxide, nitrogen dioxide, sulfur dioxide, and lead. However, despite improvements, many areas exceed air quality standards for ozone and fine particulates. These two are particularly challenging to control, as all of the ozone and most of the fine particulates are formed in the air from a wide range of precursors rather than being directly emitted from a source.

Areas that fail to meet NAAQS for one or more criteria pollutants are designated by the EPA as nonattainment areas for the relevant pollutant. These are generally major urban industrialized areas. For example, Los Angeles is a nonattainment area for ozone and fine particulates. The Clean Air Act imposes stricter rules on the construction of new sources, or the modification of existing sources, in nonattainment areas—making it much more difficult to get an NSR construction permit.[13]

Major Sources   New source review restrictions in nonattainment areas apply to major sources. The definition of major sources in nonattainment areas is based on the usual threshold of a hundred tons per year, but with some exceptions depending on the pollutant involved and the severity of the pollution. For example, in an ozone nonattainment area with extreme pollution, the threshold for "major source" gets as low as 10 tons per year of volatile organic compounds (VOCs), which are ozone precursors.

Lowest Achievable Emission Rate (LAER)   The Clean Air Act requires new sources in a nonattainment area to meet the **Lowest Achievable Emission Rate (LAER)**. This is really the most stringent level achievable. It is determined on a permit-by-permit basis, without consideration of cost. The EPA does not set uniform national standards, nor does it consider cost, feasibility, or other factors. The emission limits incorporated in a permit will reflect either the most stringent limits imposed by any state in the nation, or the lowest achieved in practice in the same class, whichever is more stringent. As a fallback, the emission restrictions in the permit must be as least as stringent as New Source Performance Standards.

Lowest Achievable Emission Rate (LAER)
A stringent, customized (not uniform) technology-based emission standard applicable to emission of criteria pollutants by new major sources in nonattainment areas

By applying the most stringent standard from *any state*, the act provides protection against the "race to the bottom" problem, similar to the protection provided by uniform national standards in other parts of the act.

Offsets   If a company wants to construct a new source in a nonattainment area, the Clean Air Act demands that the new source not exacerbate pollution. What's more, the company must actually help make progress toward reducing pollution. One way to do this is by requiring offsets. To avoid making pollution worse, the new source's emissions must be offset by a reduction of existing emissions. For example, the company applying for a permit could reduce emissions from another facility located in the nonattainment area, or it could purchase emission reduction credits from another pollution source that has reduced and "banked" its emissions. To actually help make progress toward attainment, the act requires offsets at greater than one-to-one ratio. That is, the amount of emissions eliminated must be greater than the amount of new emissions, so there will be an overall net reduction. The required offset ratio varies, depending on the type of pollutant and how much it exceeds NAAQS.

As a general rule, the offsetting reduction must occur in the same nonattainment area as the new construction. Otherwise, the goal of making progress toward attainment would be frustrated.

Additional Restrictions in Nonattainment Areas   Some other restrictions imposed by the New Source Review program in nonattainment areas include:

- If the nonattainment area has not made suitable progress toward attaining better air quality, no new construction permits will be issued.

- The permit applicant must demonstrate that benefits of the proposed new source will significantly outweigh the environmental and social costs, based on a thorough analysis of alternatives such as a different site, facility size, industrial processes, and pollution control techniques.

- The applicant must have a good record of environmental compliance. A permit may not be issued to a company that fails to comply with the Clean Air Act at other sources it controls.

Prevention of Significant Deterioration (PSD) Program

Should an area with good air quality be free to build factories and increase pollution free from any limits or controls? The law says no. Even though states in

Prevention of Significant Deterioration (PSD) Program
A program of the CAA intended to avoid excessive degradation of air quality in an attainment area

compliance with NAAQS are not subject to strict nonattainment rules, they must regulate new construction so as to preserve reasonable air quality. This is the purpose of the **Prevention of Significant Deterioration (PSD) Program**.[14]

Think of NAAQS as setting the *ceiling* for allowable ambient air pollution. The PSD program sets allowable *increments* by which ambient air pollution can increase in a year. The allowable increments vary for different pollutants. The rules are stricter in protected areas such as national parks—that is, allowable increments are smaller. Overall, the idea is to put some brakes on worsening pollution in areas with good air quality.

Restrictions on New Construction   To accomplish its goal, the PSD Program places certain requirements on new major sources or major modifications even in attainment areas. A preconstruction permit is required. There must be a preconstruction review that includes an analysis of the type and quantity of pollutants the source will emit. The permit will be approved only if the analysis demonstrates that its emissions will not result in the ambient air pollution levels exceeding allowable PSD increment limits.

best available control technology (BACT)
Ad hoc technology-based emission standard applicable to emissions of criteria pollutants by new major sources under the Prevention of Significant Deterioration program of the Clean Air Act

Further, the source must control emissions based on **best available control technology (BACT)** standards. Recall that new sources are already subject to uniform national New Source Performance Standards, based on the best adequately demonstrated emission control technology. For any criteria pollutants a proposed facility will emit in significant amounts, the EPA also imposes a BACT emission standard. The EPA makes a case-by-case decision for each facility, taking into consideration impacts on energy use, the environment and the economy, including the cost of pollution control technology. That BACT emission limit must be at least as strict as the national New Source Performance Standard that would otherwise apply. The applicable BACT emission limits, as well as other requirements such as monitoring and reporting emissions, are spelled out in the facility's permit.

Scope: Major Sources   The PSD requirements apply to *major* stationary sources. In this context, a major source means a facility that either

- Emits or has the potential to emit (after anticipated antipollution measures) 250 tons per year of any air pollutant—a more lenient definition than elsewhere; or

- For certain industries (including fossil-fuel-fired power plants, certain cement plants and certain metal smelters), emits or has the potential to emit 100 tons per year of any air pollutant (the more usual definition).

STATE IMPLEMENTATION PLAN (SIP)

Most federal environmental acts provide for joint state-federal implementation. A state may take charge of implementing the federal Clean Air Act if it has an approved **state implementation plan (SIP)**. To be approved, the SIP needs to meet all minimum requirements of the federal act and related agency regulations.[15]

state implementation plan (SIP)
A state program that meets requirements of the CAA and, with EPA approval, empowers the state to largely take over implementation of the federal act

A SIP is not so much a document as a filing cabinet. It consists of state statutes and regulations, as well as plans and other documents to demonstrate its ability to achieve federal standards. The SIP evolves, in part, to keep up when federal law evolves.

Once approved, the SIP has the force of federal law. The state becomes the lead in implementation, although the EPA or other federal agency retains an oversight role. States are motivated to adopt SIPs because they like to be in charge in their own territory.

Even if a state does not have a SIP, it can adopt and enforce state law related to the same issues as federal law. The main condition is that state law cannot conflict with or undermine federal law. In the context of environmental law, this means state laws can impose stricter standards than federal law, but they cannot relax federal standards. For example, a state could impose emission limits on an air pollutant not regulated by a federal standard. But state law could not allow emissions that exceed a federal standard.

Setting motor vehicle emission standards is one area where states are not allowed to regulate. This is an exception to the usual federal-state cooperation. (See Mobile Source Controls section later in this chapter.)

State Attainment Plan

Each state is responsible for meeting National Ambient Air Quality Standards within its borders. A state that contains a nonattainment area thus has the responsibility to address and correct the problem.

All states must have State Implementation Plans (SIPs) (see text box). A state with a nonattainment area must additionally adopt, and secure EPA approval of, a state attainment plan.[16] The attainment plan must map out how the state will come into compliance with air quality standards. The individual state has some flexibility in designing its attainment plan, but at a minimum the plan must include the requirements discussed so far in this chapter. The EPA sets deadlines for attainment. In practice, these deadlines are often missed. The consequences of failure to meet attainment deadlines varies, depending on which criteria pollutant is involved, how much ambient air pollution exceeds NAAQS, and whether the state is making good-faith and effective efforts to improve air quality. The ultimate threat faced by a state that fails to make reasonable progress toward attainment is loss of federal funding for its highways, as well as tougher offset requirements for new construction.

Emission Standards for Existing Stationary Sources   In general, the Clean Air Act does not dictate emission limits and other controls on existing industrial sources—those decisions are left up to the individual states. But for nonattainment areas, the CAA requires that states set emission limits based on **Reasonably Available Control Technology (RACT)**. This term is not well defined; the EPA does not issue uniform national RACT standards, but it does issue guidance documents that the states generally follow. A state's RACT standards must be incorporated in its State Attainment Plan, which must be approved by the EPA.

Reasonably Available Control Technology (RACT) Technology-based standards for emission of criteria pollutants by existing major sources in a nonattainment area

HAZARDOUS AIR POLLUTANTS (HAPS)

The National Ambient Air Quality Standards Program (NAAQS), discussed above, is aimed at a handful of pervasive air pollutants commonly called criteria pollutants. The other major group of air pollutants targeted by the Clean Air Act are **hazardous air pollutants (HAPs)**, also called **air toxics**. The purpose of this program is to protect public health by regulating HAPs, mainly through emission standards governing stationary sources.[17]

The HAPs program has a checkered past. Originally, the Clean Air Act gave a narrative definition of HAPs and directed the EPA to identify and regulate them. The statutory definition referred to pollutants that "may reasonably be anticipated to result in an increase in mortality or an increase in serious irreversible or incapacitating reversible illness." The act directed the EPA to identify and compile a list of pollutants meeting this definition, and to develop emission standards to protect public health with "an ample margin of safety." This approach proved unworkable for multiple reasons, including the time and effort needed to meet the requirement of establishing a standard, and the fact that there is usually no known safe level for carcinogens. This meant that the EPA could not provide an ample margin of safety unless it set the emission level at zero, which would have shut down industries and wreaked economic havoc. The EPA dragged its feet rather than precipitate such dire economic results. After twenty years and very little progress, Congress scrapped its initial approach and started over.

hazardous air pollutants (HAPs)
Any chemical on the HAP list; typically pollutants creating risk of cancer, birth defects, and specified health consequences

air toxics
Another term for hazardous air pollutants

Identifying Hazardous Air Pollutants

The official definition is simple: a hazardous air pollutant is any substance on the HAPs list. The initial list, compiled by Congress with the EPA's assistance, contained 189 substances. The act gives the EPA authority to add or delete substances from the list. With limited exceptions, a substance listed as a criteria pollutant under NAAQS cannot also be listed as a HAP. Thus, there is generally no overlap between the two lists.

Adding to the HAPs List   The act specifies the criteria for adding a substance to the list, which in essence gives us a general definition of a HAP. A pollutant may be added to the list if the EPA administrator makes a determination that it presents *or may present* a threat of adverse human health effects or adverse environmental effects,

- including but not limited to substances known or *reasonably anticipated* to be carcinogenic mutagenic, teratogenic, neurotoxic, to cause reproductive dysfunction, or to be acutely or chronically toxic;

- whether through inhalation or other routes of exposure; and

- whether due to ambient concentration, bioaccumulation, deposition, or other mechanism.

Notice that this language is precautionary—that is, Congress is telling the EPA to err on the side of health. In the face of scientific uncertainty, the act gives the EPA substantial discretion to determine whether a pollutant's potential for risk warrants its inclusion on the list. This is important when the EPA's determinations are challenged. A court will defer to the EPA's decision, so long as there is some reasonable scientific basis for it. The burden of proof is on the challenger to show there is no reasonable basis. By explicitly authorizing the EPA to consider various routes of exposure and factors such as bioaccumulation, the act removed some of the potential grounds for court challenges.

The act's protective intent tends to be frustrated, however, because the EPA cannot keep up with the chemical industry. Any proposed addition to the HAPs list requires thorough scientific review, public scrutiny through the notice and comment process, then an almost inevitable challenge in the courts. Over the years, the EPA has removed a few agents from the HAPs list in response to industry petitions, based primarily on demonstration of lack of significant community exposure. None have been added.[18] Meanwhile, an estimated two thousand new chemicals are developed every year.[19] Many may qualify for the HAPs list if and when the EPA is able to review them.

Delisting a Pollutant Anyone may petition the EPA to remove a substance from the list of HAPs. Under the Clean Air Act, the EPA will only grant the petition if it finds

- There is *adequate data* on the health and environmental effects of the substance to determine

- That it may not reasonably be anticipated to cause any adverse effects to human health or the environment

- Whether by means of emissions, ambient concentrations, bioaccumulation, or deposition of the substance

Again, the language of the statutory criterion is precautionary, indicating that the EPA should err on the side of protection. Even more important, the burden of proof is on the petitioner to show that there is adequate scientific evidence and that the evidence for delisting is strong enough that it would be unreasonable to conclude the substance might cause an adverse effect. Scientific uncertainty is common in this type of research. In this context, scientific uncertainty precludes delisting and thus favors protection.

Regulation of Hazardous Air Pollutants

The Clean Air Act establishes a two-tier system for regulating industrial emissions of HAPs. The first tier consists of **National Emission Standards for Hazardous Air Pollutants (NESHAPs)**. These are uniform national technology-based emission standards. The second tier of regulation is risk-based; it is to be triggered if technology-based emission limits prove inadequate to protect public health.

> **National Emission Standards for Hazardous Air Pollutants (NESHAPs)**
> Uniform national technology-based emission standards for hazardous air pollutants

Major Stationary Sources   The regulations described in this section apply to major stationary sources. A major source in this context is defined, more stringently than elsewhere, as one or more stationary sources in a contiguous area that are

- Under common control, and
- Emit, or have the potential to emit, either
  - Ten tons per year of any single HAP, or
  - Twenty-five tons per year of combined HAPs.

The EPA can set a lower threshold amount, based on the characteristics of the pollutants emitted—for example, potency, persistence, or potential for bioaccumulation.

Maximum Achievable Control Technology (MACT)   The act directs the EPA to promulgate National Emission Standards for Hazardous Air Pollutants (NESHAPS) for each substance on the HAPs list. The EPA must set emission

Maximum Achievable Control Technology (MACT)
A very stringent standard applicable to NESHAPS

limits based on a very stringent standard called **Maximum Achievable Control Technology (MACT)**. The act's narrative description of MACT requires standards to reflect

- the maximum degree of reduction achievable in emission of HAPs;

- including a prohibition of such emissions, where achievable;

- taking into consideration cost, energy requirements, and any non–air quality health and environmental impacts.

The CAA requires the EPA to set uniform national MACT emission standards for both new and existing sources in each industrial category. The act is more specific than usual in defining this standard. For existing sources, the MACT emission limit must be at least as stringent as the average achieved by the best-performing 12 percent of facilities in the industrial category. For *new* sources, the standard must be at least as stringent as what's achieved by the *single* best-controlled similar source. Note this involves cherry-picking among facilities. For example, one facility may be the best at controlling benzene emissions, and a different facility may be best at controlling vinyl chloride emissions.

emission floors
The stringent default setting for MACT standards based on best performance in the industry

The EPA follows a two-step process to develop numeric emission limits based on this statutory language. First it sets **emission floors**. To do so, the EPA identifies all the sources of a particular HAP within an industry and reviews their emissions. The emission level from the single best-controlled source becomes the floor for new sources. The average of the emission levels from the best-controlled 12 percent becomes the floor for existing sources. These floors are set without regard to cost.

The second step is to assess whether it is possible to achieve an emission level even lower than the floor, for example, by:

- Modifications (such as using different processes or different materials)

- Enclosing systems or processes

- Collection, capture, or treatment

- Design, equipment, work practice, or operational standards

It is at this second step that the EPA considers cost, energy requirements, and any non–air health or environmental impacts. If feasible, the EPA will set an emission standard even lower than the floor—sometimes called **beyond-the-floor limits**. This closes the loophole of an entire industry performing poorly.

beyond-the-floor limits
The second step in setting MACT standards, requiring emission limits even more stringent than emission floors if feasible; used when actual industry performance is not adequate

Residual Risk Provisions   Technology-based MACT standards are the first line of defense against HAPs. But if public health is not adequately protected by emission limits based on MACT, there is a backup defense that is risk-based. The act directs the EPA to impose even more stringent emission standards, called **residual risk standards**, as follows:

residual risk standards
Ad hoc risk-based standards invoked when MACT emission limits are inadequate to protect public health

- In general, if necessary to provide an ample margin of safety in protecting public health and the environment, taking into consideration costs, energy, safety, and other relevant factors; and

- For carcinogens, if MACT does not reduce lifetime excess cancer risk to less than one in a million.

The act specifies that residual risk standards should be based on **maximum individual risk (MIR)**. In other words, health risk must be measured for the maximally exposed individual. Conceptually, this means an individual who lives next door to a major emission source for seventy years, continuously breathing in its toxic fumes. Like MACT standards, residual risk standards are uniform national standards. This means that any stricter-than-MACT emission standard designed to protect the maximally exposed individual will apply to all similar sources—that is, to all sources in the same industrial category—regardless of geographic location, and regardless of whether anyone is actually exposed to them.

maximum individual risk (MIR)
A risk assessment concept that assumes lifetime continuous exposure

Some public health advocates have criticized the EPA for not adhering to the act's stringent risk provisions. They have challenged in court some of the EPA's residual risk standards based on a lifetime cancer risk of up to one hundred in a million for the maximally exposed individual, arguing that this violates the statutory language specifying one-in-a-million MIR risk. But courts have upheld the EPA's decision as a valid policy judgment.

Other public health experts have criticized the Clean Air Act's stringent across-the-board approach as counterproductive. First, because it disregards differences in toxicity among listed HAPs, the law gives industry no incentive to substitute a less toxic substance for a more toxic one. Second, there is an incentive for industry to switch from a listed HAP to any chemical not on the list—perhaps a new and less studied chemical. A new chemical might actually be more toxic, but not on the HAPs list because there is less information about its toxicity. There are two thousand new chemicals introduced every year, so this is not an idle concern. A third criticism of the across-the-board approach is that it disregards the difference in impact on human health based on location. The standard is the same whether emissions go over an urban area or an unpopulated desert or ocean, giving industry no incentive to consider population exposure when deciding where to situate new facilities.[20]

RISK-BASED? TECHNOLOGY-BASED?

In studying environmental health law, you'll hear standards described as either "risk-based" or "technology-based." Or maybe they'll be described as "health-based" or "feasibility-based." What's the difference?

Congress does not always use the same approach in environmental acts. Sometimes Congress focuses on the desired outcome of protective statutes. It directs the EPA to develop numeric pollution limits and other controls adequate to achieve a particular goal. The goal may be stated in very general terms requiring some interpretation by the EPA ("protect public health with an adequate margin of safety") or in quite specific terms ("not to exceed one-in-a-million lifetime risk"). In either event, using the best available science, the EPA has to figure out what exposure limits are needed to achieve the goal. Ultimately, the EPA (or the state) has to figure out what emission or effluent limits are needed to keep exposure at an acceptable level. Both the (ambient) exposure limits and the (end-of-pipe) emission limits are described as risk- or health-based, because that's where they started.

Often Congress directs the EPA to set emission or effluent limits based on what can feasibly be achieved, instead of based on the desired outcome. Usually the statutory language is ambiguous (such as "best available technology") and requires the EPA to interpret how stringent Congress wants the limits to be. The EPA uses engineering and technological expertise, and collects data from past industry performance, to determine what limitations are feasible at what cost. The limits the EPA derives are referred to as *technology-* or *feasibility-based*.

ENFORCEMENT

What happens when an industrial source violates emission limits or other require-ments? The Clean Air Act provides both civil and criminal penalties, depending on the circumstances.[21]

Civil Actions

The traditional way to prosecute violations is through civil litigation—that is, a lawsuit by the EPA against the violator. The EPA can ask the court to award civil fines of up to $25,000 per violation per day. Noncompliance by an industrial facility may involve multiple violations, for example, excessive emissions of more than one pollutant, or from more than one location at the facility. Thus, fines can add up fast. The EPA can also ask the court for an injunction—that is, an order for the violator to do, or refrain from doing, a specified action. (See text box on Injunctions, chapter 4.)

You may be surprised to learn that civil enforcement actions can be filed not only by the EPA or a state, but also by a private citizen.[22] (See text box on Citizen Enforcement Actions, chapter 4.)

Administrative Enforcement

If the total fines sought are no more than $200,000, EPA can use a more stream-lined administrative approach rather than suing in court. Essentially, the EPA administrator issues an order imposing the penalty. If the violation is contested, the violator has the option of going to court.

For minor violations, the EPA field officers can issue citations for up to $5,000 per day per violation. Field citations work essentially like traffic tickets: the violator has a deadline by which to pay or contest the citation.

Criminal Actions

A person who *knowingly* violates the act is subject to criminal fines, or even imprisonment. For example, intentional permit violations are punishable by up to five years in prison; tampering with a monitoring device, falsifying reports, and other deceptive conduct are punishable by up to two years in prison. A person who knowingly places someone in imminent danger of death or serious injury by releasing HAPs is subject to a fine up to $1,000,000 and fifteen years in prison. For repeat offenders, any of these penalties—fines or prison terms—can be doubled. Only a court can impose criminal penalties; the EPA cannot do so administratively.

ENFORCEMENT AGAINST CORPORATIONS

Industrial polluters are commonly corporations. What does that mean for enforcement of violations? In law, a corporation is treated as a legal person. Corporate violators are thus subject to fines—in fact, environmental statutes commonly impose heavier fines on corporate violators than on individual violators. For particularly egregious violations, many federal environmental acts provide criminal penalties, including imprisonment. A corporation cannot be imprisoned, but the culpable individuals within a corporation are subject to imprisonment.

Rewards

The Environmental Protection Agency is authorized by the act to pay a reward of up to $10,000 to any person who furnishes information that leads to a criminal conviction or to a judicial or administrative civil penalty for violations.

MOBILE SOURCE CONTROLS

Cars and other mobile sources are responsible for about half of our total air pollution in the United States. The EPA estimates that mobile sources account for 45 percent of all volatile organic compound (VOC) emissions, 50 percent of all nitrous oxides emissions, 60 percent of carbon monoxide emissions and 50 percent of the hazardous air pollutants in urban areas.[23] Technological advances and regulatory programs have made a difference. In terms of emissions per vehicle mile traveled, tailpipe pollution has been greatly reduced over the past forty years. At the same time, however, many more vehicles are on the road. As a result, total mobile emissions have not changed much.

The Clean Air Act bars states from regulating mobile source pollution (with two exceptions, mentioned below). This is called federal preemption, and it is a rarity in the environmental field. Usually, states are not only encouraged to jointly implement federal environmental laws, but they are also free to adopt any state laws that do not conflict with federal standards. In exercising its right of preemption here, Congress is essentially saying its mobile source laws constitute a complete and comprehensive program, from which states are not to deviate.

The Clean Air Act has three major programs to deal with mobile source pollution: new vehicle controls, inspection and maintenance requirements for in-use vehicles, and regulations on fuels. Collectively, they are commonly referred to as mobile source controls.[24]

New Vehicle Controls

The Clean Air Act imposes controls on new vehicles intended to force the auto industry to make technological advances that will reduce air pollution. This regulation consists mainly of setting national standards for tailpipe emissions. Occasionally, regulations will be enacted requiring manufacturers to install specific antipollution equipment in new cars, notably the catalytic converter and, more recently, built-in diagnostic equipment. To promote compliance, the law also requires certification and testing of new vehicles.

Tailpipe emission limits have historically been technology-forcing. That means limits are set that are not achievable with existing technology, but the effective date is delayed to give the auto industry time to develop new technology. For example, the initial requirements in 1970 included a 90 percent reduction of hydrocarbon emissions within five years. Industry has repeatedly complained that new mandates would be impossible to meet, but in each case technology was developed that could meet the lowered limit. Deadlines have sometimes had to be extended, but emissions have been significantly reduced.

Because of its extreme pollution problems, the State of California is allowed by the CAA to adopt tailpipe emission limits stricter than national standards. This is an exception to federal preemption. Other states have only two choices: they may opt to follow California standards or national standards.

Inspection and Maintenance of In-Use Vehicles

The purpose of Inspection and Maintenance (IM) regulation is to identify and require repair of in-use vehicles emitting excessive pollutants. Unlike most of the mobile source programs under the Clean Air Act, the IM program is not federally preempted. The act allows, and in fact compels, implementation by states. Specifically, any state with nonattainment areas for transportation-related NAAQS criteria pollutants must develop an IM program. The state's IM program must be included in its State Implementation Plan (SIP) and must be approved by the EPA. Typically, these programs require a passing grade on inspection testing as a condition of renewing the car's registration.

Controls on Fuels

Under the Clean Air Act, the EPA imposes various controls on the petroleum industry's production of gasoline and diesel fuel. There are some advantages to regulating fuel as compared to regulating new vehicles. It can take five or ten years lead time for significant automobile design changes to make an impact, whereas fuel reformulations can be accomplished almost immediately, and more cheaply as well. Another advantage is that fuel requirements can be tailored to meet geographic and seasonal needs—for example, the gasoline sold in ozone nonattainment areas in summer must be a special blend with low volatility. Finally, petroleum refining and distribution systems are largely centralized, which facilitates enforcement.

Fuel regulation has taken several approaches over the years to deal with various pollution problems. These include:

- Restricting additives. The first major fuel program involved reducing and ultimately eliminating lead from gasoline. Lead is an antiknock additive. It improved fuel performance, but also created pollution very harmful to health, especially in children. It also interfered with the function of the catalytic converter.

- Limiting impurities, for example, sulfur in diesel fuel.

- Decreasing volatility.

- Reducing aromatics.

- Increasing oxygen content.

- Encouraging use of alternative fuels.

ACID RAIN PROGRAM

In the atmosphere, sulfur dioxide (SO_2) and nitrogen oxides (NO_x) become oxidized and react with water vapor and other elements before falling to Earth as acid rain or other acid deposition. These acid compounds cause damage—to fish and other aquatic life, to forests, to buildings and monuments. Acid deposition in the form of fine particulates is also harmful to human health.

Congress enacted the Acid Rain Program[25] in 1990 as an addition to the Clean Air Act. The purpose is to reduce acid deposition and its adverse effects by reducing emissions of SO_2 and NO_x. Specifically, Congress set a phased goal of reducing annual SO_2 emissions by 10 million tons from 1980 levels, and NO_x by 2 million tons.

Target Sources

The Acid Rain program is focused on stationary sources—specifically, power plants fueled by fossil fuels, especially coal. Coal-fired power plants are responsible for most SO_2 emissions, and they are also major NO_x emitters.

The Acid Rain program does not address mobile sources, even though they generate about 50 percent of NO_x emissions in the United States. Provisions elsewhere in the act, such as tailpipe emission limits and fuel formulation, have helped curb NO_x emissions from mobile sources.

Reducing Stationary Source Emissions of SO_2 and NO_x

The Acid Rain Program takes innovative, results-oriented approaches, in contrast to the usual command-and-control approach of environmental regulation. The most innovative feature is the **cap-and-trade system** for SO_2 emissions.

cap-and-trade system
A market-based approach to emission control, which sets maximum total emissions allowed and permits facilities that emit less than their share to sell their unused "allowances" to other facilities

Cap-and-Trade System The Acid Rain Program introduced this as a new antipollution approach. Its effectiveness in reducing acid deposition has been welcomed by environmentalists, while its economic flexibility has been welcomed by industry. Similar approaches are being advocated for carbon dioxide in response to global climate change issues.

The *cap* of the cap-and-trade system is a permanent ceiling on SO_2 emissions from electric power plants nationwide. The cap, now fully phased in, is pegged at 8.95 million tons. This is 10 million tons below the amount actually emitted in 1980—a reduction of over 50 percent.

The advantage of a cap is that it restricts total emissions. By contrast, under traditional command-and-control approaches, emission standards typically establish separate emission limits for each source. But if the number of sources increases, so will total emissions. Similarly, if existing sources are used more, their total emissions will rise even while their emission *rates* continue steady. By contrast, the SO_2 cap ensures that total SO_2 emissions from regulated power plants will hold steady even in the face of industry growth.

The *trade* of the cap-and-trade system is a free-market approach that provides utilities with the incentive to develop cost-effective pollution reduction strategies. Rather than shares of stock, this market trades **sulfur allowances**. Each allowance permits the holder to emit one ton of sulfur dioxide in a designated year. SO_2 allowances are traded nationwide on an allowance market that works just like the stock market. A maximum of 8.95 million allowances are issued each year, which effectively caps SO_2 emissions at 8.95 million tons per year.

sulfur allowances
The commodity traded in the cap-and-trade system—each allowance authorizes emission of one ton of sulfur dioxide in a designated year

A utility that reduces its emissions—for example, through using cleaner fuel or pollution control technologies—can sell its unused allowances or bank them for future use. Conversely, a utility with more emissions than allowances must purchase additional allowances. This means that polluting directly affects the company's bottom line—a powerful incentive to pollution reduction.

One concern with nationwide trading is that it could result in hot spots—that is, localized areas of heavy emissions and higher health risks. The act addresses this problem with a prohibition: a source may not use its allowances to emit more SO_2 than consistent with standards protecting human health. This backstop prohibition appears effective: the EPA analyses show that trading has not adversely affected attainment of air quality standards.[26]

Other Features of the Acid Rain Program   For NO_x emissions, the Acid Rain Program does not use a cap-and-trade system. Nonetheless, the program strives for maximum flexibility, intended to let each utility choose the most cost-effective means of complying with NO_x emission limits and to encourage technological development to reduce compliance costs.

Regulated utilities must install continuous emission monitoring (CEM) systems and report emissions of both SO_2 and NO_x to the EPA on a quarterly basis. These requirements verify compliance and help ensure the integrity of the market-based allowance system.

CROSS-BORDER AIR POLLUTION

Some states meet federal air quality standards themselves but unintentionally sabotage the efforts of their downwind neighboring states to do so. Power plants, refineries, and other industrial plants in upwind states emit sulfur dioxide (SO_2) and nitrogen oxide (NO_x) (criteria pollutants) that are blown across state borders by prevailing winds, polluting the air of downwind states. Congress, recognizing the problem of windborne interstate pollution, included a "good neighbor" provision in the Clean Air Act. It makes each state responsible for prohibiting emissions within its borders that will significantly interfere with compliance with National Ambient Air Quality Standards (NAAQS) in other states.[27]

One early approach to local pollution tried in some upwind states was simply to build taller smokestacks. Pollution wasn't eliminated—it was just transported further downwind. This so-called solution has been rejected as a means of meeting a state's responsibility not to pollute its neighbors.[28]

The EPA has long struggled to find a regulatory program to alleviate the problem of cross-border air pollution. In 2005, the EPA attempted to address the problem by issuing a new rule called the Clean Air Interstate Rule (CAIR). This rule used a cap-and-trade system designed to reduce SO_2 and NO_x by 70 percent over a fifteen-year period. That rule was challenged in litigation. In 2008, the US Court of Appeals (District of Columbia Circuit) rejected CAIR for a variety of reasons, but let it remain in effect temporarily, so that the EPA could issue a new rule correcting the flaws.[29]

The new rule, finalized July 6, 2011, is the Cross-State Air Pollution Rule (CSAPR). This rule requires significant reductions in SO_2 and NO_x emissions from power plants in twenty-three problem states. Sources are permitted to trade emission allowances with other sources. Although the trades may occur between sources in different states, there is a strict emission ceiling in each state. This is intended to constrain sources in one state from side-stepping regulation by over-purchasing allowances from other states. To expedite the plan, the EPA has adopted a federal implementation plan (FIP) for each state covered by the rule. But the EPA encourages states to adopt their own SIPs to replace the FIP. This revised rule was struck down by the same court in August 2012.[30] Although CAIR remains in effect until the EPA can come up with a replacement that will survive a court challenge, the EPA is no closer to solving a problem that has vexed air pollution control efforts for at least three decades. An effective solution may require new legislation from Congress.

GREENHOUSE GASES

greenhouse gases (GHG)
Pollutants that cause global warming

Carbon dioxide (CO_2), methane, and other **greenhouse gases (GHG)** get their name because they have the effect of holding in heat that warms the Earth. The resulting climate change does not just make the planet warmer. It causes unpredictable variations, including more heat sometimes, more cold sometimes, more heavy storms, and other extreme weather events.

GHG have long escaped regulation by federal environmental law. That is rapidly changing. The EPA is beginning to regulate greenhouse gases under existing law, primarily the Clean Air Act. And efforts are being made by environmentalists and their supporters in Congress to pass new legislation—so far without success. For now, therefore, the EPA can only rely on the authority given it by existing statutes.

A number of states have been active in developing regulatory approaches aimed at limiting GHG emissions. California has developed a cap-and-trade program for carbon dioxide that is modeled after the successful cap-and-trade program for acid rain described earlier.[31]

Endangerment Finding

During the George W. Bush administration, the EPA declined to review and regulate GHG. A citizen action filed by several states, cities, and environmental groups led to a Supreme Court decision that the EPA must review the science and determine if GHG met the criteria of an air pollutant under the Clean Air Act.[32] Still, no official action occurred until the Obama administration. At that point, the EPA complied with the court's decision and reviewed the scientific evidence on GHG.

The Clean Air Act provides, with respect to mobile source controls:

> The [EPA] Administrator shall by regulation prescribe . . . standards applicable to the emission of any air pollutant from . . . new motor vehicles . . . which in his judgment cause, or contribute to, air pollution which may reasonably be anticipated to endanger public health or welfare.[33]

The term "air pollutant," as defined in the act, is broad. It includes "any air pollution agent or combination of such agents, including any physical, chemical, biological, radioactive substance or matter which is emitted into or otherwise enters the ambient air."[34] The term "welfare" as defined in the act explicitly includes effects on weather and climate change.

In 2009, based on the best available scientific evidence, the EPA administrator made the formal determination that six key greenhouse gases constitute a threat to public health and welfare and that the combined emissions from motor vehicles cause or contribute to the climate change problem—the **endangerment finding**. This determination triggered the CAA's mandate for the EPA to prescribe GHG emission standards for new vehicles.

endangerment finding
Formal determination by EPA administrator under the Clean Air Act that a pollutant's emissions may reasonably be anticipated to endanger public health or welfare

EPA Action

The EPA has regulations issued or in progress on several fronts. Some relate to mobile source controls; others to stationary sources under similar CAA authority.[35] All of the regulatory efforts that the EPA has under way are highly controversial. They include

- Provisions for improved fuel use and a new generation of cleaner vehicles—anticipated to reduce more than 3,100 million metric tons of (CO_2) emissions and to save more than 6 billion barrels of oil through the year 2025

- Renewable Fuel Standard program, with regulations requiring that motor vehicle fuel sold in the United States contains a minimum volume of renewable fuel—anticipated by 2022 to reduce GHG emissions by 138 million metric tons (the equivalent of annual emissions of 27 million passenger vehicles)

- National limits on the amount of carbon pollution that can be emitted by new fossil-fuel-fired power plants

- For major sources—such as power plants, refineries, and cement production facilities—including LAER and BACT requirements for GHG emissions under the Nonattainment New Source Review Program and the Prevention of Significant Deterioration Permit Programs (discussed earlier in this chapter)

- Regulations for hydraulically fractured gas wells—anticipated to reduce volatile organic compounds (VOCs) from 11,000 new wells by 95 percent, as well as reducing air toxics and methane, a potent greenhouse gas

- Based on its authority under the Safe Drinking Water Act, requirements for sequestering CO_2 in underground injection wells

CONCLUSION

The Clean Air Act and the regulations that implement it comprise a complex and often confusing patchwork. There have been repeated failures, frustrations, and do-overs. But for all that, the Clean Air Act has led to a substantial reduction in air pollution in the United States. Congress and the EPA have taken on the challenge of protecting public health and the environment from severe dangers posed by air pollution, while at the same time trying to avoid excessive economic consequences. The result is imperfect, and it is still a work in progress. But continuing that effort is essential to the health and welfare of all of us.

KEY TERMS

Air toxics

Background level

Best adequately demonstrated technology (BADT)

Best available control technology (BACT)

Beyond-the-floor limits

Cap-and-trade system

Criteria pollutants

Emission floors

Emission standard

Endangerment finding

Greenhouse gases (GHG)

Hazardous air pollutants (HAPs)

Industrial category

Lowest achievable emission rate (LAER)

Major sources

Maximum Achievable Control Technology (MACT)

Maximum individual risk (MIR)

National Ambient Air Quality Standards (NAAQS)

National Emission Standards for Hazardous Air Pollutants (NESHAPs)

New source

New Source Performance Standards (NSPS)

New Source Review (NSR)

Nonattainment areas

Nonattainment New Source Review (NNSR)

Prevention of Significant Deterioration
(PSD) program

Primary standards

Race to the bottom

Reasonably Available Control Technology
(RACT)

Residual risk standards

Risk-based standard

Secondary standards

State implementation plan (SIP)

Sulfur allowances

Technology-based standards

Uniform national standards

DISCUSSION QUESTIONS

1. Are technology-forcing standards a good idea? Why or why not?

2. The Clean Air Act makes the states—not polluters—responsible for complying with NAAQS. Does that make sense? Why or why not?

3. Why are some the EPA standards uniform nationwide, and some not? If you were in charge, by what criteria would you decide when to impose uniform national standards?

4. Why should states be barred by the Clean Air Act from regulating mobile sources? Why should mobile sources be any different than other parts of the act, where states can adopt standards stricter than federal standards?

NOTES

1. 42 USC § 7401–7671q.
2. 42 USC §7401(a)(2).
3. 42 USC §7401(b)(1).
4. 42 USC § 7602(h).
5. 42 USC § 7408(a).
6. 42 USC §7409(b).
7. These studies are called Regulatory Impact Analyses, and they are published on the EPA's website. For example, for the RIA pertaining to the NAAQS for particulates published in 2012, see www.epa.gov/airquality/particlepollution/2012/finalria.pdf.
8. For an illustrative case, see *Lead Industries v. the EPA*, 647 F.2d 1130 (D.C. Cir. 1980).

9. See United States Supreme Court opinion, *Whitman v American Trucking Assns., Inc.*, 531 US 457 (2001).

10. 42 USC § 7409(d).

11. 42 USC § 7411.

12. Concerning permitting, see 42 USC §§ 7475 and 7503.

13. Requirements for nonattainment areas are at 42 USC Part D §§ 7501–7514a.

14. Prevention of Significant Deterioration provisions are at 42 USC Part C §§ 7470–7479.

15. 42 USC § 7410.

16. 42 USC § 7502.

17. 42 USC § 4212 covers hazardous air pollutants.

18. See www.epa.gov/ttnatw01/orig189.html and www.epa.gov/ttn/atw/pollutants/atwsmod .html.

19. See, for example, National Toxicology Program: http://ntp-server.niehs.nih.gov/?objectid= 7201637B-BDB7-CEBA-F57E39896A08F1BB.

20. See, for example, Goldstein, B. D., and Carruth, R. S., "Implications of the Precautionary Principle for Environmental Regulation in the United States: Examples from the Control of Hazardous Air Pollutants in the 1990 Clean Air Act Amendments," *Duke Journal of Law and Contemporary Problems*, 2003; 66(4):247–261.

21. 42 USC § 7413.

22. 42 USC § 7604.

23. "Sources of Pollutants in the Ambient Air—Mobile Sources" available at www.epa.gov/apti /course422/ap3a.html.

24. 42 USC Subchapter II §§ 7521–7590.

25. 42 USC Subchapter IV §§ 7651–76510.

26. See, for example, www.epa.gov/capandtrade/documents/ctresults.pdf.

27. 42 USC § 7410(a)(2)(D).

28. Stack height is addressed in 42 USC. § 7423.

29. *North Carolina v. EPA*, 550 F.3d 1176, 1178 (D.C. Cir. 2008) (on rehearing).

30. *EME Homer City Generation, L.P. v. EPA*, available at www.cadc.uscourts.gov/internet /opinions.

31. Described in the website of the California Environmental Protection Agency Air Resources Board at www.arb.ca.gov/cc/capandtrade/capandtrade.htm; see also www.acc.com/legal resources/quickcounsel/UCCTR.cfm.

32. *Massachusetts v. EPA*, 127 S.Ct. 1438 (USSC 2007).

33. 42 USC § 7521(a)(1).

34. 42 USC § 7602(g).

35. See the EPA website, www.epa.gov/climatechange/EPAactivities/regulatory-initiatives.html.

Chapter 4

Clean Water Act (CWA)

WARNING
POLLUTED
WATER
Unsafe for Drinking
or Recreational Use

DIRECTOR OF PUBLIC HEALTH

DEPARTMENT OF PUBLIC HEALTH

Key Concepts

- The act protects surface waters (not groundwater) by regulating discharges from point sources, such as pipes and channels.

- The primary approach is national technology-based standards to limit effluent discharges. Stricter standards apply to new sources. Standards also vary according to type of pollutant, type of industry, and whether the facility discharges directly to surface waters or to a treatment plant.

- If technology-based standards do not achieve clean water, there are backup ambient water quality standards. These vary according to use (such as recreational use).

- The Clean Water Act relies heavily on permits to enforce standards.

On June 22, 1969, the Cuyahoga River caught fire in Cleveland, Ohio. The river was a mass of oil slicks and other pollution; in its lower stretches it showed no signs of aquatic life—not even sludge worms. The Cuyahoga had burned a dozen times from 1868 to 1952. Perhaps the difference in 1969 was that every home in America could watch the flames on television. The images of a river on fire helped spur grassroots demand for environmental protection. Three years later, Congress enacted the federal Clean Water Act of 1972.

Before 1972, water pollution control was left to the individual states, and federal law just played a supportive role. The Clean Water Act changed that: it imposed more stringent antipollution regulations, and it instituted much greater federal control.

The Clean Water Act (CWA)[1] is the main federal act protecting against pollution of surface waters, although there are two major water issues not included. The protection of drinking water is covered by the Safe Drinking Water Act; oil spill prevention and response are covered by the Oil Pollution Act. These two acts are discussed in later chapters.

The Clean Water Act's chief target is industrial pollution discharged from point sources (such as pipes). The act does not directly regulate sheet runoff, notably urban storm runoff or agricultural runoff—two intractable problems. Despite the act's shortcomings and the enormity of challenges it faces, it has succeeded in greatly improving the quality of surface waters in America. Stretches of the Cuyahoga River that were virtually dead in 1969 now support abundant aquatic life, including steelhead trout and dozens of other fish species.

SCOPE AND BASICS

This act has two names. Almost everybody calls it the Clean Water Act. But it's also known as the Federal Water Pollution Control Act, so you may occasionally see that name.

Legislative Goal

The goal of the Clean Water Act is to restore and maintain the chemical, physical, and biological integrity of the nation's waters. As part of this, the act seeks water quality that is fishable and swimmable. The act also seeks to eliminate discharge of pollutants. This latter goal was not met by the original deadline of 1985, nor has it been achieved even today. But progress has been made; pollutant discharges have been reduced, although not eliminated.

The Discharge Prohibition

The CWA makes it *unlawful for anyone to discharge any pollutant except in compliance with the act.* This key provision is commonly called the **discharge prohibition**, and it is the foundation of federal strategy against water pollution. To understand the scope and impact of the prohibition, and of the act itself, requires a few definitions.[2]

discharge prohibition
The default control measure of CWA that prohibits discharge of any pollutant not expressly allowed by a facility's permit, or in excess of the amount allowed in the permit

What's a Discharge? A *discharge of a pollutant* refers only to a discharge from a point source, meaning a confined conveyance such as a pipe or conduit. By contrast, agricultural runoff or sheet runoff from city streets—are not discharges within the scope of the CWA even though they are potentially significant sources of water pollution.

What's a Pollutant? The act's definition of **pollutant** is extremely broad. It includes dredged spoil, solid waste, incinerator residue, sewage, garbage, chemical wastes, and just about anything else you would expect—and a few you might not expect, such as heat, rock, and sand. It even includes munitions, such as shells or bombs from military exercises. If you accidentally drive your car off the end of a

pollutant
Under CWA, almost anything placed in surface waters for purposes of disposal

dock, that's not a pollutant. But if you get rid of an old, rusted jalopy by pushing it off the end of a dock, that's a pollutant.

What Waters Are Covered?   The Clean Water Act regulates discharges into navigable waters, but don't be misled into thinking it only applies to waters that ships and boats can navigate. The act defines "navigable waters" to include all **waters of the United States**—another term that is not self-explanatory. These two terms are synonymous for purposes of the act, and they basically include

waters of the United States
Surface waters subject to regulation under CWA, including interstate waters, waters subject to the tides, waters that have some connection with interstate commerce; also called "navigable waters" even if they are not really navigable

- Interstate waters: for example, any river or lake touching two or more states

- Waters used in interstate commerce; for example, a river, canal, or lake that carries vessels between states

- All waters subject to the tides—such as coastal waters of the Atlantic and Pacific Oceans

- *Intra*state waters, including wetlands, that have an adequate link to interstate commerce; for example, when fish caught there are sold in interstate commerce, or when the water body is used by interstate travelers for recreation

- Tributaries and wetlands adjacent to any of the above

The definition of waters of the United States is important, because it defines and delimits the jurisdiction of federal agencies to regulate pollution under the Clean Water Act. After the CWA was enacted in 1972, the agencies gradually expanded their interpretation to include waters whose connection to interstate commerce was less and less obvious. That trend was abruptly interrupted in 2001, when the United States Supreme Court rejected the Army Corps of Engineers' view that its jurisdiction under the CWA extended to an abandoned gravel pit that was seasonally filled with rainwater and had become a habitat for migrating birds.[3] The question of what waters are covered by the act remains a controversial and oft-disputed issue.

For convenience, this chapter often refers to waters covered by the act simply as "waters" or "surface waters." But keep in mind that not all intrastate water bodies qualify as "waters of the United States" and their status could be subject to debate. States generally have laws similar to the CWA and other federal environmental acts. So a water body found not to qualify as "waters of the United States" is not necessarily unprotected—it is still covered by state law.

Burden of Proof The discharge prohibition makes it illegal to discharge *any* pollutant *except* in compliance with the act. That means in compliance with limitations on what pollutants can be discharged and in what amounts. These limits are set forth in published regulations and, what's more, they are spelled out right in the permit issued to the individual facility. This is an effective regulatory approach, because it places the burden of proof on the discharger. In an enforcement action, it's up to the polluter to prove that its discharge was permitted, rather than up to the agency to show that there was a violation.

Major Programs

The Clean Water Act includes several programs, of which we'll discuss the following:

- National Pollutant Discharge Elimination System (NPDES) regulates direct discharges to waters of the United States, mainly by industrial dischargers

- Pretreatment program regulates industrial discharges to wastewater treatment facilities

- Dredge and Fill Permit program: regulates the deposit of fill and dredged material to surface waters, including wetlands

NATIONAL POLLUTANT DISCHARGE ELIMINATION SYSTEM (NPDES)

The **National Pollutant Discharge Elimination System (NPDES)**[4] is the centerpiece of the Clean Water Act. It regulates industrial facilities, as well as wastewater treatment plants, that discharge pollutants via point sources directly to surface waters. It uses a permit system that simplifies implementation and enforcement.

National Pollutant Discharge Elimination System (NPDES)
Major program of CWA that regulates discharge of pollutants to surface waters, including the requirement of a permit for any discharge

Some Definitions

The terms "pollutant," "discharge," and "surface waters," as used in the CWA, were explained earlier. A few other definitions will be helpful here.

Point Source Most commonly this is a pipe, but it can be any "confined and discrete conveyance." Common examples of point sources are pipes, ditches, channels, and conduits, but they also include mobile conveyances such as boats.

Direct Discharger A **direct discharger** is a facility that discharges, via a point source, directly into a river, lake, ocean, or other surface waters. Mostly, these are industrial and commercial facilities, and also include treatment facilities.

direct discharger
Under CWA, a point source that discharges effluent directly to surface waters

Publicly Owned Treatment Works (POTW) These are wastewater treatment facilities, which are operated by a municipality or other local authority. After treatment, the POTW discharges the treated waste into rivers or other surface waters. Thus, POTWs are direct dischargers (by contrast, facilities that discharge their wastes via the sewer system to a POTW are called indirect dischargers).

Permit Requirement

All direct dischargers are required to have NPDES permits. It is illegal for a facility to discharge directly to surface waters without a permit.[5]

A facility's NPDES permit specifies the types and amounts of pollutants the facility is allowed to discharge. It is illegal for a facility to discharge types or levels of pollutants not expressly allowed in its permit. Although effluent limits for each industrial category are published in regulations, the permit requirement facilitates enforcement of those controls. Spelling out the limits in the discharger's individual permit eliminates later arguments.

Permits are issued by the EPA or by states with permit programs approved by the EPA. With few exceptions, each direct discharger must apply for and obtain an individual permit. In addition to specifying the pollutant limits for the facility, the permit contains other conditions. These include important requirements for monitoring its own discharges and reporting them to the EPA or the relevant state authority. Such reporting readily reveals any violations, thus aiding effective enforcement. Penalties for violations are discussed later in this chapter. The ultimate threat is revocation of a facility's permit, without which the facility cannot legally operate.

TECHNOLOGY-BASED EFFLUENT STANDARDS

Under the Clean Water Act, the EPA promulgates technology-based effluent limits. *Technology-based* means the standards are based on the EPA's assessment of what is technologically feasible.

The act mandates various technology-based standards, which differ in their application and degree of stringency. This section will describe four major standards: best practical technology, best available technology, best conventional technology, and best available demonstrated technology. It is the EPA's task to translate these ambiguous terms into numerical effluent limits. These limits are published in tables that fill multiple volumes. When an NPDES permit is issued, it is the permit writer's job to select the appropriate **effluent standard** from those volumes, and incorporate those specific standards into the individual point-source permit.

> **effluent standard**
> A standard limiting the allowable concentration of a pollutant in discharges to surface waters

The Process of Promulgating Technology-Based Standards

The EPA looks at the actual performance of known technology and decides how low it can reasonably set effluent discharge limits. The regulations do not tell a discharger what technology it must use—just what performance it must achieve in controlling its pollutant levels.

As mentioned, the standards mandated by the act have different levels of stringency. Which standard applies depends on the type of pollutant and the type of discharger. The EPA must develop effluent limits for each standard, and for every discharger-pollutant combination. Moreover, the EPA must repeat this process for numerous different industrial categories. Because different technology-based limits apply to different industrial categories, these effluent limits are sometimes called **categorical standards**.

> **categorical standards**
> National effluent standards issued under the CWA, so called because different limits apply to different industrial categories

The effluent standards promulgated by the EPA are regulations with the force of law. Therefore, the EPA must follow the notice and comment procedures described in chapter 1, and the final regulations are subject to judicial review (see chapter 3).

The following sections describe the types of dischargers and pollutants, and the different standards applicable to them.

CATEGORICAL STANDARDS

Different industries use different raw materials and processes, and their wastes often contain different contaminants. Further, there is an unavoidable difference among industries as to how much they can feasibly reduce the contaminants in their wastes. Congress recognizes this reality, and therefore environmental acts direct the EPA to develop technology-based standards reflecting what can be achieved in each industrial category.

Under the Clean Water Act, for example, the EPA has issued effluent guidelines and standards for dairy processing, grain mills, cement manufacturing, petroleum refining, and pharmaceutical manufacturing, to name just a few. Even within an industry, the EPA must commonly consider multiple subcategories, which differ in what they can feasibly achieve. For example, the asbestos industry is divided into eleven subcategories, including asbestos-cement pipe, asbestos roofing, and asbestos floor tile. Inorganic chemical manufacturing is divided into over sixty-five subcategories. For each industrial subcategory, the EPA determines what contaminants are in its waste, and what reduction in contaminants that subcategory can feasibly achieve, under each of the multiple standards—BPT, BCT, BAT, and BADT. Those sometimes numerous standards apply nationwide to sources in the industrial the subcategory.

Types of Dischargers

The key distinctions among polluters are whether they are new or existing sources and whether they are direct or indirect dischargers. In addition, publicly owned treatment works (POTWs) are treated as a distinct group. Figure 4.1 is a simple diagram illustrating types of dischargers. The CWA is like the Clean Air Act, in that the term **new source** includes modified sources. Under both acts, a source is deemed new for purposes of an applicable regulation if it was constructed or modified after that regulation was first announced.[6]

new source
A source that was constructed or modified after an applicable standard was initially proposed

As you would expect, new (or modified) sources are subject to more stringent controls than existing sources, because new sources can readily incorporate the best and latest technology. Indirect dischargers generally have easier standards than direct dischargers, because indirect discharges will be treated by a POTW.

FIGURE 4.1 Types of Dischargers

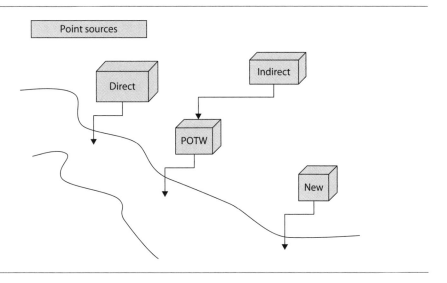

Types of Pollutants

The CWA imposes different degrees of stringency, depending on the type of pollutant. The act addresses three categories of pollutants plus a few forbidden pollutants.

Conventional Pollutants **Conventional pollutants** are the age-old public health foes, including microbial agents—the traditional targets of public sanitation and water pollution control. Their health and environmental effects are well understood. They are the types of pollutants that wastewater treatment plants can effectively treat. The act explicitly includes measurements of biological oxygen demand (BOD), an indicator of organic pollution; suspended solids; fecal coliform; and pH. The EPA has added oil and grease.[7]

Toxic Pollutants Under the Clean Water Act, the general definition of a **toxic pollutant**[8] is a pollutant that can cause death, disease, behavioral abnormalities, cancer, genetic mutations, reproductive malfunctions, and other severe effects in

conventional pollutants
Water pollutants, such as microbial agents and suspended solids, that are the traditional targets of public sanitation and water pollution control

toxic pollutant
Under CWA, a pollutant that can cause death, disease, behavioral abnormalities, cancer, genetic mutations, reproductive malfunctions, and other severe effects in humans or other organisms; defined more specifically by a list of toxic pollutants

humans or other organisms. There is a more specific definition for purposes of regulation: a toxic pollutant is anything on the EPA's official list of toxic pollutants.

There are sixty-five pollutants on the list, but many more if subcategories are counted.[9] They are organic chemical substances and metals. Some of the more recognizable examples for nonscientists are arsenic, asbestos, benzene, cadmium, chloroform, DDT, lead, and mercury. The EPA issues effluent standards only for the toxic pollutants designated on the list. If an industrial facility generates a toxic pollutant not on the federal list, the relevant state effluent standard applies. Thus, a point source's NPDES permit might include a mix of state and federal effluent standards for the various pollutants it discharges.

The EPA can add or delete pollutants from the list. In making that decision, the EPA takes into account these factors:

- Toxicity of the pollutant

- Its persistence or degradability

- Whether affected organisms are usually, or potentially, present in any regulated waters

- The importance of organisms affected

- The nature and extent of the effect on those organisms

The act requires the EPA to review the list every three years and revise it as needed, in light of new knowledge.

Nonconventional Pollutants   This is the catch-all category. Any pollutant that is not a toxic or conventional pollutant is a **nonconventional pollutant**[10] under the CWA. The Clean Water Act specifically lists the following as nonconventional pollutants: ammonia, chlorine, color, iron, and total phenols. The EPA may add a pollutant to the nonconventional list, if certain criteria are met:

nonconventional pollutant
Under CWA, a pollutant that is neither a conventional nor toxic pollutant; a catch-all category defined by an EPA list and including, for example, ammonia and chlorine

- First and foremost, the EPA must determine the substance is not a toxic pollutant as defined in the act. If it is, it must be added to the toxic pollutants list rather than the nonconventional pollutants list.

- Further, there must be sufficient data and adequate test methods to conclude that, subject to appropriate discharge limits, the pollutant will not interfere with water quality and will not pose an unacceptable risk to human health or the environment.

Forbidden Pollutants   The CWA totally bans any discharge of a few very dangerous substances:[11]

- Any radiological, chemical, or biological warfare agent

- Any high-level radioactive waste

- Any medical waste

Technology-Based Standards

There are actually multiple technology-based standards imposed by the Clean Water Act. Each standard has its own shorthand label and, of course, its own acronym. Don't be distracted by the profusion of labels and letters. The key point to grasp is that there are varying levels of stringency, based on type of discharger (such as direct or indirect) and type of pollutant. The following sections describe each standard. Table 4.1 provides an easy reference.

Best Practical Technology (BPT)   **Best practical technology (BPT)** is sort of a baseline effluent standard for existing sources discharging directly to surface waters. When enacted in 1972, BPT was the first standard Congress intended to be met, in a plan to reduce effluent discharges over time, with the ultimate goal of

best practical technology (BPT) First technology-based standard for effluent reduction under CWA

TABLE 4.1   Alphabet Soup: Technology-Based Effluent Standards

Standard	Pollutants	Sources
BPT Best Practical Technology	All: Conventional, Toxic, and Nonconventional	Existing direct dischargers (as of 1972)
BCT Best Conventional Technology	Conventional	Existing direct dischargers (after 1977)
BAT Best Available Technology	Toxic and Nonconventional	Existing direct dischargers (after 1977)
BADT Best Available Demonstrated Technology	All: Conventional, Toxic, and Nonconventional	New (and modified) direct dischargers

eliminating them. To reach that goal, Congress set 1977 as a deadline to achieve BPT, and 1989 to achieve the more stringent standards (BCT and BAT) discussed in the following sections. The 1977 deadline wasn't met. But BPT effluent limits remain on the books, forming a sort of baseline, and frequently adopted by reference in the volumes of BCT and BAT standards.

BPT applies to all contaminants (conventional, toxic, and nonconventional). The act directs the EPA to set standards that will achieve the degree of effluent reduction attainable through application of the best practicable control technology currently available for the industrial category, taking into account cost and non-water quality environmental impacts. To do this, the EPA essentially looks at the pollution-control technologies and the effluent levels of the companies within a given industrial category or subcategory. The EPA then sets BPT limits to reflect roughly the average of what the best-performing companies accomplish, using technologies typical for that industry. BPT effluent limits require the not-so-well-run companies to match the average performance of those role models.[12]

Best Conventional Technology (BCT) **Best conventional technology (BCT)** is the technology-based effluent standard applicable to existing sources discharging conventional pollutants directly to surface waters. The act directs the EPA to set standards that will achieve the degree of effluent reduction attainable through application of best conventional pollutant control technology. BCT was intended to replace BPT for conventional pollutants, as part of Congress's plan to gradually reduce and ultimately eliminate effluent discharges. BCT is potentially more stringent in that it is not necessarily tied to the techniques typically used by the industry. If an entire industry appears to be dragging its feet, the EPA can look to other industrial categories to determine what is the best control technology.

best conventional technology (BCT) Under CWA, technology-based effluent standards applicable to existing direct dischargers of conventional pollutants

The EPA must consider various factors in setting BCT standards, including cost and non-water quality environmental impacts (including energy use). The EPA must use a dual test to evaluate cost. First, is the cost to industry of the effluent reduction reasonable in relation to the benefits derived? Second, is the cost to industry reasonable compared with potential effluent reduction and cost for a POTW?[13]

Best Available Technology (BAT)   **Best available technology (BAT)** is also sometimes called "best available technology economically achievable."[14] BAT is the technology-based effluent standard applicable to existing sources discharging toxic and nonconventional pollutants directly to surface waters. The EPA must set BAT standards that will achieve the degree of effluent reduction *economically achievable* through the best available technology, taking into account cost and non-water quality environmental impacts (including energy requirements). The limit for a particular pollutant can even be set at zero—that is, total prohibition—if that is economically achievable.

best available technology (BAT)
CWA, technology-based effluent standards applicable to existing direct dischargers of nonconventional and toxic pollutants

As often happens, statutory words are not self-explanatory. What does *economically achievable* mean in practice? The EPA's interpretation, upheld by courts, is that it means economically achievable for the industrial category as a whole, not necessarily by each individual plant. If standards were set according to what the oldest, dirtiest facility could achieve, there would be no progress. BAT limits are anticipated to result in the closure of marginal facilities, but intended not to damage the overall industry. To set BAT limits, the EPA collects data on all existing sources in an industrial category to identify which plants best control a particular pollutant and how they achieve it. From that, the EPA extrapolates what best practices can achieve, and sets the limit accordingly. As with BCT, the EPA can look at technologies used outside the particular industry, if the whole industry appears to be lagging.

For any *toxic* pollutant, the EPA can impose effluent limits *stricter* than BAT if necessary to protect humans and other organisms with an ample margin of safety. By contrast, the EPA can *relax* BAT effluent limits for specific *nonconventional* pollutants within specific industries, if water quality will still be protected.[15]

best available demonstrated technology (BADT)
Under CWA, technology-based effluent standards applicable to new direct dischargers

Best Available Demonstrated Technology (BADT)   **Best available demonstrated technology (BADT)**[16] is also known as **New Source Performance Standards (NSPS)**. BADT is the technology-based effluent standard applicable to new sources discharging any type of pollutants directly to surface waters. Sources subject to this standard must achieve the greatest degree of effluent reduction achievable through application of the best available demonstrated control technology.

New Source Performance Standards (NSPS)
Standards for discharges from new sources

BADT is more stringent than BAT, for good reason. What is feasible for existing facilities consists mainly of retrofitted end-of-pipe technologies, but new facilities can incorporate the latest antipollution technologies as part of their design. In setting BADT limits, the EPA won't look at ideas still on the drawing board, but it will look at cutting-edge technologies that can reasonably be expected to work in the real world. Further heightening the stringency for new sources, the act does not specify that BADT standards be economically achievable—a major departure from BAT standards for existing sources.

As with BAT, a stricter BADT standard may be placed on a toxic pollutant, and a more lax standard may be allowed for a nonconventional pollutant, if circumstances warrant.

BEYOND TECHNOLOGY-BASED STANDARDS: WATER QUALITY SAFETY NET

What if everyone who discharges into a particular lake or river is complying with BAT standards, but the water is still polluted to an unacceptable level? It's easy to see how this could happen, for example, if there are just too many point sources discharging into the same water body. Under the CWA, if contaminant levels of the receiving waters are excessive, then pollution discharges must be reduced, even if all the dischargers are in compliance with technology-based standards. In short, if technology-based standards are not effective enough to protect health, they are trumped by risk-based standards.[17]

Water Quality Standards

How much contamination is too much? That depends on what a body of water is used for. Water in which people swim or fish needs to be cleaner than water used solely for industrial purposes. Each state is responsible for setting water quality standards within its borders, and this is a two-step process.

First, the state classifies all waters by use, such as recreation, water supply, aquatic life, or agricultural. The state isn't required to use the same classification for an entire water body. For example, a river may be divided into several segments with different uses. But the state must identify the designated use of each and every segment.

The second step for the state is to promulgate water quality standards for each designated use. These standards refer to ambient water quality, not end-of-pipeline levels. The EPA, which has far greater resources for evaluating health and environmental risks, issues guidelines for water quality standards based on use. EPA guidelines are not mandatory, but they are influential, especially since states rely on EPA funding and approvals.

Impaired Waters

States must monitor and assess all their waters to identify existing or emerging water quality problems. This enables states to identify impaired waters[18] — that is, waters for which technology-based regulations are not stringent enough to meet the state's water quality standards. A state must prioritize its impaired waters and develop **total maximum daily loads (TMDLs)** for them. You can get information about water bodies in your area online.[19]

A TMDL is a written, quantitative assessment of water quality problems in a water body and the contributing sources of pollution. It calculates the amount of a pollutant that a water body can receive and still meet water quality standards—or, less optimistically, the amount by which a pollutant needs to be reduced in order to meet those standards—and provides the basis for restorative action. The TMDL allocates pollutant load to point sources and nonpoint sources. A separate TMDL is developed for each water body-pollutant combination.

total maximum daily load (TMDL)

A written, quantitative assessment of water quality problems in a water body

If the TMDL identifies point sources as a significant source of the impairment, the restorative action may be more stringent NPDES permit limits. If the TMDL identifies nonpoint sources of pollutants as the major cause of impairment, the state can apply for EPA grants to help fund state programs for nonpoint source assessment and control. Control of nonpoint sources is a much more intractable problem. There are thousands of water bodies in the United States impaired from nonpoint sources such as stormwater and agricultural runoff, which the EPA is struggling to regulate.[20]

Congress has recognized the particular problems caused by nonpoint pollution sources to coastal waters. Legislation in 1990 called the Coastal Zone Act Reauthorization Amendments (CZARA) created the Coastal Nonpoint Pollution Control Program. This is jointly administered by the National Oceanic and Atmospheric Administration (NOAA) and the EPA. It builds on existing state coastal zone management and water quality programs, addressing runoff from six main sources including forestry, agriculture, and urban areas.[21]

ENFORCEMENT

Legislation that establishes rules of conduct must anticipate violations. Hence, Congress includes provisions for enforcement.[22] This section will discuss enforcement methods and penalties, as well as violations and defenses.

Actions and Penalties

Typically, environmental acts give the EPA (or the state agency) three avenues of enforcement—administrative, civil judicial, and criminal judicial actions. The EPA does not act as its own attorney; it is assisted in court actions by the Department of Justice.

Each environmental act sets the maximum fine or other penalty for each type of action or offense. An act typically sets a maximum *per violation*, meaning fines are imposed per day for each separate violation. For example, suppose a facility discharges two separate effluents in excess of its NPDES permit allowance, and this goes on for five days. That's a total of ten violations. If the maximum penalty is $25,000 per violation, the total fine could reach $250,000.

Administrative Proceeding For relatively minor violations, the EPA can impose administrative fines. This is the easiest approach, but also has the lowest limits. Under the CWA, the maximum penalty is $10,000 per violation, with a ceiling of either $25,000 or $125,000, depending on which of two processes the EPA selects. The two processes differ in how much procedural protection the penalized violator has. With the lower ceiling, the violator can contest the penalty only at the administrative level. If the EPA opts for the higher ceiling, the violator has the right to challenge the administrative decision in court—that is, seek judicial review.

Civil Judicial Action   For violations warranting a larger fine, the EPA can bring a civil judicial action—that is, a lawsuit. Under the Clean Water Act, the maximum civil fine a court can impose is $25,000 per violation. There is no ceiling. An alleged violator is entitled to a jury trial, but fines are set by the judge. In addition to fines, the court can grant an injunction (see following text box).

INJUNCTIVE RELIEF

An **injunction** is a court order requiring someone to do some designated act or to refrain from some designated act. The verb "enjoin" means to issue an injunction—that is, to mandate or to prohibit some action. For example, a court might enjoin the defendant company from discharging a particular pollutant into Pristine Lake—an example of an injunction *against* acting. Or a court might enjoin the defendant company to clean up pollution from Pristine Lake—an example of an injunction *compelling* some action.

injunction
A court order requiring someone to do—or refrain from doing—a designated act

One practical problem with litigation is that it takes a long time. This is especially a problem for someone seeking injunctive relief. If the defendant company's pollutant discharge is toxic to an endangered species of fish, they might all be dead before the case comes to trial. If *harm is imminent and would be irreparable*, a court can issue an immediate order to preserve the status quo—called a **temporary restraining order (TRO)**. In an emergency, a court will issue a TRO *ex parte*, meaning based on information from just one side, and without notice to the other party. The TRO is a first step, and it lasts only a few days.

temporary restraining order (TRO)
A form of injunctive relief intended to preserve the status quo for a very brief period until the parties can make initial presentations of their cases to the court

The second step is a **preliminary injunction**. Both parties give summary presentations of their positions. To grant a preliminary injunction, a court must be persuaded not only that significant harm is imminent and irreparable, but also that there is a strong likelihood the plaintiff will win at trial. A preliminary injunction preserves the status quo until trial, when each party presents its full case, including witness testimony. Once all the evidence is heard, the judge decides whether to grant a permanent injunction—the third step.

preliminary injunction
An injunction based on summary presentations, intended to preserve the status quo until there can be a full hearing before the court

Under the CWA, the mere fact of the noncompliance gives rise to liability for civil penalties. Negligence or intent are irrelevant. The violator is strictly liable, regardless of fault. Fault will, however, affect the penalty imposed for a violation.

Courts will consider several factors in deciding civil fines, such as the significance of the violation, what harm resulted to health or the environment, and whether the violator benefitted economically from the noncompliance. The duration of the noncompliance can be an important factor, particularly if it suggests the violator didn't make much effort to correct the problem. A history of violations and recalcitrance may persuade the court to impose a higher penalty. The violator's ability to pay is relevant as well, because fines are intended to deter future bad behavior. A fine of, say, $100,000 may have a tremendous deterrent effect on a small business, but wouldn't cause a major corporation to blink.

Almost all federal environmental acts, including the Clean Water Act, also provide that a private person may prosecute a civil enforcement action (see following text box on Citizen Action). A private person may not, however, pursue actions for criminal penalties nor administrative penalties.

CITIZEN ACTION

citizen action
An action in court by a private person or entity to enforce the law against a violator; allowed by most environmental acts

Most federal environmental acts allow a **citizen action** for enforcement against violators—a proceeding unique to American law. The law empowers a private citizen to step into the government's shoes and act as a private prosecutor. Typically, a citizen action is filed not by an individual, but by an advocacy organization, such as the National Resources Defense Council (NRDC) or the Sierra Club.

Essentially, the citizen files suit in court against a polluter or other violator. The citizen alleges, for example, that the defendant has discharged pollutants into a river of a type or quantity that violate its NPDES permit. A citizen can proceed only if the EPA or the state is not prosecuting the violation(s). This is not a rare occurrence—there are many more violations than the government agencies have resources to prosecute. Thus, allowing citizen enforcement actions fills a gap.

Where does a private citizen get the evidence to prove a violation? That can be easier than you would think. The defendant's NPDES permit, specifying what it is allowed to discharge, is public information. So are the defendant's monitoring reports showing what it actually discharged. A simple comparison of the numbers can prove a history of violations.

If the plaintiff wins the case, the court typically imposes a fine, and some-times an injunction—the same as it would in an enforcement action by the EPA. The plaintiff does not get to keep the fines—they go to the public treasury. However, the court grants an award to the successful citizen prosecutor as compensation for attorney fees. This is important, because litigation can be very expensive. If a plaintiff wants to recover damages—such as compensation for property damage—that must be done through a tort lawsuit, not a citizen's action.

As in any court suit, the plaintiff must have **standing**. For a citizen group, such as NRDC, at least some of its members must have standing. Standing essentially means a sufficient stake in the matter to ensure a vigor-ous litigation effort. That stake need not be an economic interest—it could be any interest which is adversely affected by the violation. For example, perhaps some of the Sierra Club's mem-bers like to fish or swim in Pristine Lake, and the defendant's violations cause contamination or unpleasant odors or other interference with those activities. Those facts could support standing on the part of the members, and of the Sierra Club acting in their behalf.

standing
Eligibility to file a lawsuit that depends on one's having a sufficient stake in or connection to the matter

Criminal Penalties   Federal environmental acts typically provide for criminal fines and even imprisonment, if warranted by the violator's conduct. The severity of the penalty will depend on how bad the conduct was. Under the Clean Water Act, a court can impose penalties as follows:

- Negligent violations: up to $50,000 per day; up to one year in prison

- Knowing violation: up to $100,000 per day; up to three years in prison

- Knowing endangerment (meaning the violator knew there was a signifi-cant risk of death or serious injury): up to $250,000 per day; up to fifteen years in prison

- False statements or tampering with monitoring devices: up to $20,000; up to four years in prison

Enforcement Strategy

The Clean Water Act is a good model for an effective enforcement strategy. In particular, the National Pollutant Discharge Elimination System (NPDES) facilitates the identification and proof of violations. A discharger's NPDES permit clearly establishes what pollutants it may discharge and in what amounts. Dischargers are also required, by law and by permit, to monitor and report their discharges, including any noncompliant discharges. Simply comparing the reports with the permit provides proof of violations.

The CWA imposes no-fault liability for noncompliance with a permit. Negligence or other fault can affect the penalty imposed in a civil action, but the discharger is strictly liable regardless of fault. Thus, to prove a violation, there is no need to show intent or other complicating factors. There are only very limited grounds a noncompliant discharger can cite in its defense, and the discharger bears the burden of proof. All of this makes it relatively easy for the EPA—or a private person in a citizen action—to prevail in an action for civil penalties.

PRETREATMENT PROGRAM FOR INDIRECT DISCHARGERS

For most of us, our wastewater goes down the drain, flows through a series of pipes, and ends up in a public sanitary sewer system operated by the municipal wastewater authority where it is treated and then discharged into a river or lake. These municipal facilities are called **publicly owned treatment works (POTWs)**. Because they are point-sources discharging directly into surface waters, POTWs must have NPDES permits and comply with all of the requirements discussed previously in this chapter.

POTWs are not limited to treating just residential wastes. Many commercial and industrial facilities also dispose of their wastewaters through the sewers to POTWs. These are called **industrial users (IUs)**. Because industrial users do not discharge directly to surface waters, they are not subject to the BCT/BAT/BADT requirements discussed above. Instead, they are classified as **indirect dischargers**, reflecting the fact that their wastewater detours for treatment by a POTW before discharge to surface waters.

Discharging industrial wastewater to a POTW is not a magical solution to water pollution. Most POTWs are designed to

publicly owned treatment works (POTW)
Water treatment facility owned by a local or other governmental entity

industrial user (IU)
An industrial point-source that discharges effluent waste to a POTW

indirect discharger
Under CWA, a point-source that discharges to a water treatment facility (POTW) rather than directly to surface waters

treat only conventional, biodegradable wastes, not unconventional or toxic wastes. Depending on the amount and nature of contaminants, wastewater from industrial users can pose risks to the POTW—such as killing the bacteria that are crucial to the biodegradation treatment process. Industrial wastewater can also pose a risk to the receiving waters. For example, toxic pollutants can pass through the treatment plant into streams, poisoning fish and endangering humans who eat them.

To protect against these risks, the Clean Water Act's **pretreatment program** requires industrial users to treat wastewaters *before* discharge to the sewer system in prescribed circumstances.[23] Basically, the goal is that pretreatment by the industrial user plus treatment by the treatment plant produces wastewater clean enough to meet BAT standards for discharges to surface waters.

pretreatment program
Clean Water Act program requiring pretreatment of waste before discharge to a POTW, if the waste would otherwise cause the POTW to exceed effluent limits

Pretreatment Requirements

There are various types of regulatory controls imposed on industrial users of POTWs. All of them serve the same two fundamental goals: preventing disruption of POTW operations and preventing harmful contamination from reaching the receiving waters.

General Prohibitions   This type of control consists of federal regulations applicable to all industrial users nationwide. They prohibit any discharge that would cause a POTW to violate its own permit due to **interference** or **pass through**. Interference means an IU discharge that disrupts or inhibits the POTW's treatment processes or sewage sludge management. Pass through refers to a discharge from an IU of any contaminant that the POTW cannot effectively treat, which therefore passes through the POTW and contaminates the receiving waters. This is especially relevant to toxic pollutants.

interference
Under the CWA, an industrial discharge to a POTW that disrupts or inhibits the POTW's treatment operations

pass through
Under the CWA, the discharge by an industrial user to a POTW of any contaminant the POTW cannot effectively treat, which therefore passes through the POTW and contaminates the receiving waters

Specific Prohibitions   In addition to the two general prohibitions, EPA regulations applicable to all industrial users nationwide impose certain restrictions that are very specific: no pollutants that pose fire or explosion hazards; no pollutants that will cause corrosive structural damage to the

POTW; no solid or viscous pollutants that would obstruct flow; no heat that could inhibit biological activity; no pollutants that could cause acute worker health and safety problems.

National Categorical Standards   This type of control applies to specified industrial categories that produce troublesome wastes. The EPA has developed numerical effluent standards that apply nationwide to all industrial users within the relevant industrial category. The EPA bases these numerical effluent standards on the average performance of POTWs in pollutant removal. Thus, effluent limits require the industrial user to remove or reduce contaminants to a level that *average* POTW treatment can ensure discharges that comply with BAT standards. If a POTW consistently achieves a *better-than-average* level of removal, its industrial customers may qualify for a less stringent pretreatment standard.

Local Limits   A POTW may establish local limits that are more stringent than federal standards, to ensure that it can comply with its own NPDES permit, or for reasons such as limiting outdoor air emissions or protecting its workers from toxic fumes. Local limits are generally implemented through contracts between the POTW and its industrial users. As with any environmental law, the POTW has no authority to prescribe standards *less* stringent than those established by federal law.

Implementation and Enforcement of Pretreatment Program

Although the EPA and the states retain oversight authority, the Pretreatment Program is largely implemented at the municipal level. A POTW with a federally approved pretreatment program is authorized to implement and enforce the Clean Water Act's Pretreatment Program.[24] The requirements for industrial users of the POTW are spelled out in their individual permits or agreements with the POTW. The POTW has the power to prosecute violators in court. Depending on the circumstances, civil or criminal fines may be imposed, as well as injunctive relief.

DISCHARGES OF FILL AND DREDGED MATERIALS

The Clean Water Act does not regulate dredging per se—dredging is covered by the federal Rivers and Harbors Act, which governs navigation. But the CWA regulates the *discharge* of dredged material or fill into surface waters.[25]

Whether discharged material constitutes fill or pollutants depends on the purpose of the discharge. If the purpose is to create dry land from an aquatic area (such as Kips Bay in Manhattan) or to change the contours of a lake bed (perhaps to make a safer swimming area at a lake resort), the material would clearly be deemed fill, and a **dredge and fill permit** is needed. But material—even material of the exact same composition—would be deemed a pollutant subject to NPDES requirements if the discharger's purpose is really just to get rid of it. Conceptually, the distinction between pollutants and fill is easy to understand, but in practice there are gray areas. The issue is sometimes subject to intense debate because NPDES permits impose more stringent requirements than dredge and fill permits.

dredge and fill permit
A permit issued by the Corps of Engineers and required for the deposit of fill or dredged material into surface waters

Wetlands

Like all of the Clean Water Act, dredge and fill requirements apply to waters of the United States, including wetlands. Many of the controversies that arise from dredge and fill regulation involve wetlands, and these permit requirements are among the most important legal protections of wetlands.

For much of our history, destroying wetlands for development was accepted without question. Land usable for agriculture, industry, commerce, and even for recreation and residences, was valued by our society; swamps were despised as breeding grounds for disease. In more recent times, we've become aware that wetlands perform important functions, including protecting the quality of adjacent waters through filtration of pollutants, absorption of floodwaters, and providing a valuable ecosystem, including habitat for aquatic animals. As a result, wetlands are now seen as worthy of legal protection.

Identification of what is or is not a wetland for permit purposes is often subject to debate. Generally, wetlands are defined as areas that are normally inundated or saturated by surface or groundwater sufficient that they can and do support aquatic vegetation. Detailed criteria are spelled out in a government manual.[26] Determination of whether those criteria are met typically requires an expert survey, and experts do not necessarily agree. In one case involving a twenty-thousand-acre tract of forested land in Louisiana, there was a dispute over what percentage of the tract was wetlands. Three different surveys reached three very different conclusions. The US Fish and Wildlife Service said 100 percent; the EPA said 80 percent; and the US Army Corps of Engineers said 35 percent.[27]

An area does not need to be saturated year-round to qualify as wetlands; seasonal saturation can suffice. Wetlands are included within the scope of the act if they are adjacent to water bodies or tributaries that qualify as waters of the United States. Nonadjacent wetlands are also within the scope if they have their own connection to interstate commerce, for example, wetlands that are used to irrigate crops sold in interstate commerce. In general, regulation of discharges of dredged material or other fill to wetlands is quite stringent.

The Permitting Process

This program of the Clean Water Act is jointly implemented by the EPA and the US Army Corps of Engineers ("the Corps"). Basically, the Corps is the authority that issues or denies permits, whereas the EPA sets the standards and guidelines for getting a permit. The EPA also has authority to veto a permit issued by the Corps. The partnering of these two agencies can give rise to tensions at times, because of their differing emphases. Historically, the Corps is oriented toward development, whereas the EPA is oriented toward protection of health and the environment.

404 permit
A dredge and fill permit

With few exceptions, the Clean Water Act requires a permit for the discharge of dredged or fill material into waters of the United States. This dredge and fill permit is frequently called a **404 permit**—a reference to the relevant CWA section number.[28] A very few activities are exempt from the 404 permit requirement, for example, plowing and other normal farming practices. Further, the Corps has issued blanket 404 permits covering designated activities that involve only minor discharges, such as bank stabilization or backfilling of utility lines. But most projects that involve discharge require an individual 404 permit.

public interest review
Inquiry conducted by the Corps of Engineers to determine whether to issue a 404 permit

Public Interest Review Applications for individual 404 permits are submitted to the Corps, which conducts a **public interest review** to decide if the permit should be granted. In this review, the Corps evaluates the impacts on the public interest of both the proposed construction activity and the planned long-term use. The Corps looks at anticipated economic and environmental impacts—impacts on things like water quality, fish and wildlife, aesthetics, flood damage prevention, and energy—and balances the benefits and detriments to the public. Commonly this means balancing economic benefits against environmental harm.

Although the Corps decides whether to issue a 404 permit, it must apply guidelines issued by the EPA. These EPA guidelines prohibit dredge and fill activities if there is a practicable alternative that would cause less adverse impact to the aquatic ecosystem. In deciding whether an alternative is practicable, the Corps looks at cost, technology, and logistics in light of the overall project purposes. The types of alternatives considered include changes in the project location, scope, design, and methods of construction. Another alternative the Corps must always consider is the "no project" alternative—that is, whether the permit should be denied because the project's purpose and public benefits are outweighed by the harm.

The most basic question is whether the proposed project is water-dependent, or if it could just as well be done in a nonaquatic location. If the project is not water-dependent, there is a presumption under EPA guidelines that a practicable alternative exists, unless the applicant clearly demonstrates otherwise. This presumption applies whether the project involves wetlands or other waters.

There is a second hurdle specifically for wetlands. The EPA guidelines create a presumption against allowing work in wetlands. Thus, where wetlands are involved, a heavy burden is placed on the applicant to show that there are no practicable alternatives. The applicant's burden includes showing substantial public need and benefits, such that the "no project" alternative is not practicable.

If the Corps is persuaded to issue a 404 permit for a wetlands discharge, EPA guidelines require that damage be minimized, and that any unavoidable damage be mitigated. Mitigation essentially means restoration of the damaged wetlands where possible, or creation of new, artificial wetlands to offset the loss—generally on an acre-for-acre basis. Promises and requirements of mitigation are written into the 404 permit.

As part of the process, the Corps is required to consult with the EPA and the US Fish and Wildlife Service for input concerning their respective areas of expertise. The Corps must also consult with the affected state. A 404 permit may not be issued unless the state certifies the project will not violate applicable laws and regulations, including water quality regulations. Issuance of a 404 permit is also subject to the National Environmental Policy Act (NEPA), which may require an Environmental Impact Statement (EIS).

Penalties for Violations

Discharges made without a 404 permit, or which do not comply with a duly issued permit, are violations of the Clean Water Act. Violators are subject to penalties up to $25,000 per day for each violation. A court can also issue injunctive relief, such as an order to stop discharges. The most onerous penalty is an order for restoration. This can include requiring the discharger to restore the water flow and bottom contours to their previolation condition. Restoration can be expensive and difficult. It is usually reserved for aggravated offenses, such as willfully continuing to discharge after being ordered to desist by the Corps or a court.

But That's My Private Property!

The Clean Water Act's restrictions on development apply to privately owned wetlands, not just public lands. The property investors and commercial developers most affected probably realize this. But it often comes as a surprise to students, who are shocked that property owners can be prevented by the act from using their own land. What is the scope of this situation? And what, if any, recourse does the private owner have?

Scope of Wetlands   There are slightly over 100 million acres of wetlands in the contiguous forty-eight states, representing about 5 percent of the total land surface. Seventy-five percent of these wetlands are privately owned. So there is a large volume of private property impacted by wetlands restrictions and, not surprisingly, a lot of controversy and litigation when permits are denied. Wetlands regulation is even more controversial in Alaska, which has about 175 million acres of wetlands, covering over 40 percent of the state's area.[29]

regulatory taking
Depriving a person of the benefit of their private property by operation of a regulation, such as restrictions on the development of wetlands

Is There Any Recourse?   Under the Due Process Clause of the US Constitution, the government may not deprive a person of property without due process of law. The government may take private property for a public purpose—for example to build a military air base—but it must follow the rules of due process, and it must compensate the owner for the property taken. Originally, this protection was applied only to physical takings. But courts have come to recognize the concept of a **regulatory taking**, where a governmental regulation interferes with the ordinary rights of a property owner.

The policy issue, in terms of our present context, is this: if the law is going to protect wetlands for the public interest, should the cost be borne by the public or by the individual owner? The general rule is that private property may be regulated to some extent, but if restrictions go too far, there must be compensation. Minor infringements won't qualify; an infringement that essentially renders the property valueless will qualify; but there is a lot of gray area in between.

Thus, denial of a 404 permit needed for development may require compensation to the property owner, depending on the facts of the individual case. A court typically asks what fraction of the tract cannot be developed due to the denial of the permit. There are no absolute rules, but the larger the percentage of wetlands comprising the property, the more likely a court will rule that denial of the permit constitutes a taking, so that the owner is entitled to compensation. The court also considers whether the owner had reasonable, investment-backed expectations of developing the property. If the owner knew of the potential problem at the time of purchase, and especially if the purchase price was low as a result, a court is unlikely to award compensation.

CONCLUSION

Surface water is a vital resource that is easily damaged by pollutants. The Clean Water Act has been reasonably successful in controlling pollutants from industrial point sources. But non-point-source contamination, such as storm runoff and agricultural sheet runoff, remain intractable problems.

The EPA is the primary federal agency responsible for implementing the Clean Water Act. The Army Corps of Engineers, however, is integrally involved in the portion of the act pertaining to dredge and fill operations. State governments are involved in implementing the entire Clean Water Act. Federal-state cooperation is particularly important in water protection, as many intrastate bodies of water are not subject to federal jurisdiction. States play an active role, both in implementing federal law and in providing further protections through state law. Local governmental entities also play an important role, particularly in the operation of POTWs and enforcement of regulations for the protection of POTWs.

The CWA relies heavily on permit systems—both NPDES and dredge and fill permits. These permit programs are effective tools for enforcement of environmental protections.

KEY TERMS

404 permit

Best available demonstrated technology (BADT)

Best available technology (BAT)

Best conventional technology (BCT)

Best practical technology (BPT)

Categorical standards

Citizen action

Conventional pollutants

Direct discharger

Discharge prohibition

Dredge and fill permit

Effluent standard

Indirect discharger

Industrial category

Industrial user (IU)

Injunction

Interference

National Pollutant Discharge Elimination System (NPDES)

New source

New Source Performance Standards (NSPS)

Nonconventional pollutant

Pass through

Pollutant

Preliminary injunction

Pretreatment program

Public interest review

Publicly owned treatment works (POTW)

Regulatory taking

Standing

Temporary restraining order (TRO)

Total maximum daily loads (TMDLs)

Toxic pollutants

Waters of the United States

DISCUSSION QUESTIONS

1. Review how the CWA allocates the burden of proof, both in the NPDES program and the dredge and fill program. Do you find it fair? Effective? As you study other environmental acts, think about who has the burden of proof in what circumstances, and how that matters in the effectiveness of health and environmental protections.

2. The CWA also provides other tools for enforcement, including permits, monitoring, and reporting requirements. Do they seem effective? Why or why not? As you study other environmental acts, think about what tools they use, and which tools seem likely to work best.

3. Is it appropriate for government to restrict what people can do with their private property? Should owners be allowed to do whatever they want on their own property? Is it any business of their neighbors? Of the community as a whole? Of the federal government? Why or why not?

NOTES

1. 33 USC §§ 1251–1387; for an overview of the act by the EPA see www.epa.gov/agriculture /lcwa.html.

2. Terms are defined in 33 USC § 1362.

3. *Solid Waste Agency of Northern Cook County v. US Army Corps of Engineers*, 121 S.Ct. 675 (USSC 2001).

4. 33 USC § 1342.

5. 33 USC § 1311(a).

6. 33 USC § 1316(a)(2).

7. 33 USC § 1314(a)(4); 44 FR 44501, July 30, 1979.

8. 33 USC § 1317(a); information on the EPA website is available at http://water.epa.gov /scitech/methods/cwa/pollutants-background.cfm.

9. The list appears in the Code of Federal Regulations at 40 CFR 401.15.

10. 33 USC § 1311(g).

11. 33 USC § 1311(f).

12. 33 USC §§ 1311(b)(1) and 1314(b)(1).

13. 33 USC §§ 1311(b)(2)(E) and 1314(b)(4); see *American Paper Institute v. EPA*, 660 F. 2d 954 (Court of Appeals, 4th Cir. 1981), interpreting 33 USC § 1314(b)(4) for an example of a case where the court rejected the EPA's interpretation of the statute.

14. 33 USC §§ 1311(b)(2)(A) and 1314(b)(2).

15. 33 USC §§ 1311(n) and (g).

16. 33 USC § 1316.

17. 33 USC § 1313.

18. See, for example, EPA, Impaired Waters and Total Maximum Daily Loads at http://water .epa.gov/lawsregs/lawsguidance/cwa/tmdl/intro.cfm.

19. http://water.epa.gov/lawsregs/lawsguidance/cwa/tmdl/index.cfm.

20. See EPA, TMDLs, and Stormwater at http://water.epa.gov/lawsregs/lawsguidance/cwa /tmdl/stormwater_index.cfm; see also Birkeland, "EPA's TMDL Program," originally published in 28–2 *Ecology Law Quarterly*, at 297 (2001), available online from the National Agricultural Law Center at http://new.nationalaglawcenter.org.

21. See, for example, http://coastalmanagement.noaa.gov/nonpoint.

22. 33 USC § 1319.

23. 33 USC § 1317(b); 40 C.F.R. Part 403.

24. 33 USC § 1319(f).

25. 33 USC § 1344.

26. *Federal Manual for Identifying and Delineating Jurisdictional Wetlands*, an Interagency Cooperative Publication of Fish and Wildlife Service, Environmental Protection Agency, Department of the Army and Soil Conservation Service (January 1989), available at http://digitalmedia.fws.gov/cdm/ref/collection/document/id/1341. There has been controversy around the manual and proposals for revisions. See, for example, Walker and Richardson, Virginia Water Resources Research Center, Virginia Polytechnic Institute and State University Special Report No. 24, "The Federal Wetlands Manual: Swamped by Controversy" (1991).

27. *Avoyelles Sportsmen's League v. Marsh*, 715 F.2d 897 (5th Cir., 1983).

28. Section 404 of the Clean Water Act is the same as 33 USC § 1344. All federal statutes have dual designations. The designation § 404 comes from the initial numbering of sections in the Clean Water Act as enacted by Congress. But all statutes are codified—that is, incorporated into, and published in, the United States Code—which has its own numbering system. The Clean Water Act is in Title 33 of the Code, which covers Navigation and Navigable Waters. Hence, CWA § 404 becomes 33 USC § 1344. What can be very confusing is that both numbering systems exist side by side and are used interchangeably.

29. Alaska Wetlands Initiative Summary Report, issued jointly by the EPA, Department of the Army, US Fish and Wildlife Service, and National Marine Fisheries Service (NOAA), available at http://water.epa.gov/grants_funding/wetlands/facts/upload/alaska.pdf, 2.

Chapter 5

Safe Drinking Water Act (SDWA)

Key Concepts

- The act takes a highly precautionary approach to keep our drinking water safe and reliable.

- Water utilities are responsible for removing contaminants from water, regardless of whether the contaminants are there naturally or resulted from human activity.

- Consumers have the right to know about the quality of their drinking water.

Historically, once people started living in close proximity in cities and towns, they started suffering epidemics of water-borne intestinal diseases such as cholera, typhoid fever, and others. With no other ready explanation, they believed these diseases came from *miasmas*—an undefined, evil quality of air, especially misty, dank air. So their main defense was to close their windows and drain their swamps. What they didn't understand was that their own dense populations were the source of the problem. Human excretory wastes fouled the drinking water with disease-causing microbes and parasites. Scientific discoveries of the cause and transmission of these diseases enabled preventive approaches. The field of sanitary engineering made rapid advances in technology to appropriately handle excretory wastes. People could then have safe drinking water, uncontaminated by human wastes.

When we turn on our kitchen tap in the United States, we take for granted that the water will be clean. This doesn't happen automatically, and it certainly doesn't happen all over the globe. If the topic of safe drinking water seems boring, it is because you have it. Our water is safe thanks only to behind-the-scenes actions dealing with numerous threats. Before the water reaches us, someone has to treat and disinfect it. Someone also has to maintain and ensure the safety of the mains and pipes that bring the water to our homes. Moreover, the lakes, streams, and wells that provide the water must be protected against contamination.

The primary federal law that provides this protection is the Safe Drinking Water Act (SDWA).[1] Its goal is to assure a safe supply of drinking water. To accomplish this goal, it requires identification, monitoring, and control of harmful contaminants before the water is piped to our homes. The act also has anti-pollution provisions for the protection of source waters, both surface and ground (subsurface) waters. The other major federal act protecting water is the Clean Water Act, covered in the previous chapter.

The SDWA is implemented by the EPA and the states. The principal regulated community consists not of polluters, but of utilities, specifically **public water systems (PWSs)**. These utilities didn't put contaminants into the water, but they are responsible for taking them out, in compliance with the standards set under this act.

public water system (PWS)
A water utility (whether publicly or privately owned) that has at least fifteen connections or serves at least twenty-five individual customers

WHO IS REGULATED: PUBLIC WATER SYSTEMS

What Is a Public Water System (PWS)?

This statutory term is deceptive. As used here, *public* does not necessarily mean publicly owned. A PWS can be either municipally or privately owned. Under the SDWA, a public water system is a utility that provides water for human consumption, through a delivery system (pipes), and serves at least twenty-five customers. That means twenty-five individuals, not households. Alternatively, a water system qualifies as *public* if it has at least fifteen connections—for example, households, schools, and offices—regardless of the number of individual users. Thus size, not ownership, determines if a water utility is a public water system. More information about public water systems, where they get their water, and how many people they serve, is given later in this chapter.[2]

The EPA is not authorized to regulate private drinking water wells that have fewer than fifteen service connections and serve fewer than twenty-five persons. Nor does the act apply to bottled water, which is regulated by the Food and Drug Administration.

Regulatory Approach

Public water systems are unique among utilities in that their product is taken into the body and is essential to life.

Certification   A public water system must be certified by the state where it operates. Each state adopts its own certification standards. However, states are expected to meet at least minimum certification standards set by EPA guidelines.[3]

Supportive Approach   A PWS is responsible to monitor and treat or remove contaminants from the water it delivers to its customers, to ensure its safety as drinking water. How well the public water system does its job obviously has a direct impact on public health. Whereas certification and regulation of other utilities is aimed mainly at controlling unintended side effects, such as pollution or fire, a PWS is closely regulated in the performance of its basic functions.

When other utilities—or other industries in general—do not meet environmental standards, the ultimate threat is to close down their operation. But closing down a PWS would leave its customers with no water supply. Therefore, government provides substantial assistance, including financial, technological and educational assistance, to help public water systems comply with standards. Such support is especially needed by small rural water systems.

WHAT CONTAMINANTS ARE REGULATED?

Contaminants are selected for regulation by the EPA based on the best available science.[4] The intent is to focus government resources where they will do the most good in terms of protecting health. Regulation can apply to any substance capable of contaminating water, regardless of whether it is a microbial, chemical, or physical agent.

Regulatory Criteria

The Safe Drinking Water Act authorizes the EPA to regulate any contaminant that meets all three of the following criteria:

- It may have an adverse effect on human health, and
- The frequency and levels at which it occurs create public health concerns, and
- Regulation "presents a meaningful opportunity for health risk reduction."[5]

The first criterion embodies the precautionary nature of the act: the EPA need not wait for scientific proof, or for people to get sick, before it can regulate a suspect contaminant. The second and third criteria embody the practical nature of the act. It doesn't matter that a substance is dangerous if nobody is exposed to it; the EPA is not authorized to regulate a contaminant that is too scarce to pose a risk. Nor is the EPA to issue regulations if they won't do any good—for example, if there is no known technology for treating the contaminant.

How a contaminant gets into the water is *not* a criterion for regulation. Safe drinking water standards apply to contaminants that occur naturally as well as those that result from human activity.

Contaminant List

Contaminants that have been determined to meet the regulatory criteria are identified on a **Contaminant List** maintained by the EPA.[6] This is the official list of regulated contaminants. The list contains close to ninety contaminants that present an actual or anticipated danger to health. These are the contaminants that a PWS must monitor and treat in compliance with the standards discussed later in this chapter. The list is not static—the act specifically provides for periodic review and update.

Contaminant List
Official list of contaminants subject to regulation under SDWA

Updating the Contaminant List

Selecting new contaminants for regulation is almost reminiscent of auditioning actors for a starring Broadway role. But here, the bad actors win.

The Candidates   Under the act, the EPA maintains a second list called the **Contaminant Candidate List (CCL)**. These are contaminants that are not regulated, but which are likely suspects for future regulation. As of this writing, there are 116 contaminants on the candidate list. A PWS is not required to treat the listed candidates, but it is required to monitor up to thirty of them, designated by the EPA, to see if frequency and concentration might warrant closer scrutiny.

Contaminant Candidate List (CCL)
List of contaminants not regulated under SDWA, but identified by EPA as potential additions to the Contaminant List

To meet the challenge of new and worrisome contaminants, the act mandates reviews every five years to update the Contaminant Candidate List, and, if appropriate, the Contaminant List as well. (This five-year requirement does not limit the EPA's authority to take action between reviews.)

Auditions for New Candidates   For the five-year update of the Contaminant Candidate List, the EPA enlists broad participation—asking for suggestions from scientists, including its own National Drinking Water Advisory Board, and even soliciting nominations from the public. With this input, the EPA creates a large slate of contenders. After an initial screening, the EPA focuses on the most worrisome nominees for a more detailed evaluation, based on public health risk and the likelihood of occurrence in drinking water. When it updated the CCL in 2009, the EPA started with about 7,500 contenders, from which it selected 116. The EPA's decision to include or omit a contaminant from the Contaminate Candidate List is not subject to judicial review.

Auditions for New Regulated Contaminants   The other step of the EPA's five-year responsibilities is to review five or more candidates to determine whether they should be added to the official Contaminant List and become regulated. The EPA, in consultation with the EPA Science Advisory Board, selects the five or more candidates that present the greatest public health concern. In making the selection of which candidates to review, particular attention is paid to at-risk subpopulations, such as infants, children, pregnant women, the elderly, and the chronically ill. The EPA evaluates the selected candidates in depth to determine whether they meet the three criteria described above—that is, adverse health effect, occurrence, and meaningful possibility of reducing risk through regulation. The conclusion of this in-depth evaluation is a formal decision by the EPA administrator, called a *regulatory determination*. If the EPA administrator determines that a candidate meets the criteria, it is added to the Contaminant List and the next step is to develop standards as discussed below. If the EPA administrator determines *not* to regulate, that is a final decision subject to judicial review.

NATIONAL DRINKING WATER REGULATIONS

How much of any given contaminant is allowed in the drinking water that reaches our taps? The act gives the EPA the task of setting standards to protect public health (primary standards) and public welfare (secondary standards).[7]

Primary Standards

The EPA sets standards for the protection of health, called **National Primary Drinking Water Regulations (NPDWR)** or simply *primary standards*. The act prescribes a two-step process to establish legally enforceable primary standards.

National Primary Drinking Water Regulations (NPDWR)
Regulations under SDWA for the protection of human health

Maximum Contaminant Level Goal (MCLG)   For each contaminant, the act directs the EPA to set the **Maximum Contaminant Level Goal**, meaning the ceiling needed to avoid any known or anticipated adverse health effect, with an adequate margin of safety. The act explicitly tells the EPA not to consider cost in setting the MCLG. Notice that this is a health-based standard—that is, based on the desired health outcome. Notice also that the legislative mandate is very precautionary.

Maximum Contaminant Level Goal
The level of a contaminant in drinking water that would lead to no adverse health effects

For carcinogens and microbial contaminants, it is EPA policy to set the MCLG at zero, because at least theoretically one single molecule is sufficient to cause disease, and one single microbe can divide until a sufficient number is present to cause disease. For noncarcinogenic organic chemicals, the EPA calculates the MCLG based on the **reference dose (RfD)**—that is, the maximum daily exposure, lifetime, without adverse health effects. The RfD is based on available epidemiological and toxicological studies and is published in the EPA's **Integrated Risk Information System (IRIS)**.

reference dose (RfD)
The maximum daily exposure, lifetime, shown not to cause adverse health effects

What is important to understand about the MCLG is that it is *an ideal, not an enforceable limit.* The ideal safe level is impossible to achieve, at least for carcinogens. So the MCLG serves as the first step to establishing the enforceable standard.

Integrated Risk Information System (IRIS)
EPA database of scientific information pertaining to risk from environmental agents

Maximum Contaminant Level (MCL)   The enforceable limit—the actual primary standard—is called the **maximum contaminant level (MCL)**. The MCL is based on the MCLG; specifically, the EPA sets the MCL as close to the MCLG as is feasible. Under the act, *feasible* means the level that can be achieved with the use of the best available technology, treatment techniques, and other means, taking cost into consideration. Notice that these are technology-based standards—that is, standards based on feasibility. Notice also this is the stage where cost is considered. The EPA balances costs and benefits in setting MCLs.

maximum contaminant level (MCL)
Allowable level of a contaminant in drinking water

For carcinogens and microbial contaminants, there can be a significant difference between what is ideal (MCLG) and what is feasible (MCL). For noncarcinogenic organic chemicals, MCLG and MCL are often identical.

Treatment Techniques For some contaminants, it's not feasible to set a numeric MCL, for example, due to difficulty measuring actual concentration. In such cases, the EPA may prescribe a specific **treatment technique** that public water systems must use for that contaminant. This is an enforceable standard, just like an MCL. (See the following text box on *American Water Works v. EPA*.)

treatment technique
An enforceable standard, prescribing a specific method of treatment that the EPA may issue if a numeric standard is deemed unfeasible

Additional Regulatory Requirements In addition to setting allowable limits on contaminants in drinking water, National Primary Drinking Water Standards impose further detailed responsibilities on public water systems, including:

- Monitoring requirements (specifying location, frequency, and methodology for sampling)

- Methodology for analyzing samples

- Record keeping and reporting requirements (discussed later in the chapter)

AMERICAN WATER WORKS V. EPA[8]

The SDWA allows the EPA to prescribe a particular treatment technique as the primary drinking water standard for a contaminant if a numeric maximum contaminant level (MCL) is not economically or technologically feasible. The EPA adopted a treatment technique as the standard for lead contamination. The Natural Resources Defense Council (NRDC) challenged the EPA's standard. The NRDC argued that lead in drinking water could be measured, so it was feasible and therefore mandatory for the EPA to adopt an MCL.

The EPA disagreed that *feasible* simply means measurable. The EPA interpreted feasible to mean that an MCL could be accomplished *consistent with the overall public health purposes of the act*. Lead gets into drinking water because it is leached from old lead pipes through which it flows. Compliance with a lead MCL would require public water systems to use aggressive corrosion control techniques. While reducing the amount of leached lead, such techniques could increase levels of other harmful contaminants, to the overall detriment of public health. The EPA concluded that an MCL was not feasible, and prescribing a particular corrosion control technique would best protect public health. The court upheld the EPA.

There was a second issue in the same case. The EPA exempted transient non-community public water systems from the lead standard. NRDC argued that a primary standard must apply to all public water systems, and the exemption was therefore improper. The EPA reasoned that lead poses a significant health risk only with chronic exposure. Applying the standard to a transient noncommunity system would therefore have no appreciable public health benefit, but it would be highly burdensome for these systems, many of which are quite small. The court expressed general approval of the EPA's explanation.

Secondary Standards

The primary standards just discussed are intended to protect human health. The Safe Drinking Water Act also directs the EPA to establish **National Secondary Drinking Water Standards** to protect the public welfare. These apply to contaminants that can make consumers unwilling to use the water, even if it does not endanger health. For example, some contaminants cause adverse aesthetic effects (such as unpleasant taste, odor, or color) or cosmetic effects (such as discoloration of teeth or skin).

National Secondary Drinking Water Standards
Regulations under SDWA for protection of public welfare and the environment

The EPA sets secondary standards, reflecting how much of a contaminant can be in drinking water without causing adverse effects. Unlike primary standards, *National Secondary Drinking Water Standards are not enforceable as federal limits*. Aesthetic and cosmetic impacts are regulated by the individual states, not the federal government. The EPA secondary standards serve as guidelines. They are followed by many states, either explicitly as numeric standards, or as implied standards for descriptive rules (such as rules against offensive odor or taste).

The remainder of this discussion will focus on primary, not secondary, standards.

Process for Setting Standards

Adoption of National Primary Drinking Water Regulations is subject to the usual notice and comment process. The act emphasizes both precaution and transparency in the setting of drinking water standards. To set an MCLG, the EPA conducts a risk assessment based on the best available science. This risk assessment is public information, and it must be clear and comprehensible.

To set an MCL, the EPA must do a cost-benefit analysis. It must take into consideration both quantifiable and nonquantifiable costs and benefits. In weighing the pros and cons, it must consider the effects of the contaminant on the general population, but also on subpopulations such as infants, the elderly, pregnant women, and persons with chronic illnesses. This analysis is public information.

Primary standards are subject to judicial review. The EPA's risk assessment and cost-benefit analysis—often the most controversial aspects of rulemaking—cannot be challenged as interim steps, but only as part of judicial review, after the final standard is published. On review, a court will reject a regulation only if it finds the agency action was arbitrary and capricious.

The act requires the EPA to review primary standards at least every six years for adequacy to protect public health. More frequent reviews and revisions are at the EPA's discretion.

KEEPING CONSUMERS INFORMED

A public water system is held highly accountable to its customers.[9] This is partly through incident reports. Any time a PWS violates an MCL or a treatment technique or a requirement for testing or monitoring, it must give notice to all customers. If the violation has the potential for serious human health effects, the notice must be given within twenty-four hours.

consumer confidence report (CCR)
A detailed water quality report and disclosure statement that a PWS must provide annually to each customer

On a yearly basis, a PWS must send all its customers a **consumer confidence report (CCR)** (also called a water quality report), giving detailed information on the quality of the water it delivers to them, including any risks. Among other things, the CCR must provide the following information:

- Identify the water source, and provide any assessments that have been done of the source water

- Report the detection of any contaminants subject to mandatory monitoring

- Disclose any monitoring results that may raise health concerns

- Disclose any violations of drinking water regulations

Both the incident reports and the annual reports require an unusually high degree of transparency. Requiring so much public disclosure makes sense, given the direct impact on the health of customers of any tainted water coming out of their taps.

A CLOSER LOOK AT PUBLIC WATER SYSTEMS

What does Giles Flea Market in New Tazewell, Tennessee, have in common with the multimillion-customer City of Chicago Department of Water Management? Answer: they are both public water systems.

There is tremendous diversity among public water systems. Distinctions include how many customers they serve and what type of customers. Public water systems are classified in several ways, and regulation varies for the different classifications. This section describes some classification criteria and a few interesting statistics.

Classification by Size

The EPA classifies public water systems based on the number of consumers served. There are five size classes, ranging from very small (five hundred or less) to very large (over one hundred thousand). These numbers don't give the full picture—the very large category includes metropolitan systems with millions of customers. The very small systems serve as few as twenty-five individuals.

Classification by Who Drinks the Water and How Often

Besides classifying by size, the EPA has defined three types of systems, reflecting who is drinking their water and how regularly.[10] Some contaminants can cause acute health effects from short-term exposures. For example, cryptosporidium causes acute diarrheal disease. It caused an epidemic in Milwaukee in 1993 in which at least a hundred people died and hundreds of thousands were sickened. By contrast, other contaminants mainly impact health through chronic, long-term exposure. These include, for example, neurotoxins such as lead and mercury. Because of this difference, the EPA distinguishes between three types of public water systems, based on factors reflecting exposure, namely whether the PWS provides water year-round, and whether it is consistently the same people drinking that water (see table 5.1.).

TABLE 5.1 Types of Public Water Systems

Type of System	Who It Serves	Regularity of Service
Community	Fixed customer base	Year-round
Nontransient noncommunity	Fixed group	At least 60 days per year, but not year-round
Transient noncommunity	Transient visitors	At least 180 days per year; can be year-round

Community Water Systems PWSs that serve year-round residential communities are called **community water systems**. Their consumers are exposed consistently and over long periods to the water delivered to their taps. Community water systems must therefore be concerned with contaminants whose impacts occur from chronic long-term exposures, as well as contaminants that commonly cause acute effects from short-term exposure. Accordingly, community water systems are the most highly regulated class of public water system. There are approximately fifty thousand community water systems in the United States.

community water system
A public water system that serves a fixed customer base year-round

Noncommunity Public Water Systems There are various public (or quasi-public) facilities that provide drinking water to at least twenty-five consumers, even though that isn't their main function. These may be schools, factories, churches, restaurants, motels, highway rest stops, and so forth. The key is whether such a facility provides drinking water from its own water supply (usually a well). Facilities that use their own water, rather than buying already-treated water from an independent regulated PWS, are regulated under the SDWA as noncommunity public water systems. They are deemed PWSs because they function like PWSs—namely in supplying water for people to drink. As such, they are required to provide a safe and adequate water supply to the people they serve.

Noncommunity public water systems are classed as transient or nontransient. A **nontransient noncommunity water system** is one that supplies water to the same people at least sixty days per year total (not necessarily continuous). Examples are schools and places of employment. There are slightly less than twenty thousand nontransient noncommunity water systems in the United States. Because the same people are consistently exposed to the drinking water at such facilities, regulations must be concerned with chronic as well as acute exposures.

nontransient noncommunity water system
A public water system that serves a fixed group of people at least sixty days per year, but not year-round

A **transient noncommunity water system** is one that provides water at least six months per year, but not consistently to the same people. Examples are hotels and restaurants. Because exposure is transient, the primary regulatory concern is protection against those contaminants that can cause acute illness from short-term exposure. (See previous text box on *American Water Works v. EPA*.) In round numbers, there are eighty-eight thousand of these systems in the United States.

> **transient noncommunity water system**
> A public water system that serves transient visitors at least 180 days per year

A Few More Interesting Statistics

In comparing the types of public water systems, the number of systems is not necessarily an indication of the number of people drinking the water[11] (this is illustrated in table 5.2). For example, there are a huge number of transient noncommunity systems, but most are very small and together they serve a small fraction of the population.

Similarly, with respect to classification by size, the number of systems is no indication of the population served—it's more of a reverse indication. Among community water systems, over half are in the *very small* class, but they serve only 2 percent of residential customers. By contrast, only 1 percent of community water systems are in the *very large* class, but they serve 46 percent of all PWS residential customers (see table 5.3).

TABLE 5.2   Number of Systems and Drinkers, by Type of PWS (2010 Statistics with Numbers Rounded)

Type of Public Water System	Number of Systems	Number of Drinkers
Community water system	50,000	298,000,000
Nontransient noncommunity	18,000	6,000,000
Transient noncommunity	88,000	13,000,000

TABLE 5.3   Percentage of Systems and Drinkers by Size of CWS

Community Water System Size	Percentage of Systems	Percentage of Drinkers
Very small (500 or less)	55	2
Small (501–3,300)	27	7
Medium (3,301–10,000)	9	10
Large (10,001–100,000)	7	36
Very large (over 100,000)	1	46

SOURCE WATER

Source water is untreated water used to provide public drinking water.[12] It can be surface water (from rivers, streams, or lakes) or groundwater (from underground aquifers). Source water is pumped by a public water system to its treatment plant, where the water is treated in preparation for public consumption.

Where Does the Water Come From?

The great majority of community water systems use groundwater (subsurface water). But the great majority of consumers drink treated surface water. This reflects the fact that most large urban communities are served by a relatively small number of PWSs that draw their water from reservoirs and other surface sources. To illustrate, table 5.4 gives comparative figures for community water systems.

For noncommunity water systems, both transient and nontransient, there is no such inversion. The percentage of noncommunity systems that use groundwater is very high (well over 90 percent). The percentage of consumers served by groundwater is also high (over 80 percent).

Protection of Source Water

Even though drinking water is treated before reaching our taps, protection of source water is an important goal under the act.[13] Groundwater is in need of protection from chemicals that migrate through the soil and reach drinking water aquifers. Surface water is even more vulnerable, because it is open to the atmosphere, and thus to contamination from air pollutants and surface runoff containing chemical and physical agents, as well as animal fecal matter. Protecting source water from contamination helps reduce the cost of treatment and helps reduce risks to public health.

To be effective, protective measures must be tailored to local factors. Thus, state and local governments, and water utilities themselves, play a crucial role in

TABLE 5.4 Systems and Drinkers by Type of Water Source (2010 Statistics with Numbers Rounded)

Community Water Systems	Groundwater	Surface Water
Number of systems	40,000 (77%)	12,000 (23%)
Number of drinkers	88,000,000 (30%)	209,000,000 (70%)

source water protection. The act requires states to have EPA-approved programs for assessment and protection of source waters serving public water systems.

BEAVER FEVER

Giardiasis, also known as Beaver Fever, is caused by a protozoan that lives in the intestines of animals and humans. It is the most commonly reported cause of water-borne disease outbreaks in the United States. The Centers for Disease Control's nationwide surveillance, based upon data gathered from the forty-five states and five other jurisdictions for which giardiasis is a reportable illness, records about twenty thousand cases a year, which is a significant underestimate of the total. Children are more likely to be affected than adults. About three-quarters of the outbreaks are due to inadequate surface water treatment, usually in smaller rural community water systems.[14] Problems like this illustrate the importance of protecting source waters.

Source Water Assessment Each state must have an EPA-approved program for assessing all sources—both groundwater and surface water—serving public water systems. The state's **source water assessment** is intended to

source water assessment
Assessment by each state of surface and groundwater sources serving public water systems

- Delineate the boundaries of the water source

- Inventory existing or potential sources of contamination within the delineated area

- Determine the susceptibility of the water supply to contamination

Source water assessments are publicly available. You can obtain information about your local drinking water, including source water, at http://water.epa.gov /drink/local.

Source Water Protection Each state must also have an EPA-approved program for the protection of drinking water sources. Using information from the source water assessment, protective actions are designed to manage potential sources of contamination, so as to minimize the threat to drinking water sources. Protective measures might consist, for example, of local zoning restrictions on certain types of development in locations that could threaten source water. Similarly, state authorities could deny or impose conditions on permits required under the Clean Water Act for construction or effluent discharge. Another important element of the source water protection programs is the development of a contingency plan for responding to emergencies. Source water protection programs vary from state to state. Some impose mandatory requirements on local governments and public water systems. Others promote and rely on voluntary action.

THE HYDRAULIC FRACTURING EXCEPTION[16]

hydrofracturing or "fracking"
A technology to obtain fossil fuels bound in rock strata deep underground by injection of pressurized fluids

Hydraulic fracturing (**hydrofracturing or "fracking"**) is a technology that increases production of natural gas by freeing gas trapped in deep underground shale formations. Hydrofracturing involves a major and rapidly expanding use of underground injection, yet it is specially exempted from regulation by the Safe Drinking Water Act's Underground Injection Control Program. What's the story?

The hydrofracturing process involves high-pressure injection of water combined with sand and chemicals (commonly called "fracking fluid") into deep underground wells. Current hydrofracturing for shale gas uses upward of five million gallons of water for each hydrofracture, and there may be as many as a dozen hydrofractures in different directions from the same well pad. If done successfully, chemicals are injected deep underground far below the level of groundwater and appear unlikely to cause contamination, although groundwater has been compromised by hydrofracturing agents through failure of the well casings or other industrial incidents at or close to the surface. About 20–50 percent—perhaps 1–2.5 million gallons—of the injected fracking fluid returns to the surface relatively quickly. This immediate return is commonly called "flowback." After the initial flowback, a smaller amount of fluid—perhaps fifty gallons per day—continues to surface throughout the life of the well. This slower continual return is often called "produced water." In addition to the sought-after hydrocarbons and the original fracking fluid chemicals, the flowback and produced water contain significant amounts of brine, iron, radionuclides, and other potentially harmful agents. This is because these agents exist naturally underground, and they are soaked up by the fracking fluid, creating a hazardous mixture. As a result, these return flows contain more—and much more dangerous—chemicals than the original fracking fluid.

How to safely handle and dispose of flowback and produced water is a major challenge for the industry. Underground injection of flowback and produced water works well in certain geological areas, such as in Texas, but not in others, such as in Pennsylvania. Disposal above ground presents more potential risk than the initial injection of fracking fluid. As part of the flowback and produced water, those chemicals have the potential to enter and contaminate drinking water aquifers.

So why isn't the injection of fracking fluid, flowback, and produced water regulated by the Safe Drinking Water Act's Underground Injection Control Program? Originally, it was. But in 2005 Congress created a special exemption for the hydrofracturing industry. This is often called the Halliburton Loophole. The exemption was proposed by the Bush administration, in accordance with the recommendation of its specially appointed National Energy Policy Development Group. This special task force was led by then–vice president Richard B. Cheney, former head of the Halliburton Company, a leader in the shale gas hydrofracturing industry. The task force was criticized by many for its lack of transparency. Nonetheless, it succeeded in getting the exemption that applies only to this one industry. This is an illustration of how our laws can be influenced by the push and pull of special interests.

Underground Injection Control Program   Underground injection is a technology that places fluids deep underground, where they are more or less trapped in porous mineral formations. This technology is used for various purposes, including waste disposal, storage of natural gas, and carbon dioxide sequestration.

To protect source water against contamination, injection activities are regulated through the **Underground Injection Control Program**.[15] The program is mandated by the act and jointly implemented by the EPA and states with approved programs. Under program regulations, any of the following would violate the Safe Drinking Water Act:

Underground Injection Control Program
SDWA program to protect source waters from contamination by regulating the placement of fluids deep underground

- Any injection activity—for example siting, construction, operation, or abandonment—that endangers underground drinking water sources

- Escape of any fluids from the well or intended injection zone

- If any fluids directly or indirectly injected into a drinking water aquifer cause a PWS to violate a primary drinking water standard or otherwise adversely affect public health

Sole Source Aquifer Protection Program   Some communities are dependent on a single aquifer to supply all or most of their drinking water, with no feasible alternatives available. Such a community can request a **sole source aquifer (SSA)** determination.[17] This is a formal determination by the EPA administrator that an aquifer is the sole or principal (at least 50 percent) drinking water source for the area, contamination of which would create a significant hazard to public health. Being designated a sole source area automatically creates special protections for that aquifer in connection with any activities involving federal dollars. Specifically, any project involving federal funds must be submitted to the EPA for review. If the EPA administrator determines that the project indeed poses such a risk of contamination, it must either be redesigned to the EPA's satisfaction or lose federal financing. Note that this program does not apply to projects paid for entirely by private, state, or local money, or some combination thereof.

sole source aquifer (SSA)
Designation for a water source that is the sole or principal (at least 50 percent) supplier of water to a community

ENFORCEMENT

Although public water systems are the main group regulated by the Safe Drinking Water Act, they are not the main targets of enforcement efforts. In general, PWSs strive to meet drinking water standards. When violations occur, the approach of EPA and state authorities tends to be supportive rather than adversarial.

The real targets of enforcement efforts are polluters who endanger source water. Some violations are from legitimate and productive industrial activities that simply lack adequate precautions. The most culpable violations arise from intentional acts, such as illegal dumping of hazardous wastes.

Enforcement Actions

The Safe Drinking Water Act provides the usual enforcement tools, with some extra muscle added.[18] As with other acts, the EPA (and states with approved programs) can take administrative action to impose fines, or they can initiate a judicial enforcement action. In judicial actions, as usual, the court has power to impose fines, injunctive relief, and even criminal penalties for really egregious conduct. Further, as with most environmental acts, the Safe Drinking Water Act authorizes citizen enforcement actions. Thus, for example, a community whose water supply is contaminated by an industrial polluter can file a court action seeking fines and injunctive relief to protect their water source. Unique to this act, there is one additional category of potential enforcers: a public water system may bring an enforcement action against polluters of its source water.

States with approved programs have **primacy**—that is, primary responsibility for enforcement. But the EPA still retains oversight and enforcement powers. If the EPA perceives a problem, it notifies state authorities and gives them the opportunity to address it. But if the state does not take the action that the EPA deems necessary, then the EPA can step in and take over enforcement despite the state's primacy status. Thus, the EPA plays a combined umpire/backstop role in primacy states. In nonprimacy states, the EPA handles enforcement responsibilities alone or in cooperation with state authorities.

primacy
Primary responsibility for enforcement; SDWA gives primacy to states with approved programs

Emergency Enforcement Actions

The act gives the EPA extra muscle: extensive emergency powers.[19] This EPA authority exists in all states, regardless of primacy.

What Constitutes an Emergency?   In the words of the act,[20] the EPA's emergency powers are triggered on receiving information that

- "a contaminant . . . is present in or is likely to enter a public water system or an underground source of drinking water" or

- "there is a threatened or potential terrorist attack (or other intentional act designed to disrupt the provision of safe drinking water or to impact adversely the safety of drinking water supplied to communities and individuals)," and

- such occurrence "may present an imminent and substantial endangerment to the health of persons," and

- "state and local authorities have not acted to protect the health of such persons."

Notice the precautionary nature of the statutory language *("or is likely to enter," "potential," "may present")*. Notice also that no formal finding by the administrator is required—just the receipt of information. This substantial degree of discretion entrusted to the EPA reflects the extreme concern about potentially dire consequences—*imminent and substantial endangerment*—and the need to act quickly to avert them.

EPA Emergency Powers Are Extensive　Once its emergency powers are triggered, the EPA may take such actions as it deems necessary to protect public health. This includes the power to issue orders necessary to protect the health of the affected community, including an order requiring those who caused (or contributed to) the endangerment to provide alternative water supplies. The EPA may also file a civil action asking the court to grant a restraining order or other relief. But it is the extensive authority to issue its own orders that gives the EPA real power in this context. The EPA is expected to consult with state and local authorities, but only to the extent the administrator deems "practicable in light of such imminent endangerment."

EMERGENCY ENFORCEMENT: *TRINITY AMERICAN V. EPA*

Courts are highly deferential to the EPA if its emergency orders are challenged. In a 1998 case in North Carolina, toxic chemical wastes dumped over many years were found to have migrated to an aquifer supplying drinking water wells on adjacent land, making the wells unsafe for use. The EPA used its emergency powers to order the industrial dumper, Trinity American Corp., to test water supply wells within a designated area every ninety days, and to provide safe drinking water, until the EPA was satisfied that the wells no longer contained unsafe levels of contaminants. If the EPA determined that a well could not consistently provide water meeting primary standards, then the EPA's order required Trinity to provide a permanent alternative source of safe drinking water.

When Trinity petitioned for judicial review, the federal court upheld the EPA's order. The court observed,

Congress intended to confer completely adequate authority to deal promptly and effectively with emergency situations. . . . So EPA can act promptly and effectively when a threat to public health is imminent, courts must ensure that the agency's power under the act remains relatively untrammeled.[21]

On review, a court will uphold an agency action authorized by statute unless it is *arbitrary and capricious*. Among other reasons for this deferential standard, a court is not well equipped to evaluate competing technological and scientific evidence (see discussion of judicial review in chapter 2). With respect to an emergency order, the court pointed out still another reason for deference: that having to defend its decision in court could divert the EPA's time and resources needed to address an emergency. The court found there was at least *some* rational basis for the EPA's decision, and it did not need to look further.

CONCLUSION

You can think of the SDWA as a campaign to assure the public of safe, healthful water. There are two major fronts in this struggle. The first is the removal of unsafe levels of microbial, chemical, and physical contaminants from the water delivered to our taps. The EPA with the states determine acceptable limits, and it is the job of POTWs to achieve those levels by treatment of raw source water. POTWs are not the polluters, but they are the regulated group in this part of the act.

The second major front is the protection of source waters. If source waters become too contaminated, POTW treatment might not be able to provide safe water to our taps. Source waters are vulnerable to a wide array of threats, from air pollution to leaky waste sites, and from mining activities to bioterrorism. Protecting source waters requires diligent monitoring and enforcement.

KEY TERMS

Community water systems

Consumer confidence report (CCR)

Contaminant Candidate List (CCL)

Contaminant List

Hydrofracturing (fracking)

Integrated Risk Information System (IRIS)

Maximum contaminant level (MCL)

Maximum contaminant level goal (MCLG)

Nontransient noncommunity water system

Primacy

National Primary Drinking Water Regulations (NPDWR)

Public water system (PWS)

Reference dose (RfD)

National Secondary Drinking Water Regulations

Sole source aquifer (SSA)

Source water assessment

Transient noncommunity water system

Treatment technique

Underground Injection Control Program

DISCUSSION QUESTIONS

1. This book focuses on regulatory programs, but most environmental acts also have provisions for governmental research grants tailored to promote the legislative goals. If you were Congress, what research projects would you support related to safe drinking water?

2. In your own words, explain the interplay of risk-based versus technology-based standards in the SDWA. What problem is this duality intended to solve, and does it appear to be an effective solution?

3. Imagine an outbreak in your specific community of diarrheal disease for which health authorities believe there may be transmission through tap water. Who has the authority to act and under which laws? How might this differ in different states? How might this differ if the suspected cause of the outbreak was recreational water?

NOTES

1. 42 USC § 300f—300j-26.
2. For definitions, see USC § 300f.
3. USC § 300g-8.
4. USC § 300g-1; see also http://water.epa.gov/scitech/drinkingwater/dws/ccl/basicinformation .cfm.
5. 42 USC § 300G-1(B)(1)(A).
6. The list of contaminants and their maximum limits is available at http://water.epa.gov/drink /contaminants/index.cfm.
7. USC § 300g-1.
8. *American Water Works v. EPA*, 40 F.3d 1266 (CADC 1994).

9. 40 CFR Part 141, Subpart Q.

10. The Centers for Disease Control and Prevention (CDC) gives a nice description at www.cdc .gov/healthywater/drinking/public.

11. Statistics in this section are from the EPA's "Fiscal Year 2010 Drinking Water and Groundwater Statistics," available at http://water.epa.gov/drink/standards/hascience.cfm.

12. 42 USC § 300h—300h-8.

13. See http://water.epa.gov/infrastructure/drinkingwater/sourcewater/protection/index.cfm.

14. Yoder, J. S., et al., Giardiasis surveillance—United States, 2009–2012; *Morbidity and Mortality Weekly Report 61* (SS05): 13–23, Sept 7, 2012); EPA, Giardia: Drinking Water Fact Sheet, link available at http://water.epa.gov/drink/standards/hascience.cfm.

15. 40 C.F.R. Parts 144–148; also see http://water.epa.gov/type/groundwater/uic.

16. 42 USC § 300h(d)(1). For discussion of this controversial exemption, see, for example, "The Halliburton Loophole," *New York Times*, November 2, 2009, available at http://www .nytimes.com/2009/11/03/opinion/03tue3.html; "Safety First, Fracking Second," *Scientific American*, October 19, 2011, available at www.scientificamerican.com/article.cfm?id=safety -first-fracking-second; and D. A. Hines, "The 'Halliburton Loophole': Exemption of Hydraulic Fracturing Fluids from Regulation Under the Federal Safe Drinking Water Act," March 8, 2012, available at http://energy.wilkes.edu/PDFFiles/Laws%20and%20 Regulations/Halliburton%20Loophole%20Essay%20Final.pdf.

17. 42 USC § 300h-3(e); see also § 300h-6.

18. 42 USC § 300h-2.

19. 42 USC § 300i.

20. 42 USC § 300i-1.

21. *Trinity American Corporation v. United States Environmental Protection Agency*, 150 F.3d 389 (CA4, 1998).

Chapter 6

Comprehensive Environmental Response, Compensation, and Liability Act (CERCLA or "Superfund Act")

Key Concepts

- Cleaning up hazardous wastes that harm health and the environment—whether the wastes are newly released or historical. Remedies are selected based on risk.

- Paying for cleanups. Broad, no-fault liability for "potentially responsible parties," with the Superfund as a backup.

- Emphasis on informing and involving the public.

In the 1890s, William T. Love set out to build a model community near Niagara Falls, New York. His vision included a canal intended to provide hydraulic power. By 1910, when the dream failed, Love Canal was just a partial ditch. From the 1920s until after World War II, the ditch was used as a dumpsite for wastes, including over twenty thousand tons of hazardous chemicals.

Much of that came from Hooker Chemical Company, which took over in the 1940s. Hooker was not a fly-by-night dumper. It took protective measures that were standard at the time, including draining the canal, lining it with a thick layer of clay, and placing the wastes in barrels. In the early 1950s, Hooker covered the wastes with twenty feet of soil and warned that the site should be sealed off to protect against contact with people or animals. But the City of Niagara Falls wanted the land and pressured Hooker to hand it over. Within a few years, it became a neighborhood of a hundred homes and two schools.

As early as the 1960s, there were instances of escaping chemical wastes. The big disaster came in 1978, triggered by a record rainfall. Barrels rose to the surface of the saturated ground. There were puddles of leaked chemicals in the streets, schoolyards, and basements of homes. High rates of disease were reported by residents, including cancers and birth defects. The area was evacuated, but too late to prevent significant exposure to toxic chemicals.

Bad as it was, Love Canal was just the tip of the iceberg. Officials estimated there were hundreds, if not thousands, of old dumpsites bad enough to endanger public health. One contemporary article called these old dumpsites "time bombs with burning fuses—their contents slowly leaching out. And the next victim could be a water supply."[1]

Congress needed to respond quickly with federal legislation that could deal both with these old dumpsites and with new spills of toxic chemicals—estimated at over three thousand per year. There were three big questions. For the questions of how to "fix" the damage, and how to pay for it, Congress responded with the Comprehensive Environmental Response, Compensation, and Liability Act (CERCLA), enacted in 1980.[2] The third big question—how to prevent future contamination of the environment by improper disposal of hazardous wastes—is addressed in the Resource Conservation and Recovery Act (see chapter 7).

OVERVIEW AND DEFINITIONS

CERCLA has two focuses: responding to spills and other releases, and allocating liability for the costs of a response. Basically, the act provides for federal control of the response and private liability for the costs.

One important feature of CERCLA is the Superfund, created to ensure that funds were available for immediate, effective governmental response to emergencies. The Superfund can be used to finance governmental response actions, subject to reimbursement from responsible parties.

CERCLA deals with the release or threatened release of hazardous substances from a vessel or facility into the environment. Those terms, as used in CERCLA, need some explaining.[3]

What's a Hazardous Substance?

The term **hazardous substance**, for purposes of CERCLA, is very broad. The definition incorporates by reference the lists of substances regulated under several other federal environmental acts, such as the Clean Air Act and Clean Water Act. In addition, the EPA can add any substance that "may present substantial danger" if released into the environment. The EPA has designated about two thousand hazardous substances under this authority. In addition, here are some general concepts:

hazardous substance
Definition varies from act to act, with much overlap. Generally defined by toxicity and other characteristics

- *Mixtures*: If a hazardous substance is mixed with a nonhazardous substance, the entire mixture becomes a hazardous substance. For example, if a hazardous substance is spilled on the ground and migrates through the soil, all of the contaminated soil is deemed to be a hazardous substance. This also means that you can't avoid hazardous waste rules just by diluting the waste.

- *Not just waste*: The contents of a hazardous waste disposal facility are an obvious example of hazardous substances. But CERCLA is not limited to the release of hazardous *wastes*. It encompasses the release of any hazardous substance, including commercially useful chemicals—for example, if a tank truck overturns and spills toxic chemicals. Once released, though, even useful chemicals become waste, and the release site is referred to as a hazardous waste site.

- *Petroleum exception*: In short, CERCLA's definition of "hazardous substance" encompasses almost anything you might think of, but with one major exception. Petroleum and natural gas are generally excluded (with limited exceptions). Petroleum is addressed by the Oil Pollution Act and the Resource Conservation and Recovery Act.

What's a Release?

Almost any time a hazardous substance is freed from its normal container into the environment is deemed a *release* under CERCLA. The statutory definition includes "any spilling, leaking, pumping, pouring, emitting, emptying, discharging, injecting, escaping, leaching, dumping or disposing into the environment." In fact, the definition is so broad that the hazardous substance does not even have to escape from its container. The term "release" includes "the abandonment or discarding of barrels, containers, and other closed receptacles containing any hazardous substance or pollutant or contaminant."[4]

A release can be instantaneous, such as from an explosion at a chemical factory or from a tank truck overturning. Or it can be a slow drip from a cracked pipe. It can be invisible—such as a leak from an underground storage tank. It can be accidental, such as a spill of valuable chemicals. Or it can be intentional, such as "midnight dumping" of hazardous wastes by somebody knowingly breaking the law.

Volume Is Not a Criterion A release in any quantity is still a release. Volume is relevant only to reporting requirements (discussed later in this chapter), not to the definition of a release.

Age Is Not a Criterion CERCLA is not limited to recent releases. A release might have happened long ago, even before CERCLA existed. Nonetheless, if there is hazardous substance contamination, it falls under CERCLA jurisdiction. Both the cleanup requirements and liability provisions apply, even if the release was legal at the time it first occurred. In that sense, there is no statute of limitations for CERCLA.

Threatened Release

The *threat* of release is not defined in the act, but courts give the term its commonsense meaning. Typically, if there is a hazardous substance at a facility, which the owners-operators have shown themselves unwilling or incompetent to control, that will be deemed a threatened release so as to justify EPA's exercise of its CERCLA powers. An example would be the storage of toxic wastes in an improper container, such as a corroded tank.

What Is Not a Release?

Like most statutory provisions, there are exceptions and exclusions, often because they are covered by other statutes. For example, CERCLA does not apply to motor vehicle exhaust, nuclear material from a nuclear incident, a workplace release that does not migrate beyond the workplace, the normal application of fertilizer, or the application of registered pesticides.

From a Vessel or Facility

CERCLA applies to any release or threatened release *from a vessel or facility*. A vessel includes watercraft and virtually any makeshift contrivance that will transport something on water. (The rest of this chapter will use the word "facility" to broadly include vessels as well.)

The word "facility" is broadly defined to include almost every source imaginable. It encompasses not just buildings and other structures, but also pipes, storage containers, equipment, ditches, motor vehicles, airplanes, and much more. Lest there be any doubt of its intended breadth, the statutory definition ends with a catch-all: "any site or area where a hazardous substance has been deposited, stored, disposed of, or placed, or otherwise come to be located." The only potential sources of a release not included are consumer products in consumer use.

Into the Environment

For CERCLA to apply, the release or threatened release must be "into the environment." This is broadly defined to include surface waters, groundwater, the drinking water supply, soil (surface and substrata), and the ambient air.

REPORTING RELEASES OF HAZARDOUS SUBSTANCES

Whether a release is new or has lain undiscovered for years, the authorities cannot react until they know about it. Hence, reporting of releases is an important function addressed by the act.

Mandatory Reporting by Facility

Anyone in charge of a facility (or vessel) involved in a release must report to the National Response Center (NRC) as soon as a release occurs or is discovered.[5] The

reportable quantity
Under CERCLA, the threshold amount that triggers the duty to report a release

releaser's obligation to report is triggered only if the release is a **reportable quantity**. How much is a reportable quantity? It varies, depending on the type of hazardous substance involved, and sometimes depending on the medium into which it is released (land, water, and so forth).

The act imposes stiff civil and criminal penalties for failure to report, including up to three years in prison for a first offense.

Discovery by Others

Many releases are discovered by someone other than the releaser, often years or decades after the initial event. For example, federal, state, or local authorities may discover a release in the course of a governmental inspection. As a direct result of CERCLA liability provisions, investigations by expert consultants are becoming more routine in connection with property sales or development. These investigations are specifically looking for evidence of hazardous substance releases.

RESPONDING TO A RELEASE OF HAZARDOUS SUBSTANCES

National Response Center (NRC)
A clearinghouse for reports of pollution events under multiple environmental laws

Reports of all releases go to the **National Response Center (NRC)**. The NRC serves as the clearinghouse for reports of pollution events under multiple environmental laws. CERCLA applies to both new and old releases. New releases should be reported as soon as they occur. Past releases should be reported as soon as discovered.

When a release is reported, the EPA or another federal agency is appointed as lead agency. State and local participation is handled through standing emergency response committees established under the Emergency Planning and Community Right-to-Know Act. The lead agency may conduct the response, or the affected state if it has the capability. Alternatively, a responsible party may do so, usually with persuasion or compulsion from the EPA.

A framework for responding to releases is provided by the National Contingency Plan (NCP), [6] which applies both under CERCLA and the Oil Pollution Act (OPA) (see text box on National Contingency Plan in chapter 8).

Assessment and Ranking

The magnitude, severity, and urgency of the release are key to determining what response measures to take. Typically, there is a rapid initial assessment to determine if there is immediate danger to health or the environment that requires emergency response measures. Subsequently, there may be more thorough inspections and assessments, depending on the circumstances.

Hazard Ranking System   One important assessment tool is the **Hazard Ranking System (HRS)**.[7] EPA assigns scores to hazardous waste sites, based on several factors. The scoring helps in comparing different release sites and deciding which need the greatest attention. Some of the key criteria are

Hazard Ranking System (HRS)
Scoring system for hazardous waste sites, which helps focus responses where most needed

- How toxic is the substance?

- How much was released?

- What is the size of the population potentially exposed?

- Could the release contaminate drinking water or otherwise endanger public health?

National Priorities List (NPL)
A list of the hazardous waste sites posing the greatest danger to human health or the environment, and therefore priority cleanup sites

National Priorities List (NPL)   The **National Priorities List**[8] is a list of the worst hazardous waste sites, in terms of danger to human health and the environment. These sites get the most thorough investigation and response. Most sites on the National

Priorities List are there because they got a high score on the EPA's Hazard Ranking System. Some sites get listed even without a high score; for example, each state can designate its own worst site.

The EPA's decision to add a site to the NPL is a formal agency action subject to public notice and comment requirements. The decision is also subject to judicial review, although court challenges are usually unsuccessful. The people likely to resist listing are the property owners and other responsible parties, because listing requires a more intensive and costly cleanup and affects property values. On the other hand, state and local authorities may support listing because it can give access to Superfund financing (the Superfund is discussed later in this chapter).

Remedial Investigation and Feasibility Study (RI/FS)   Hazardous waste sites are subject to various assessments at various times, and with varying goals, depending on the needs of the situation. The **Remedial Investigation and Feasibility Study (RI/FS)**[9] is the most rigorous type of assessment, and it typically costs $1 million or more. It is conducted for sites that, based on preliminary assessments, merit long-term remediation action. In its remedial investigation (RI), the EPA determines the acceptable long-term exposure levels—essentially, how clean the site needs to be—based on how dangerous the substance is and what populations or resources are exposed. The feasibility study (FS) evaluates various response actions to see which could achieve the level of "cleanness" dictated by the RI. The feasibility study doesn't select a specific remedy, but essentially identifies and evaluates candidates according to the so-called Nine Criteria for remedy selection, described in the following section.

Remedial Investigation and Feasibility Study (RI/FS)
Under CERCLA, steps in determining the appropriate response plan for a hazardous waste site

removal action
Under CERCLA, a limited and typically temporary response, intended to quickly protect against acute danger from a hazardous release

remediation
Under CERCLA, a long-term and relatively thorough cleanup of a hazardous waste site

Response Actions: Removal or Remediation

The term "response" generally connotes containment, cleaning up, and restoring a site to a more or less "safe" condition. There are two alternative types of response, referred to in the act as a **removal action** and **remediation** actions.[10] These two approaches are not mutually exclusive, in that it's possible to have removal followed by remediation (but not the reverse).

Removal   Essentially, removal is a short-term response intended to quickly protect against acute danger from a release or threatened release, but not intended to provide permanent solutions. The name "removal" is unhelpful. It would be more descriptive to call it a temporary or "limited emergency" action. Circumstances that might trigger a removal action include immediate endangerment of humans, risk to drinking water supplies, bad weather that threatens to worsen the release, and threat of fire or explosion.

Because of the need for speed, the EPA itself often conducts removal actions. An agency-conducted removal is paid for by the Superfund (subject to later reimbursement by the responsible parties). A removal action financed by the Superfund is normally limited to one year and maximum $2 million in expenditure.

Remediation   The second type of response, remediation, is a long-term, more thorough, and more expensive cleanup approach. Its goal is to permanently eliminate or neutralize the hazard. It might cost a few million dollars, or tens of millions or more; there is no upper limit. Remediation may occur instead of or in addition to removal actions, depending on the circumstances.

Unlike removal actions, there is no uniform limit on the cost and duration of EPA-conducted remediation actions. There are, however, other restrictions. The EPA cannot undertake remedial action (using Superfund money) unless the site is listed on the National Priorities List. Further, the EPA cannot undertake remediation without the involvement of the state where the release site is located. This includes a commitment by the state to pay 10 percent of the remediation costs, and further to assure maintenance of the site after remediation is completed.

What Response Measures Are Available?

There are many possible response measures,[11] and the EPA selects one or more to fit the needs of a particular site. The array of response measures includes:

- Fencing the site or posting signs to limit access

- Capping contaminated soil with a clay cover to reduce migration of contaminants

- Drainage controls to reduce migration due to precipitation (such as storm runoff) flowing onto or away from the site

- Excavation and removal of highly contaminated soil

- Removing tanks or other containers that are leaking or pose a threat of release

- Applying chemicals to slow a release or mitigate its effects

- Onsite treatment or incineration

- Providing alternative water supplies

- Evacuating residents

Most of these methods might be utilized in either removal or remediation actions. Actions that permanently eliminate or reduce the danger are preferred. Methods such as on-site treatment and incineration are preferred over excavation, which simply moves the contamination problem somewhere else.

Developing a Response Plan: The Nine Criteria

Nine Criteria

Under CERCLA, the criteria considered in selecting remediation measures for a hazardous waste site

In remediation actions (and to the extent time permits in removal actions), the EPA selects response measures tailored to site-specific circumstances and designs a response plan. The plan is based on the analysis in the RI/FS (particularly the feasibility study), and is memorialized in a Record of Decision (ROD). The factors that EPA considers in reaching its decision are called the **Nine Criteria**.[12] The criteria are divided into three groups: required, balancing, and to be considered.

Required Factors   To be selected, remediation measures must meet two threshold criteria:

1. *Protectiveness*: Under the law, a remediation remedy must be sufficiently protective so that exposure to the finished site does not cause adverse health effects even to sensitive individuals. The EPA performs a complex risk assessment to determine acceptable numeric exposure levels that can be tolerated at the site after cleanup.

2. *ARARs*: This is an acronym that stands for any legally *applicable or relevant and appropriate requirement* under other federal laws or laws of the state where the site is located (if more stringent). For example, if the Clean Water Act has a standard applicable to the substance released, that would be an ARAR. A remedy must meet all ARARs.

Balancing Factors   When there are multiple remedies that satisfy both the protectiveness and ARARs criteria, the EPA will balance five additional factors in making its selections:

3. Will the remedy be *permanent* or at least *effective in the long term?*

4. How much will it *reduce volume, toxicity, and mobility* of the contaminants? (On-site treatment and incineration, for example, are preferred over simply excavating the contaminated soil and moving it someplace else.)

5. *Short-term* effectiveness. This includes potential risks and impacts on the community, cleanup workers, and the environment during implementation, and how long implementation will take.

6. How easy or difficult will it be to *implement?*

7. Is it *cost-effective?* In addition to the cost of remediation measures, the agency must consider ongoing costs of operating and maintaining the site.

Other Factors to Be Considered   CERCLA promotes public involvement, and so two additional factors will be considered:

8. *State acceptance* of the remedy

9. *Community acceptance* of the remedy

Community Involvement   People have an urgent desire to be informed and to be heard when their community is threatened by a hazardous release. The regulations make a serious effort to promote transparency and public participation, as reflected in the last two of the nine criteria. The state's and community's views must be sought and considered—though they are not as important as the required and balancing factors. How much communication is practicable depends on the circumstances. At a minimum, the lead agency is required to immediately notify affected individuals, state and local officials, and (if appropriate) civil defense and emergency management agencies, giving them information about the release and the agency's response actions.

The degree of public participation necessarily varies depending on the urgency of government action. Where time permits, the agency must actively solicit public input through interviews of local officials, residents, public interest groups, and others. Before a long-term remediation plan can be adopted, the agency must give public notice and the opportunity to submit written comments. In addition, the agency must hold a public meeting in the affected area, so that neighbors and other interested parties can have their say.[13] The EPA takes stakeholder involvement seriously and promotes community engagement even more broadly than mandated by the act.

AGENCY FOR TOXIC SUBSTANCES AND DISEASE REGISTRY

Agency for Toxic Substances and Disease Registry (ATSDR)
A federal agency within the Public Health Service whose responsibilities include the health component of CERCLA

Congress, in CERCLA, created a new public health agency to study, evaluate, and advise on health aspects of hazardous waste sites. This is the **Agency for Toxic Substances and Disease Registry (ATSDR)**. On the federal organization chart, ATSDR is within the Public Health Service, which is part of the US Department of Health and Human Services (HHS). ATSDR has a variety of tasks under CERCLA, working in cooperation with the EPA, the Centers for Disease Control and Prevention (CDC), which is also part of HHS, and other federal agencies, as well as state and local officials. ATSDR has many joint functions with the CDC Center for Environmental Health, including being headed by the same individuals.

CERCLA also gives two specific functions to the National Institute of Environmental Health Sciences (NIEHS): training of workers involved in hazardous waste, and developing research centers to advance understanding of the potential risks of agents.

Evaluating Sites and Hazardous Substances

National Toxicology Program (NTP)
An interagency program, headed by NIEHS, whose mission is to evaluate agents of public health concern

ATSDR works with the EPA, the National Toxicology Program, and other agencies to evaluate hazardous waste sites, the substances located at those sites, and the threats they pose to public health. The **National Toxicology Program (NTP)** is an interagency program, headed by NIEHS, whose mission is to evaluate agents of public health concern, using its expertise in toxicology and molecular biology. ATSDR conducts periodic screening and survey programs for the purpose of determining relationships between exposure to toxic substances and illness. It evaluates hazardous substances based on the information thus developed and other scientific evidence.[14]

Substance Priority List   Together, ATSDR and EPA evaluate the hazardous substances most commonly found at sites on the National Priorities List (NPL), and determine which are posing the most significant potential threat to human health, based on a combination of their frequency, toxicity, and potential for human exposure at NPL sites. CERCLA directs the two agencies to maintain a prioritized list of at least a hundred of these worst-threat substances, to be reviewed and revised at least annually. This list is referred to as the **Substance Priority List (SPL)**. As of 2011, it ranked 275 substances, with arsenic, lead, and mercury at the top of the list.[15]

Substance Priority List (SPL)
A list of substances at National Priorities List sites posing the greatest risk to health

TOXICOLOGICAL PROFILES

Toxicological profiles are useful descriptions of the potential health effects of environmental agents. Each profile is prefaced by an overview of the findings in language suitable for use by community members. Each profile also contains a compendium of the various state and federal environmental and workplace standards set for the agent of concern. ATSDR maintains a toxic substances portal with links to each toxicological profile: www.atsdr.cdc.gov/toxprofiles/index.asp.

Toxicological Profiles   ATSDR established and maintains the **National Disease Registry**—a registry of serious diseases and illnesses—as well as a registry of persons exposed to toxic substances. Based on peer-reviewed scientific research and its own registries and investigations, ATSDR prepares a **toxicological profile** for each substance on the Substance Priority List. As part of this process, ATSDR, in consultation with EPA, evaluates whether existing information is adequate, and what additional toxicological testing might be needed for any of the substances. The specific concern is to identify the health effects associated with each substance, and the type and level of exposure that may present significant

National Disease Registry
A registry of serious diseases and illnesses maintained by ATSDR

toxicological profile
An evaluation and compilation of information by ATSDR on each hazardous substance on the Substance Priority List

risk of adverse health effects. Where there are gaps, CERCLA directs ATSDR to ensure that an appropriate research program is initiated, in cooperation with the National Toxicology Program. CERCLA provides that the cost of such research be borne by the manufacturers and processors of the hazardous substance in question.[16]

Public Health Assessments of NPL Sites   ATSDR performs a *public health assessment* of each hazardous waste site listed on the National Priorities List (NPL), and some sites not yet on the list. ATSDR starts by reviewing the toxic substances at a site and site-related environmental data, such as the presence of ground or surface water. The assessor estimates the dose of a substance to which people in the community might be exposed, and also factors in reports of actual exposures. Further, the assessor evaluates cases of disease in the community that might be related to exposure. The purpose of the assessment is to evaluate whether exposures to substances at the site may be at harmful levels, and therefore whether action is needed to reduce exposure levels. If an assessment shows significant risk to human health, CERCLA directs the executive branch to use its public health authority to eliminate or reduce exposure as needed, including steps such as provision of alternative water supplies or relocation of residents. ATSDR works with and shares information with the affected state and community, as well as the EPA. The EPA uses these assessments in determining whether to add a site to the NPL, and in prioritizing responses.[17]

Community Outreach

Part of ATSDR's mission is to provide medical care and testing to individuals exposed to toxic substances in a public health emergency. In such emergencies, exposed individuals are eligible for admission to Public Health Service hospitals and other services.

Regardless of whether there is an emergency, state and local officials can consult with ATSDR on health issues relating to exposure to hazardous substances. Consultations to individuals may be provided by states in cooperation with ATSDR.

THE SUPERFUND

Congress created the Superfund in the effort to enable a sure and swift response to releases that endanger health and the environment.

What Is the Superfund?

The **Superfund** is a trust fund created primarily to support EPA in the exercise of its powers under CERCLA. Superfund monies can be used for several purposes, summarized below. Most notably, it provides bridge funding for cleanup projects, subject to later reimbursement from those designated *responsible parties* under CERCLA's liability provisions. Further, it covers **orphan sites (shares)**, which no one is available or able to pay for.

Superfund
A trust fund the EPA can use as bridge funding for cleanups under CERCLA. The term is also used to refer to CERCLA as a whole

orphan sites (shares)
Orphan sites (shares); under CERCLA, hazardous waste sites for which no legally responsible party is available or able to pay cleanup costs

What Can the Superfund Be Used For?

The fund can be used for the following purposes:[18]

- *Government-conducted response actions, under certain conditions*: If the site is urgent enough to justify removal action, the EPA can use the Superfund. But there is a limit of $2 million for removal activities. The EPA can also use the Superfund to finance governmental remediation actions, but only if the site is severe enough to be listed on the National Priorities List. There is no statutory dollar limit on the use of Superfund monies for remediation of an NPL site.

- *Reimbursement to third parties for response expenses*: Someone who participates in appropriate response activities approved by the EPA can be reimbursed from the Superfund. However, anyone designated a responsible party under CERCLA's liability provisions is not entitled to Superfund reimbursement (but can seek contribution from other responsible parties—see the following).

- *Damage to natural resources*: In addition to cleanup costs, another cost of spills is the damage they cause to natural resources. If the damaged resources are owned by government (federal or state) or by an Indian tribe, the Superfund can be used to compensate them. But the Superfund is a backup to be used only if it is impossible to recover from the responsible party—for example, if the responsible company has gone out of business or is bankrupt. Superfund compensation is not available for damage to private property (but a private owner can file a tort lawsuit seeking compensation).

- *Enforcement costs*: The EPA uses the Superfund to finance actions to hold responsible parties liable for costs. In cases where the government does not itself undertake the response, enforcement includes persuading or compelling responsible parties to do so.

Where Does the Superfund's Money Come From?

Superfund tax
A tax (no longer in effect at the time of this writing) on oil and chemical companies that was originally the source of some funding for the Superfund

Originally, the Superfund was funded primarily by a feedstock tax on oil and chemical companies, commonly called the **Superfund tax**. The idea was that companies reaping the profits from these products should help pay for the messes their products sometimes make.

The Superfund tax expired at the end of 1995 under a *sunset* provision. This means that Congress put an expiration date on the original law, so that it would automatically lapse unless renewed by Congress. Although legislation to renew the Superfund tax has been proposed regularly in Congress, it has never passed.

Until and unless the Superfund tax is reenacted, there are only two sources of income to the Superfund. First, when the EPA collects reimbursement from responsible parties for response costs, that money goes back into the Superfund. These collections fall far short of need. So most of the money now going into the Superfund comes from the second source: general tax revenues. This means the burden of paying for government-conducted cleanups falls on all of us as taxpayers rather than on the oil and chemical industries. Moreover, the amount of funding authorized by Congress has decreased. As a result, response actions are perceived to be slower and less thorough than before December 1995.

LIABILITY

The liability provisions are a major part of CERCLA.[19] Congress's policy is that the financial consequences of a release or threat of release fall on the parties responsible for it, rather than on society as a whole. Sometimes the results are harsh and seem unfair, especially when someone whose responsibility is relatively small bears all or most of the cost.

Liability for What?

CERCLA imposes liability on potentially responsible parties for the cost of response and for damage to natural resources.

Response Costs   When the government conducts and pays for response actions (from the Superfund), EPA can sue a potentially responsible party to recover reimbursement. This is called a **recovery action**. That money goes back into the Superfund. When a state or (innocent) private party participates in approved response activities, CERCLA gives them the same right to seek reimbursement from a responsible party.

CERCLA also gives EPA authority to issue an **abatement order**.[20] This refers to an order to a potentially responsible party to undertake a response action if it may be necessary to abate imminent endangerment to public health or the environment. EPA can also go to court for a judicial abatement order, but the authority to issue an administrative order is a more powerful enforcement tool. If a responsible party doesn't comply, EPA can impose stiff administrative penalties—up to $25,000 per day. Although the responsible party can challenge the administrative order in court, it cannot do so immediately. CERCLA does not allow for judicial review until EPA decides to file an enforcement or recovery action in court. By then, the responsible party could have racked up a huge amount in fines. Further, if the responsible party loses its challenge, it is liable for up to treble damages. Thus, even if the targeted party believes it has a valid defense, there is a strong incentive to agree to a settlement with the EPA.

recovery action
Under CERCLA, an action against responsible parties to recover response costs advanced from the Superfund

abatement order
Under CERCLA, an order to a responsible party to undertake response action

Damage to Natural Resources   The federal government, a state, or an Indian tribe is entitled under CERCLA to payment from a potentially responsible party for contamination or loss of natural resources. The money recovered is to be used for restoration or for the purchase of replacement resources.

If the government or tribe collects compensation to replace or restore a natural resource, it cannot also collect for cleanup of the same natural resource. In other words, CERCLA does not allow double recovery for the same harm.

Potentially Responsible Parties

potentially responsible parties
The universal term for parties liable under CERCLA for response costs and other harm from hazardous releases

The parties liable under CERCLA for response costs and other harm are universally referred to as **potentially responsible parties** or PRPs. It comes as a shock to some people that, to be held responsible, a party need not have actively participated in the disposal or release of the hazardous substance. The general idea is that each category targeted by CERCLA as potentially responsible parties had some control over the hazardous substance at some time, and therefore could have averted the release or at least minimized the harm. There are four categories of PRPs: owners and operators; former owners and operators; arrangers; and transporters.

Current Owners and Operators   The current owners and operators of the facility or vessel are liable, *even if the contamination was there before they acquired ownership or control.* To appreciate the impact, remember that the term *facility* includes any site where a hazardous substance has come to be located. This means you don't have to own or operate a dirty industrial plant to be a responsible party. You could be an ordinary person who buys property where a dirty industrial plant operated fifty years ago and left contamination behind.

The law recognizes a defense for an "innocent purchaser," meaning an owner who did not know or have reason to know of some key fact when the property was acquired. But that defense is limited in the context of hazardous waste sites. To be "innocent" under CERCLA, owners must prove they were unaware of the contamination at the time of acquisition, *despite conducting "all appropriate inquiries" into the previous ownership and uses of the property consistent with good commercial or customary practice*, commonly called due diligence.[21] As a result, hiring an environmental consulting firm to do a due diligence investigation prior to purchase has become standard practice, and banks will not lend without it. But owners who acquired their property before due diligence investigations became customary are not "grandfathered," even if they purchased before CERCLA was enacted. Absent due diligence, a property owner is not protected by this defense, no matter how long ago the property was purchased.

The innocent purchaser defense, however, protects even without due diligence in limited circumstances. For example, an individual who inherited the property can claim the defense. So can a bank that acquired the property through foreclosure on a mortgage (and had no other participation). Beyond that, there are some limited exceptions for federal, state, and local governments.

Former Owners and Operators

Anyone who owned or operated a facility *at the time of the disposal* is a PRP. Courts are split on what this means, due to differing interpretations of the word "disposal." Some courts say that any continued *migration* of contaminants through the soil or groundwater constitutes disposal. Other courts limit disposal to the *introduction* of contaminants at a site. But even this more lenient interpretation can be harsher than appears at first sight. For example, if a long-abandoned underground storage tank is slowly leaking contaminants into the soil, the movement from tank to soil would qualify as the introduction of contaminants at the site.

Arrangers of Disposal or Transport

An arranger is anyone who, by contract or otherwise, helps arrange for the transport or disposal of hazardous substances.

A generator of hazardous wastes—for example, a manufacturing company that generates hazardous wastes as a byproduct of its manufacturing processes—is an arranger. So are brokers who arrange for sale or disposal of hazardous substances.

Arrangers are PRPs under CERCLA. Even if they scrupulously comply with all rules governing transport and disposal of hazardous substances, arrangers are still liable if the hazardous substances go astray—for example, if there is a leak from a hazardous waste disposal facility. If the disposal facility is licensed and reputable, the arranger is still liable. If the leak doesn't occur until twenty years later, the arranger is still liable. In fact, the leak doesn't even have to involve the particular waste the arranger dealt with. If any hazardous substance escapes a disposal site, then all arrangers who contributed to the site are liable. Otherwise, EPA might be unable to hold any arranger liable, as there is no "fingerprint" to say whose waste leaked.

Transporters

A transporter is anyone who accepts hazardous substances for transport to a disposal or treatment facility. Generally, this means commercial waste haulers. If a contaminant is released while in custody of the transporter, the transporter is a PRP. If a contaminant goes astray after reaching its destination, a transporter is not routinely liable. But if the transporter recommended or in any way helped select the treatment or disposal facility, then the transporter is a PRP.

Liability Is Broad

CERCLA gives the EPA heavy weapons for enforcing liability against PRPs in court. The act imposes strict liability. Moreover, a PRP who had paid once may find the issue of liability reopened. Liability can be "retroactive" in the common meaning (if not the legal meaning) of that word. Finally, liability is joint and several.

Strict Liability   This means that a responsible party is liable regardless of fault. It doesn't matter—and the EPA therefore does not have to prove—that the defendant actively participated in the discharge, or that the defendant was negligent or otherwise culpable. The EPA does not even need to show that any action of the defendant "caused" the release. To trigger liability under CERCLA, the only requirements are (1) a release or threatened release of hazardous substance from a facility that (2) caused the EPA (or other plaintiff) to incur response costs, and (3) the defendant fits CERCLA's broad definition of potentially responsible party.

Reopening Liability   A PRP might spend millions of dollars to clean a site to EPA specifications, but that does not guarantee freedom from future liability.

reopener
Refers to CERCLA provision for reopening a settled case and imposing further liability if future circumstances necessitate further cleanup of a hazardous waste site

There are inherent uncertainties about the long-term effectiveness of remediation measures. Settlements with EPA have a **reopener** provision, allowing EPA to impose further liability if information comes to light indicating that additional cleanup is needed to protect the public.[22] This could occur, for example, if containment measures once judged effective have started to fail, or if new scientific studies show that residual contamination once thought acceptable in fact poses a significant health risk.

"Retroactive" Liability   PRPs are liable for response costs regardless of when the release occurred. Even if the release predated the enactment of CERCLA, they are still liable. Courts have held that CERCLA is not retroactive in a legal sense, because it deals with the *present* effects of past actions.

Joint and Several Liability   For many hazardous waste sites, there are multiple PRPs. This is especially true when there is leaking from a hazardous waste disposal facility, where hundreds of companies may have disposed of waste. At multi-party sites, CERCLA imposes **joint and several liability** on all responsible parties. This means that EPA (or other plaintiff) can collect 100 percent of the liability from any PRP (who can then seek contributions from other PRPs).

This concept of joint and several liability applies commonly in all kinds of lawsuits where there are multiple defendants. Although it might seem unfair to the defendant, a different rule would place a heavy burden on plaintiffs. In order to collect the full amount, a plaintiff would have to chase down all defendants, some of whom might be insolvent. Further, it might be difficult or impossible for the plaintiff to prove what percentage each defendant should pay. As between an innocent plaintiff and a responsible defendant, the law places the burden of unfairness on the defendant.

In practice, courts and mediators frequently do *not* impose liability jointly and severally in recovery actions by the EPA. But the prospect of joint and several liability gives the EPA a powerful tool to get PRPs to cooperate. Many cases are settled rather than going to trial. In a settlement, one of the things PRPs can negotiate is how they will share liability amongst themselves.

joint and several liability
A legal rule that allows a plaintiff to collect 100 percent of the liability from any one of multiple defendants

What If a Potentially Responsible Party Pays More Than Its Fair Share?

A PRP who has been compelled to pay more than its share can file a lawsuit against other PRPs for **contribution** (partial reimbursement).[23] However, any PRP who has previously reached a settlement with EPA is shielded from liability for contribution. Thus, being the lone holdout when other PRPs are settling is a risky strategy for a PRP.

The court is not required to allocate CERCLA liability equally among the PRPs. The court will consider fairness and mitigating factors in apportioning liability, including:

contribution
Partial reimbursement paid by one defendant to another defendant who, under the principle of joint and several liability, has paid more than its share of a judgment

- Volume contributed by each
- Relative degree of toxicity
- Extent of involvement
- Exercise of care
- Cooperation with government officials

Contribution from other responsible parties is the only recourse for a defendant who overpays. A responsible party cannot be reimbursed from the Superfund for overpayments.

Orphan Share

What if some responsible parties are bankrupt, defunct, or just cannot be identified? This is a common problem, especially when hundreds of companies contributed wastes to a hazardous waste disposal facility. The share attributable to an unavailable responsible party is called an orphan site (or share).

Because responsible parties are jointly and severally liable for 100 percent of costs, the remaining responsible parties are stuck with liability for any orphan shares if the case goes to trial. This provides an incentive for responsible parties to cooperate with the EPA, find other PRPs, and reach a settlement rather than go to trial. As part of a settlement, the EPA can carve out the orphan share, so the settling parties don't have to foot that part of the bill. If all the responsible parties settle, the EPA has authority to pay the orphan share from the Superfund. If one of the responsible parties refuses to settle, and then loses in court, it will be liable for all costs not collected in the settlement, including the entire orphan share.

BROWNFIELDS

Picture an ugly, abandoned factory, surrounded by weeds and chain-link fence, windows broken, a bane to the neighborhood. This is probably a brownfield—an unanticipated and undesirable side effect of CERCLA.

brownfields
Contaminated sites from past industrial activity that nobody will buy due to cleanup liability, that have therefore been left idle and unproductive

Brownfields are sites that are contaminated from past industrial or commercial activities. Commonly, the state has taken ownership for nonpayment of property taxes. The sites sit idle because potential purchasers and redevelopers are afraid of getting snared into CERCLA liability. Instead, those companies build new facilities in new areas, which often means using up desirable "greenfields" for industrial purposes.

Besides being eyesores, brownfields create lots of other problems for the local community. They can shelter drug dealing and other criminal activity. They lower property values. Because they are unproductive, they do not contribute to the community's tax base. Further, because they don't get cleaned up, they are a continuing source of potential hazardous exposure.

Congress and the EPA, as well as states, have made some efforts to address this problem. In part this involves steps to ameliorate potential liability and thus promote cleanup and redevelopment of brownfields. In addition, there is a grant program to support remediation in communities without other means to pay. Remediation grants normally may not exceed $1 million, and they may be awarded to state and local governmental bodies, Indian tribes or Alaska Native corporations.[24]

But progress is slow. There are estimated to be four hundred thousand brownfields in the country, which could cost over $600 *billion* to clean up. In general, the sites are small individually, but collectively they are a huge problem.

CONCLUSION

CERCLA has made considerable progress in cleaning up hazardous waste sites. However, the task remains far from complete, due in part to Congress's discontinuation of the Superfund tax, and its reduction of funds available to EPA for this purpose. Particularly challenging are the legacy of brownfields, which often are located in inner cities or other disadvantaged communities, and for which appropriate redevelopment should be a high priority.

In the authors' view, one of the ways CERCLA has been most effective involves prevention rather than treatment. Many companies handle hazardous substances with greater care now—sometimes going beyond what is required by various environmental laws—because they know a release will subject them to CERCLA's broad liability rules.

CERCLA's emphasis on prioritizing sites and selecting remedies based on risk—that is, cleaning up the more hazardous sites first—has been successful. Further, this strategy has spurred innovative approaches to risk assessment, which is a benefit in implementing many environmental acts.

KEY TERMS

Abatement order	Orphan sites (shares)
Agency for Toxic Substances and Disease Registry (ATSDR)	Potentially responsible parties
	Recovery action
Brownfields	Remedial Investigation and Feasibility Study (RI/FS)
Contribution	
Hazard Ranking System	Remediation
Hazardous substance	Removal action
Joint and several liability	Reopener
National Disease Registry	Reportable quantity
National Priorities List	Substance Priority List (SPL)
National Response Center (NRC)	Superfund
National Toxicology Program (NTP)	Superfund tax
Nine Criteria	Toxicological profile

DISCUSSION QUESTIONS

1. Are there any brownfields or other hazardous waste sites in your community? What impacts do they have on a community? Should government (at any level) help disadvantaged communities in dealing with these sites? Why and how?

2. Hypothetical scenario: Joe's Truck Stop was a large gas station owned and operated for many years by Joe Small as a franchisee of a major oil company. Twenty years ago a new highway was built that diverted truck traffic, and Joe went out of business. Joe sold the property to Thomas Land Company, a real estate developer. Thomas demolished the service station, subdivided the land into lots, and built homes on the lots. One of the homes was purchased by Fred Firstowner. Last year Fred moved and sold his home to Brenda Buyer. Authorities recently discovered there is hazardous contamination in the soil, which they attributed to leakage from the service station's underground fuel storage tank. Under CERCLA, which parties are liable for cleanup costs? If you could rewrite CERCLA, would you make any changes to that?

3. In Europe, approved remediation is sometimes limited to sealing and/or fencing a site to prevent human exposure. Should our law permit this? Under what circumstances, and who gets to decide?

4. If you were Congress, would you reactivate the Superfund tax on oil and chemical companies to provide funding for the Superfund? Or continue to take the money from general tax revenues? Or find someone else to pay? Or do away with the Superfund?

NOTES

1. Beck, Eckardt C., "The Love Canal Tragedy," *EPA Journal*, January 1979, available at www.epa.gov/aboutepa/history/topics/lovecanal.

2. 42 USC §§ 9601–9675.

3. Definitions are at 42 USC § 9601.

4. 42 USC § 9601(22).

5. 42 USC §§ 9603, 9602.

6. 40 CFR Part 300.

7. 40 CFR Part 300, App. A.

8. 40 CFR Part 300, App. B.

9. 40 CFR 300.430.

10. 42 USC § 9604.

11. See 40 CFR Part 300, App. D.

12. 42 USC § 9621; 40 CFR 300.430.

13. 42 USC § 9617; see also § 9613(k)(2)(B).

14. NTP's website is at http://ntp-server.niehs.nih.gov.

15. The Substance Priority List is available at www.atsdr.cdc.gov/SPL/index.html.

16. 42 USC § 9604(i)(3) and (5); www.atsdr.cdc.gov/toxprofiles/index.asp.

17. 42 USC § 9604(6); generally see www.atsdr.cdc.gov/publications/CitizensGuidetoRisk Assessments.html; for links to public health assessments and health consultations, see www.atsdr.cdc.gov/hac/PHA/index.asp.

18. 42 USC § 9611.

19. See generally 42 USC § 9607.

20. 42 USC § 9606.
21. 42 USC § 9601(35)(B).
22. 42 USC § 9622(f)(6).
23. 42 USC § 9613(f) and § 9622(h)(4).
24. 42 USC § 9604(k).

Chapter 7

Resource Conservation and Recovery Act (RCRA)

Key Concepts

- Cradle-to-grave (and beyond) responsibility: regulation of hazardous waste handling, disposal, and postdisposal.

- Manifest tracking system and shared responsibility of all participants for proper waste handling.

- Disfavor of land disposal; preference for recycling or treatment that reduces risk.

- Financial responsibility for liability and cleanup, extending thirty years beyond closure of a disposal facility.

Love Canal (see chapter 6) motivated Congress on two fronts. CERCLA (the Comprehensive Environmental Response, Compensation, and Liability Act) addressed how to clean up Love Canal and the hundreds of other hazardous waste sites that had accumulated due to poor disposal practices. The Resource Conservation and Recovery Act (RCRA)[1] deals with how to manage and dispose of hazardous waste to avoid creating any more Love Canals. Although RCRA was first enacted in 1976, Congress beefed it up following the Love Canal disaster.

The best way to protect health and the environment from hazardous wastes is to prevent exposure. RCRA's first line of defense is to contain and isolate such wastes in a controlled setting designed to minimize the risk of escape. To achieve this, the act takes a systematic "cradle-to-grave" approach with respect to handling and disposal of hazardous wastes. Tracking and other key features of this approach are discussed in this chapter.

RCRA's systematic approach has been reasonably effective. But escape can still occur, whether due to human error, unavoidable events such as a tornado, or other causes. So RCRA contemplates backup strategies. Some wastes can be treated to reduce toxicity, so they will do less harm if they escape. Treatment can also, in some cases, reduce mobility, so that escaped contaminants cannot spread as far. Another strategy is to discourage land disposal in favor of other methods, such as incineration, that reduce the volume of waste that might escape. Land disposal is subject to stringent regulation, for example, disapproving locations where there is high risk to groundwater and requiring installation of redundant detection and alarm systems for leaks.

Besides regulating disposal of wastes, RCRA also tackles another source of hazardous contamination: leaking underground storage tanks. RCRA has been fairly effective both in dealing with the problem of hundreds of thousands of preexisting buried tanks and in making new tanks safer.

Another stated goal of RCRA is to reduce the amount of hazardous waste generated in our society. But the act does not provide effective means to accomplish this goal, so little progress has been made.

RCRA is implemented by the EPA and by states with approved programs. To be approved, the state program must be at least as stringent as federal law.

WHAT IS A HAZARDOUS WASTE?

Definitions[2] play a key role in the implementation and enforcement of RCRA, and in the efforts by some people to escape its requirements. This chapter will discuss the definition and nature of hazardous wastes at some length before addressing how they are regulated.

In the most simplistic terms, a hazardous waste is a solid waste that is hazardous. As used in RCRA, the term "hazardous" is fairly straightforward, but the term "solid waste" is a bit counterintuitive.

What Is a Solid Waste?

Under RCRA the term *solid waste* encompasses pretty much all materials to be discarded, for example, spent material, sludge, by-products, commercial chemical waste, and scrap metal. The surprising aspect is that solid waste includes not just solids, but also liquids and containerized gases. Essentially, it encompasses wastes intended for land disposal—as opposed to air disposal (such as smokestack emissions regulated by the Clean Air Act) or water disposal (such as discharges to surface waters regulated by the Clean Water Act).

Hazardous waste is a subset of solid waste. The other categories are municipal waste (which includes household waste) and industrial waste. RCRA establishes federal control over hazardous waste. The act leaves nonhazardous solid wastes under the primary control of the states, with federal support and guidelines.[3]

Exception: Materials to be recycled or reused are a notable exception from the definition of solid waste. This exception has been exploited by some as a loophole to avoid the high cost of compliance with RCRA. This is discussed further in the next section.

What Makes a Solid Waste "Hazardous"?

hazardous waste
Under RCRA, a solid waste that is hazardous

RCRA defines **hazardous waste** as "a solid waste . . . which because of its quantity, concentration, or physical, chemical or infectious characteristics may

(A) cause, or significantly contribute to an increase in mortality or an increase in serious irreversible, or incapacitating reversible, illness; or

(B) pose a substantial present or potential hazard to human health or the environment when improperly treated, stored, transported, or disposed of, or otherwise managed."[4]

listed waste
A substance on EPA's hazardous waste list and therefore a RCRA hazardous waste by definition

EPA has translated this broad statutory language into a concrete two-part definition. Hazardous wastes include anything on a list created by EPA (**listed waste**), as well as anything that has certain harmful characteristics (**characteristic waste**).

Listed Hazardous Wastes   The EPA has substantial discretion in deciding what to include on its list of hazardous wastes.[5] The factors that the EPA considers include whether the waste is corrosive, ignitable, reactive, or toxic.

characteristic waste
A waste deemed hazardous, even if not listed as such by EPA, due to characteristics of corrosivity, ignitability, reactivity, or toxicity

These factors relate to the hazard (type of harm) a waste can cause, and they are the same qualities that can make something a characteristic waste. In deciding whether to list a waste, EPA also considers additional factors that make it more likely that humans, animals, or the environment will be exposed to the waste; that is, its persistence in the environment and whether it bioaccumulates.

Defining hazardous wastes by means of a list is an important tool of effective environmental protection. It means the EPA doesn't have to analyze every waste stream from every waste generator, which would be almost impossible in our society today. Instead, the many wastes common enough to be on the list are hazardous wastes by definition. Each listed waste is given an identifying code number (ID code).

While listing is a common and helpful way of defining substances subject to regulation, there is a weakness. The list is finite; the possible types of hazardous waste seem infinite in number. A new waste, or a waste slightly modified so that it no longer qualifies under an ID code, would escape regulation if the list were the only definition. So the EPA has a backup definition.

Characteristic Wastes   A characteristic waste[6] is any solid waste having any of the following characteristics:

- Corrosivity

- Ignitability

- Reactivity

- Toxicity

Sometimes these are referred to by the initials **CIRT wastes**. Because toxicity is much different from the other characteristics, you will also see references just to CIR wastes. The EPA has standards that spell out how corrosive, ignitable, and so forth a waste must be to be deemed a characteristic waste—sometimes referred to as the "characteristic level." Below the characteristic level, a CIR waste is not deemed a *hazardous* waste.

CIRT wastes
Shorthand term for characteristic wastes, the initials standing for corrosivity, ignitability, reactivity, and toxicity

Loopholes and Exceptions

Compliance with regulations for the management and disposal of hazardous waste is very costly. A waste generator can avoid that cost if its wastes don't fit the definition of "hazardous waste." Thus, generators try to find loopholes, which EPA tries to close.

The Mixture Rule   A common environmental mantra is that *dilution is not the solution to pollution*. Reflecting this dictum, EPA adopted the *mixture rule*.[7] This rule says that a hazardous waste, when mixed with another solid waste, is still a hazardous waste. There is good reason for this rule: mixing does not reduce toxic burden; it just results in more total waste to cope with. Thus, dilution by mixture can be harmful, not helpful, to environmental protection.

The mixture rule applies to listed wastes and to toxic characteristic wastes. CIR wastes are different—mixing can actually mitigate their harmfulness. Thus, wastes identified as hazardous solely because of their corrosive, ignitable, or reactive characteristics are exempt if they fall below characteristic levels due to mixing.

The Derived-From Rule   Some hazardous wastes can be destroyed by incineration. But the ash left behind may itself be toxic. The same is true when hazardous waste changes its physical form in other ways. Rather than having to analyze such changes on a case-by-case basis, EPA adopted the derived-from rule.[8] This rule says that a solid waste derived from a hazardous waste is still a hazardous waste. As with the mixture rule, CIR wastes may be exempt if the derivative falls below characteristic levels.

The Contained-In Policy   This policy applies when a hazardous waste spreads into soil, groundwater, or other medium, for example, due to a leak. In that event, the entire contaminated matrix is considered a hazardous waste. This is because there is no practical way to unmix the contaminant from the medium.[9]

In essence, the contained-in policy complements the mixture rule in closing loopholes. Under the mixture rule, you can't escape hazardous waste status by mixing with another solid waste. Under the contained-in policy, you can't escape hazardous waste status by mixing with a nonwaste medium such as soil or groundwater.

Recycle Exemption   RCRA encourages recycling. Because they are not discarded materials, recycles don't meet the definition of solid waste. And because hazardous waste is a subset of solid waste, recycles are automatically excluded from the definition of hazardous waste, no matter how hazardous they are. But distinguishing whether something is a legitimate recycle—or a discard masquerading as a recycle—is a difficult challenge that has led to a lot of litigation and confusing regulations.

Recycles, including hazardous recycles, are not regulated under RCRA. RCRA imposes no requirements for safe handling and storage of hazardous recycles. Further, RCRA does not provide for monitoring to make sure they are really used as recycles, nor set any deadline after which they will lose their recycle status. States may have laws regulating hazardous recycles. But once a hazardous material is classified as a recycle, it falls off RCRA's radar—a potentially huge loophole.

As a result, if a purported recycle program is really a sham, or if a good faith plan to recycle goes awry, hazardous materials may reside indefinitely in an uncontrolled condition and location, with none of RCRA's protections for public health and the environment. For this reason, the EPA (and the courts) may scrutinize a hazardous waste generator's purported recycle plan to determine whether it is genuine. Basically, the EPA tries to determine the generator's intent: will it really recycle the hazardous materials? Or is this just a ruse to discard hazardous waste without complying with costly regulations? Generally, hazardous material is recognized as a legitimate recycle (and therefore escapes regulation) if it fits into one of the categories in List 1, and does not fall into any of the categories in List 2.[10]

List 1: To be a legitimate recycle, hazardous material must be

- Directly used as an ingredient in a production process, or

- Used as an effective substitute for a commercial product, or

- Returned to the production process directly and without further treatment.

List 2: A hazardous material is not a recycle if it is

- Used as fill, or otherwise placed on land in a manner that is essentially disposal, or

- Burned as a fuel, or

- Accumulated speculatively for indefinite future use.

Exclusions   RCRA and EPA regulations exempt a number of substances from the definition of hazardous waste.[11] Therefore, those items are not subject to regulation under RCRA, even though they are discards that may be both voluminous and toxic.

One exception is for household hazardous waste, such as paints, pesticides, fertilizers, and batteries. Although each household's waste is miniscule, the aggregate of all household wastes is a large quantity and a large problem. But it is a problem that would be difficult to control by regulation at the federal level.

Other exceptions apply to various special interests, some possibly due to difficulties of regulation, some in deference to other governing statutes, some perhaps due to political influence. In the agricultural industry, irrigation returns are exempt, as well as certain wastes used as fertilizer. Drilling wastes from oil and gas exploration and production are excluded, as are some mining wastes. The list goes on, and it's something of a hodgepodge.

CRADLE-TO-GRAVE REGULATION

RCRA calls for "cradle-to-grave" regulation,[12] meaning from the time a hazardous waste is generated by some industrial process until the time it is finally disposed of, and even beyond disposal. The major tools of hazardous waste regulation are permit requirements, packaging and labeling standards, a tracking system for waste, and shared responsibility among everyone who handles the waste, including generators, transporters, and disposal facilities.

Some general requirements apply to all categories of hazardous waste handlers. All must train their workers in proper handling of hazardous waste. All must file notification with the EPA and thereby obtain an identification number. Thus, each individual waste handler has its own identification code, just as each listed hazardous waste has its own identification number. Although there are variations among the different categories, all handlers must keep detailed records of the hazardous wastes they handle, including source, ID codes, quantities, and disposition.

Besides requirements that apply to all hazardous waste handlers, there are additional regulatory requirements for each category of waste handler. These are discussed in the following sections.

Generators

Anyone whose activities create hazardous wastes is a *generator*, subject to certain requirements under RCRA. It is the generator's responsibility to identify any hazardous wastes in its waste stream, using analytic methods prescribed by the EPA. The generator is responsible for proper handling of hazardous wastes, which includes proper containment and labeling of containers.

The generator is not allowed to accumulate hazardous wastes for more than ninety days. The generator must make arrangements for its hazardous wastes to be picked up before the deadline by an authorized transporter and delivered to an authorized disposal facility. In some cases, there may be intermediate stops at a treatment facility or a temporary storage facility. If so, these must be authorized facilities, and the generator must make all arrangements before the waste load begins its journey. For each load, the generator must create a hazardous waste manifest to document and accompany the load.

Requirements are somewhat less stringent for small generators, particularly those generating less than one hundred kilograms per month of hazardous waste.

hazardous waste manifest

The list and itinerary that must document and accompany every load of hazardous waste disposed of under RCRA

The Tracking System

For each load of hazardous wastes, the generator must create a tracking document called a **hazardous waste manifest**. In the manifest, the generator records the ID code and quantity of each type of hazardous waste in the load. The manifest also serves as an itinerary for the load, listing the identification number of the transporter, the disposal facility, and any intervening facilities the load will be taken to. The generator signs the manifest to certify that all information is true and accurate, and that the generator has complied with regulatory requirements.

The transporter, the disposal facility, and any intervening facilities are each responsible to check the load and verify that it matches the manifest. Each handler is required to sign the manifest, certifying that it is the authorized handler identified in the manifest, that it has verified the load against the manifest, and that it has otherwise complied with requirements. One of those requirements is that hazardous wastes cannot be accepted from or delivered to anyone except the authorized waste handler identified in the manifest. In this manner, all handlers of a load share responsibility for proper handling and disposal.

The manifest must accompany the load of hazardous waste throughout its journey. There are, however, multiple copies. The generator and each subsequent handler keeps a copy of the manifest.

A major goal of the tracking system is to make sure the waste reaches a proper disposal facility, where it will be isolated to the extent possible from the environment. To make sure the waste doesn't go astray on its journey, there is one final step. After receiving the waste and signing the manifest, the disposal facility returns the final copy of the manifest to the generator, confirming the load has reached its destination. The law allows forty-five days for that circle to be completed. If the final manifest copy from the disposal facility is not back within forty-five days, the generator must notify EPA. In essence, when the transporter picks up the waste, the generator sets an alarm that will go off in forty-five days if the confirming manifest isn't back yet.

Transporters

Like all waste handlers, transporters of hazardous waste must be registered and have identification numbers. Their responsibilities are relatively light compared with generators and especially with disposal facilities. They can only accept hazardous waste from an authorized facility. They must confirm that the load matches the manifest, and that it is properly packaged and labeled. They must deliver it only to the authorized facility designated on the manifest. Delivery must be prompt: a transporter cannot hold hazardous wastes for more than ten days. The transporter must handle the waste properly; it is not allowed, for example, to mix wastes together. The transporter must sign the manifest, which is certification of compliance with all requirements.

In the event of any spills of hazardous waste in its possession, the transporter must notify the EPA and is responsible for cleanup of the spill.

TSD Facilities

TSD facility

General term referring to any treatment, storage, or disposal facility for hazardous wastes under RCRA

A **TSD facility** is not a single type of facility. Rather, this is an acronym referring to treatment, storage, and disposal facilities for hazardous waste. All TSD facilities must have EPA permits,[13] but the permit requirements and other rules differ for each type of facility. This section will briefly touch on treatment and storage facilities. Most of the section will focus on disposal facilities, which are the most heavily regulated.

Treatment Facilities   A treatment facility is one that uses any process to change the physical, chemical, or biological character of hazardous waste, so as to make it less of a danger. Typically, the treatment is aimed at making the waste less toxic, less mobile, or both. Incineration is a common method of treatment, which has the dual benefit of destroying hazardous organic constituents and reducing the volume of waste. Hazardous waste incinerators are subject to stringent design and operating standards under RCRA. Further, the EPA strictly regulates their air emissions as part of its goals under the Clean Air Act.

Storage Facilities   A storage facility is a facility that holds hazardous waste temporarily, either before treatment or before final disposal. There are a variety of storage methods, such as containers, tanks, surface impoundments, and waste piles. There are detailed EPA regulations governing the design and operation of each type of storage. The length of time wastes can be held, as well as other requirements, can vary depending on the nature and quantity of the hazardous waste and other factors.

Disposal Facilities   A hazardous waste disposal facility is a facility where hazardous waste is intentionally placed on or into the land. The wastes are generally intended to remain there permanently, even after closure of the facility. Design and operating requirements are intended to minimize the risk of hazardous wastes escaping from the disposal facility into the surrounding environment, both during operation and after closure of the facility. Because some escape is all but inevitable, RCRA also imposes financial responsibility requirements, to cover cleanup and liability during the facility's operation and for thirty years after closure.

The most familiar type of disposal facility is the hazardous waste landfill. Some other types, such as surface impoundments, can be storage or disposal facilities. But to be used as disposal facilities, they must meet far more stringent requirements. Liquid hazardous wastes are commonly disposed of in underground injection wells—another type of land disposal. Because underground injection of hazardous wastes poses a potential threat to drinking water resources, these facilities must comply with regulations under the Safe Drinking Water Act as well as RCRA.

Land Disposal: Minimizing Risk of Escape and Minimizing Risk If It Escapes

RCRA assumes (correctly) that any hazardous waste disposed of on land will eventually get into the environment. Land disposal is so disfavored that RCRA imposes a general prohibition commonly referred to as the **land ban**. Land disposal is not prohibited entirely, but it is subject to stringent requirements. For one thing, land disposal of some hazardous wastes is prohibited unless it is first treated to reduce toxicity and/or mobility. Most of the land ban requirements are intended to isolate and prevent migration of hazardous wastes.[14]

land ban
Common term for stringent restrictions on land disposal of hazardous wastes

The goal—unattainable but toward which the EPA strives—is to isolate hazardous wastes so that they will not endanger public health or the environment. Regulation under RCRA makes every effort to make the confinement of wastes as effective as possible. It begins with the requirement that generators place wastes in prescribed containers, properly sealed. Further, the disposal facilities where those containers will come to rest are subject to design specifications requiring safeguards such as strong and redundant bottom and sides, and bottom lining intended to prevent groundwater contamination.

There are many other design and operation requirements for land disposal facilities. Some of these are physical, such as drainage control and systems to collect leachate. Others are technological, such as systems to monitor the groundwater and detect any leaks.

There are other requirements that apply generally to all TSD facilities, but most rigorously to land disposal facilities. These include personnel training and inspections. Further, they must keep detailed records itemizing the type and quantity of waste received, date and method of disposal, and its location within the facility. Additionally, there are security requirements, mainly to prevent unauthorized entry.

Every hazardous waste disposal facility must have an operating permit. The permit spells out the specific requirements applicable to the individual facility. This facilitates enforcement by eliminating any room for confusion or ambiguity.

Land Disposal: Preparing for Contingencies All of this regulation is aimed at isolating hazardous wastes as much as possible, but also to be prepared when isolation fails. For example, the monitoring systems are designed to raise an alarm if leaks or other contingencies are detected. As another example, treatment requirements that make wastes less toxic or mobile mean that, if they escape, they won't go as far or do as much harm as untreated wastes.

What happens when something goes wrong? A fire or explosion or other accidental release? Contingency planning and preparation are required of every disposal facility as a condition of getting and keeping its operating permit. The facility is required to have specified safety equipment, which must be regularly tested and maintained. The facility must inform local fire and police departments and local hospitals of the types of hazardous waste and the facility's layout. And the layout must facilitate emergency response—for example, aisles must be wide and unobstructed so that crews and equipment can maneuver.

The detailed records required for a disposal facility become particularly important in some types of contingency. For example, if there is an explosion or fire within a facility, knowing exactly what is located where can be critical for emergency response.

RCRA also pays attention to the potential financial consequences when isolation fails. Disposal facilities are required to establish financial responsibility, for example, by posting a bond. The facility's potential responsibility extends to both cleanup costs and liability claims.

Where Will You Put It? The issue of where hazardous waste disposal facilities should—or should not—be located is fraught with controversy. Most people will agree that disposal facilities, like factories, highways, and drug rehabilitation centers, serve a valuable purpose. But nobody wants to live near one. These necessary but unpleasant facilities are sometimes called **LULU**, a catchy acronym for *locally undesirable land uses*. When the question arises of where to put a LULU, the typical response is **NIMBY**, meaning "Not in my back yard!"

Given that nobody wants a disposal facility in their own neighborhood, where do we put them? The EPA's main concern is to further the purposes of RCRA. Recognizing that no isolation system is foolproof, it's desirable to avoid locations where escape of hazardous wastes would be particularly injurious—for example, near drinking water supplies or residential neighborhoods.

LULU
Locally undesirable land use, such as a hazardous waste disposal facility

NIMBY
"Not in my back yard"—the common response to the question of where to put a LULU

All disposal facilities must have an operating permit. In addition to facilitating enforcement, this requirement serves two other important purposes. For one, it enables EPA to identify and limit these facilities. For proposed new facilities, this gives EPA leverage to influence location.

Another important purpose served by the permit requirement is transparency and public participation. The issuance of a permit is subject to public notice and comment requirements, as well as judicial review. This gives the community a chance to speak out—and perhaps to influence EPA or the courts—about the proposed location or any other concerns.

Closure of Disposal Facilities Hazardous wastes last virtually forever, but disposal companies do not. What happens when a TSD facility closes? There is no perfect protection, but RCRA makes an effort. As a requirement of its operating permit, every TSD facility is required to have an approved closure and post-closure plan. This is intended to provide for both physical safety and financial responsibility. At closure, as during a facility's operation, RCRA's goal is to protect health and the environment—especially groundwater—by minimizing the risk of wastes escaping into the environment.

One closure option is to remove all hazardous wastes and decontaminate the site—sometimes called a "clean closure." This approach is usually required for certain types of surface disposal facilities, such as tanks and waste piles. The other option is to close the facility with wastes *in situ* as a hazardous waste landfill, which is subject to stringent (but not foolproof) regulatory safeguards.

ENVIRONMENTAL JUSTICE

environmental justice
Refers to the disproportionate burden of adverse environmental impacts on minority and other disadvantaged communities

The issue of **environmental justice** can arise in many contexts, but it especially relates to the perception that hazardous waste landfills are disproportionately located in poor and minority communities. The concept of environmental justice can be stated in a nutshell: is our society foisting off all its undesirable, unhealthful facilities onto disadvantaged neighborhoods? This is a significant ethical question with no easy answer. If a neighborhood is not poor when a hazardous waste landfill is constructed, it soon will be; property values will decline and everyone who can afford to do so will move away. On the other hand, wealthier neighborhoods generally have more political power to resist being saddled with such facilities.

The granting of a hazardous waste facility permit is now subject to requirements of public notice and comment. Thus, community members who feel their neighborhood is burdened with more than their fair share of undesirable facilities have the opportunity to speak out. But this is not a guarantee against such facilities being built mostly in minority areas. Although it would be illegal for the permitting authority to discriminate on racial grounds, alleged discrimination is hard to prove. The fact of disparate impact on minority communities is not enough; an opponent of the permit would have to prove discriminatory intent—a very difficult burden of proof.

Efforts to protect minority communities are more likely to succeed if there is federal funding involved. An executive order issued by President Clinton in 1994, and reaffirmed by subsequent presidents, requires that a federal agency, "to the greatest extent practicable, shall make achieving environmental justice part of its mission by identifying and addressing, as appropriate, disproportionately high and adverse human health or environmental effects of its programs, policies, and activities on minority populations and low-income populations."[15]

The responsibility imposed by this order on federal agencies is reminiscent of the National Environmental Policy Act (NEPA), which requires federal agencies to take environmental impacts into account in the decision-making process. The executive order does not guarantee any particular outcome, but at least it makes officials think about the problem.

There are detailed design and construction requirements for the final cover of a hazardous waste landfill. These specifications for the cover deal with long-term concerns such as minimizing migration of liquids, minimizing erosion, and withstanding settling and subsidence. Once closure is complete, the law requires ongoing monitoring and maintenance for thirty years—the **postclosure** period. Postclosure requirements include continuance of leak detection and groundwater monitoring systems, as well as maintenance and repair of any damage from erosion, subsidence, or other causes.

postclosure
Refers to a thirty-year period following closure of a hazardous waste disposal facility; RCRA imposes physical and financial responsibilities for this period that must be secured by a bond or similar means

Who does this after the facility closes and the operator is long gone? That is covered by the closure and postclosure plans and the financial responsibility requirements that must be in place from the time the facility begins operating. The liability insurance, bond, or other financial instruments provided by the operator must be adequate to pay for postclosure monitoring and maintenance, as well as for any needed cleanup and damage claims, throughout operation and the postclosure period.

These are good safeguards. But thirty years of postclosure care may be a lamentably short time, when you consider that some of these hazardous wastes can remain hazards for hundreds of years.

Corrective Action   When there is a release of hazardous waste, either within a TSD facility or migrating offsite, EPA has broad authority to order corrective action.[16] For example, EPA can order remediation, impose financial responsibility, and even suspend or revoke a facility's operating permit. Facilities must comply with such orders under the law and also as a condition of their permits.

This is the only part of RCRA that addresses response to past harm rather than prevention of future harm. To some extent, it overlaps with the Comprehensive Environmental Response, Compensation, and Liability Act (CERCLA). In fact, sometimes simultaneous response actions under both acts are required at a single site. But there are differences between the two acts. Notably, only the TSD facility is liable for costs—unlike the broad liability under CERCLA. RCRA covers petroleum wastes, whereas CERCLA does not. RCRA is much less detailed in its requirements than CERCLA, leaving more to EPA's discretion. EPA generally takes a more flexible and less onerous approach under RCRA. RCRA corrective action sites tend to be much smaller but more numerous than CERCLA sites.

WASTE MINIMIZATION

Although most of RCRA and its attendant regulations deal with safe handling and disposal of hazardous waste, the act has a second explicit goal: reducing the amount of such waste created by our highly technological and material society.

Waste minimization is a worthwhile goal, but the act does nothing to implement it. The only relevant requirement is that every generator must have a written program to reduce the quantity and toxicity of its hazardous waste "to the degree determined by the generator to be economically practicable."[17] Every hazardous waste manifest certifies in the fine print that the generator has such a written program. But as environmental protection, this requirement is toothless. The adequacy of the written program and the reasonableness of the proposed reduction are left to the generator's discretion. What's more, the generator has no obligation whatsoever to implement its written program, nor even commit to doing so in the future.

In short, the act only pays lip service to the goal of waste minimization. The only real incentive for a generator to reduce hazardous waste is the stringent requirements under RCRA that make hazardous waste management and disposal so expensive.

ENFORCEMENT

RCRA is implemented by the EPA and by states with approved programs. The act mandates periodic inspections of waste handling facilities. It also authorizes unscheduled inspections and the taking of samples. In addition, courts have upheld EPA in ordering facilities to conduct monitoring and analysis if EPA has determined that waste at the facility may present a substantial hazard to health and the environment.

RCRA provides enforcement measures similar to other federal environmental acts. These include administrative measures (fines and—more drastically— permit revocation) and judicial enforcement (fines, injunctions, and criminal prosecutions). Like CERCLA, RCRA gives EPA authority to seek abatement or other injunctive relief against anyone whose handling, transport, storage, treatment, or disposal practices create an imminent and substantial endangerment to health or the environment. In practice, EPA takes a pragmatic approach to enforcement. Most enforcement action is administrative, and most problems are dealt with informally—that is, by EPA working cooperatively with the facilities it regulates.

Like most federal environmental acts, RCRA provides for citizens' enforcement actions and whistleblower protection. (See text box on Citizen Actions in chapter 4 and text box on Whistleblower Protection in chapter 10.)[18]

UNDERGROUND STORAGE TANKS

In 1984, just four years after RCRA was first adopted, Congress enacted the Underground Storage Tank (UST) Program,[19] and incorporated it into RCRA. At that time, there were estimated to be over two million of these tanks in the country, containing petroleum and hazardous substances. Hidden from sight, many of these tanks suffered corrosion, structural failure, overflows, and other problems. Silent leaks contaminated soil, as well as ground and surface waters that supply much of the country's drinking water.

To illustrate the magnitude of the problem, over half a million releases had been confirmed as of early 2012 from leaking underground storage tanks (LUST). At that time, most of those releases had been cleaned up, pursuant to the UST Program. Further, of the two million tank systems existing in 1984, about 75 percent have been closed.

RCRA's UST Program provides comprehensive regulation of underground storage tanks, both new and old. It is implemented by EPA and by states with approved programs. As usual, the state standards must be at least as strict as federal standards.

Definitions

The UST component of RCRA has its own statutory definitions of key terms.

UST Systems   The program regulates UST systems—underground storage tank systems—that are used to contain regulated substances. *UST system* is defined as one or more tanks plus connected pipes. To qualify as *underground*, the system need not be entirely buried; it just needs to have at least 10 percent by volume below the ground surface. Connected pipes are an integral part of a UST system, subject to the same regulation and counted toward the 10 percent measurement.

Regulated Substances   The UST Program only applies to tank systems containing *non*-wastes. (Tanks containing hazardous wastes are regulated by the hazardous waste provisions of RCRA.) There are two categories of regulated substances under the UST Program. First, the term includes hazardous substances as defined in CERCLA. Second, it includes petroleum and petroleum-based substances (which CERCLA does not).

Regulatory Requirements

The UST Program provides for comprehensive regulation of both old and new underground tank systems.

Inventory   Each state is responsible to create an inventory of UST systems and monitor them. Anyone installing a new UST system must notify the state, which adds the new system to its inventory. The UST Program requires that preexisting USTs be identified and registered, so they too can be included in the inventory.

Standards for Design, Operation, and Closure   All new underground tank systems must meet detailed design standards, for example, corrosion-resistant materials and devices to prevent overfilling. For some particularly hazardous substances, double-hulled tanks are required. Because it is impossible to guarantee the integrity of a tank, the regulations provide for additional layers of protection. These include systems to detect erosion or leaks. Preexisting UST systems either must be brought up to certain design and operating standards or closed.

An owner or operator closing an underground tank must notify the state. Further, closure must comply with approved methods, such as cleaning and filling or removing the empty tank.

Dealing with Releases   Because of the difficulty in detecting underground leaks, the regulations require action if there is even *suspicion* of a leak. Both leaks and suspicions of leaks must be reported. Any suspicion must be investigated, typically by testing the tank for tightness. For any actual release, the owner or operator must take corrective action. Short-term requirements focus on limiting the size of the release and dealing with any acute dangers such as explosive vapors. Long-term corrective actions might include measures such as excavation or cleanup of soil and repair or removal of the tank.

Even though the UST Program has been in effect since 1984, we cannot be certain that all preexisting tank systems have been discovered and registered. Some old tanks have been abandoned and forgotten, but may still contain regulated substances. When a preexisting system is identified, it must be inspected to determine whether there has been any past leaking, and corrective action must be taken for any environmental damage. There is no grandfathering of releases.

Underground Storage Tank Fund The UST Program establishes a Leaking Underground Storage Tank Fund, somewhat analogous to the Superfund under CERCLA. The fund can be used for cleanup of orphan sites—that is, leaking tank systems for which no solvent owner or operator can be identified.

CONCLUSION

RCRA's main focus is the safe handling, treatment, storage, transport, and disposal of hazardous wastes. It uses an innovative tracking system that makes each participant jointly responsible to ensure that protective rules are followed. In addition, it sagely anticipated that hazardous wastes will escape, and employs redundant safeguards to minimize the adverse impacts when the inevitable happens. In general, the act has been effective in preventing and curtailing releases of hazardous wastes that would pose a risk to health and the environment. The act's program for regulating underground storage tanks that contain petroleum or hazardous substances has also been quite effective.

But there are areas where RCRA needs improvement. One of these is its waste minimization program. Lip service is paid to recycling and waste minimization, but the EPA is given no authority to really do anything. Another shortcoming is the thirty-year limit on responsibility after closure of a hazardous waste disposal facility. No matter how much waste has been disposed at a site, how dangerous it is, and how long the danger will persist, the facility's owner/operator is off the hook thirty years after closing the facility.

KEY TERMS

Characteristic waste	Listed waste
CIRT wastes	LULU
Environmental justice	NIMBY
Hazardous waste	Postclosure
Hazardous waste manifest	TSD facility
Land ban	

DISCUSSION QUESTIONS

1. Assume a proposal for a hazardous waste site to be located a half-mile from your home. What is your reaction? What if it's a half-mile from your workplace?

2. Congress is reluctant to meddle in private companies' internal production decisions, which is a major reason RCRA does not actually require recycling and other measures to minimize generation of hazardous waste. Given the abundance and dangers of hazardous wastes, is it time for Congress to put some teeth into waste minimization? How? Should there be enforceable limits on generation of hazardous waste, just as there are on industrial discharge of water pollutants? Should there be economic incentives for research that leads to new waste minimization techniques?

3. Who should be responsible for balancing the value to a disadvantaged community of the jobs provided by a LULU, such as a hazardous waste disposal facility, with the obvious negative consequences of the LULU?

NOTES

1. 42 USC §§ 6901–6992k.
2. Definitions are at 42 USC § 6903.
3. 42 USC Subchapter IV §§ 6941–6949a.
4. 42 USC § 6903(5).
5. 42 USC § 6921(b)(1); the lists of hazardous wastes are codified at 40 CFR 261, Subpart D.
6. Characteristics of hazardous waste are covered at 40 CFR §§ 261.21–261.24.
7. 40 CFR § 261.3(a)(2)(iv).
8. 40 CFR § 261.3(c)(2)(i).
9. 40 CFR § 261.3(d)(2).
10. See Applegate and Laitos, *Environmental Law: RCRA, CERCLA, and the Management of Hazardous Waste*, Foundation Press (2006), 42–43.
11. 40 CFR § 261.4(b).
12. Hazardous waste management standards for generators, transporters, and TSD facilities are covered in RCRA at 42 USC §§ 6922, 6923 and 6924 respectively; and in EPA regulations at 40 CFR §§ 262, 263 and 264.

13. 42 USC § 6925.

14. 42 USC § 6924(d)–(k).

15. Executive Order 12898 of February 11, 1994, §1–101. Published in the *Federal Register*, 59(32), February 16, 1994, available at www.archives.gov/federal-register/executive-orders/pdf/12898.pdf.

16. 42 USC §§ 6924(u), (v) and 6928(h); see also www.epa.gov/correctiveaction/resource/guidance/gw/gwhandbk/hwhandbk/htm.

17. 42 USC §§ 6922(b)(1) and 6925(h).

18. For this section, see 42 USC §§ 6928 and 6971–6973.

19. 42 USC §§ 6991–6991m.

Chapter 8

Oil Pollution Act (OPA)

Key Concepts

- Preplanning, nationally and locally, and including all levels of government plus industry, to optimize effectiveness and coordination in spill response.

- Stringent penalties and liability.

- Responsibility of the oil industry, through a tax for the Oil Spill Liability Trust Fund, to help pay for cleanup and losses.

In the predawn hours of March 24, 1989, Captain Joseph Hazelwood radioed fateful words to the US Coast Guard: *We've fetched up hard aground on Bligh Reef.* The oil supertanker *Exxon Valdez* had strayed from shipping lanes and grounded. The tanker proceeded to spill eleven million gallons of North Slope crude oil into Prince William Sound—an environmental disaster that riveted the attention of the American public. The following year, 1990, Congress enacted the Oil Pollution Act (OPA),[1] a comprehensive oil spill prevention and response regime. Legislation for this purpose had been debated in Congress for twenty years, but it did not get enacted until a catastrophe galvanized public demand for environmental protection.

OVERVIEW

The OPA seeks to promote health and the environment by protecting our navigable waters from oil and other hazardous pollution.

Scope

The OPA is aimed at preventing oil spills, ensuring effective response when spills occur, and imposing stringent penalties and liability on those responsible for spills. It applies to spills of oil and hazardous substances on navigable waters and shorelines. In addition to oil, OPA covers spills of hazardous substances on navigable waters (which are covered by CERCLA on land). The OPA greatly increased federal oversight of maritime oil transportation and environmental safeguards, such as

- Requirements for vessel construction and crew licensing
- Mandated contingency planning

- Enhanced federal response capability

- Greater enforcement authority

- Increased penalties and liability

Some of these provisions had existed previously in the Clean Water Act, but the OPA is far more comprehensive and strict. After enactment of OPA, oil spill statistics in the United States notably improved, at least until the blowout of the BP *Deepwater Horizon* well in the Gulf of Mexico in 2010.

Implementation

Emergency response is a multi-agency, multilevel effort. The US Coast Guard is assigned major responsibilities. The EPA and the National Oceanic and Atmospheric Administration (NOAA) also play important roles. State and local authorities are also involved (see discussion of spill response later in the chapter).

Key Definitions

Regulation is aimed at facilities and vessels that are involved with—and therefore may spill—oil or hazardous substances. A vessel is broadly defined as any "watercraft or other artificial contrivance used, or capable of being used, as a means of transportation on water," other than a vessel owned or operated by a government for noncommercial purposes. A **facility** is even more broadly defined to mean "any structure, group of structures, equipment or device (other than a vessel) which is used for one or more of the following purposes: exploring for, drilling for, producing, storing, handling, transferring, processing, or transporting oil. This term includes any motor vehicle, rolling stock, or pipeline used for one or more of these purposes."[2]

facility
Under OPA, any structure, equipment, or device (other than a vessel) used in handling or other activities involving oil

SPILL PREVENTION

The OPA contains comprehensive regulations concerning equipment, personnel, and operations designed to help prevent spills. The major equipment requirement is that all new tanker vessels be built with double hulls. Existing single-hulled tankers are to be phased out.

Alcohol use was an issue in the *Exxon Valdez* oil spill, and the new personnel regulations reflect concern with drug and alcohol impairment. Requirements include mandatory drug and alcohol testing; background investigation for licensure; and potential loss of licenses for drug and alcohol violations by personnel in safety-sensitive jobs. Other regulations restrict vessel crews' work hours to avoid fatigue-related mishaps.[3]

Operational provisions address a variety of matters, including when and where a tanker must have a pilot or tug escorts; when the use of automatic pilot is allowable; and improvements to vessel traffic systems.[4]

SPILL RESPONSE

Response to an oil spill consists of containment, removal, and, commonly, dispersal of the oil with chemical dispersants. (The response to a CERCLA hazardous substance can be more complex, depending on the characteristics of the substance.) Assuring that spill response is fast, well organized, and maximally effective is a major focus of the OPA. This section describes some of the main features.[5]

Notification

The spiller is required to notify authorities immediately of any spill, large or small. Failure to do so invokes severe penalties, as described later in the chapter.

Equipment

The equipment needed for spill response is to be strategically placed and ready for rapid mobilization, so that it can quickly reach any location where a spill occurs. This is largely the responsibility of vessel and facility owners, which must ensure, by contract or otherwise, the availability, readiness, and preplacement of response resources. The regulations set specific time limits. For example, vessel owners must be prepared to mobilize response equipment within two hours. Their equipment should be able to reach a spill in a port area within twelve hours. Longer time limits are allowed for inland or offshore spills that are less accessible.

Governmental authorities also have a role in rapid marshaling of response equipment under the OPA. *Local area committees*, made up of federal, state, and local agencies, are involved in emergency planning. One of their responsibilities is to keep tabs on all available response equipment in their area, no matter if it's privately or publicly owned. If a spill occurs, the committee's equipment census lets authorities know exactly what is available and where.

Personnel

Requirements relating to response personnel are analogous to those for equipment. Owners of vessels and facilities are responsible to provide response crews that are trained, drilled, and ready for immediate mobilization to a spill. In addition, local area committees maintain a list of all federal, state, local, and private personnel in their area who can be called up in case of a spill. Coast Guard strike teams, specially trained and equipped to deal with oil spills, can be called in to help.

Lines of Authority

Confusion about lines of authority and responsibility can paralyze a response effort. The OPA makes it very clear that the federal government is in charge, both of public and private response activities. Depending on their assessment of what is needed, federal authorities may simply direct and monitor efforts, or they may "federalize" the response—that is, actively conduct and pay for the response (subject to later reimbursement as discussed in the section on liability for costs, below). One federal official, designated the **federal on-scene coordinator (FOSC)**, is appointed to direct response operations. The on-scene coordinator is the ultimate authority at any spill site.

federal on-scene coordinator (FOSC) The federal official designated to direct all response operations at a particular cleanup site

Planning

Vessels and facilities must have contingency plans for spill response, demonstrating their preparedness and capability to respond to a spill. The plan must, for example, identify the response equipment and personnel available for compliance with OPA requirements. It must describe how the response personnel are trained and drilled. The plan must identify who will be the point person with authority to act for the owner-company in the event of a spill. A plan must be approved by federal authorities, as must any changes to the plan. In addition, vessels and facilities are subject to inspection to ensure they are complying with their plans.

National Contingency Plan
A framework for response to spills and other contingencies, addressing the roles of federal, state, and local officials

On the government side, there are multiple entities with response functions, all of which engage in planning. There is an overarching plan called the **National Contingency Plan** that addresses response duties of governmental agencies at all levels—federal, state, and local, in addition to port authorities. As part of the plan, there is a national surveillance and notice system, designed to relay immediate warning of threatened or actual spills to state and federal officials.

There is a network of local area committees, made up of federal, state, and local agencies, which develop and maintain local area contingency plans. Their plans identify locally available response personnel and equipment, whether public or private. In addition, the plans contain information about the local area, such as sites of special economic or environmental importance. Local plans are integrated with national planning, with the plans of other local area committees, and with vessel and facility plans to enable coordination and cooperation. All this networking and integration is important, because oil spills do not respect state and local boundaries.

There are other governmental entities, some with specific missions and some engaged in coordinating contingency planning and response. But this partial summary should convey the importance OPA places on planning and readiness.

NATIONAL CONTINGENCY PLAN (NCP)

The National Contingency Plan (NCP)[6] is a framework for responding to spills or releases, on land or water, of oil or hazardous substances. It consists of regulations adopted by the EPA pursuant to both the Comprehensive Environmental Response, Conservation, and Liability Act (CERCLA), and to the Oil Pollution Act (OPA).

Individual spills and releases vary greatly, for example, in volume, type, and toxicity, as well as sensitivity of location. Therefore, regulators cannot prescribe a one-size-fits-all response approach. Instead, the NCP establishes the organizational and procedural foundation for effective response. There are three organizational levels:

- The **National Response Team (NRT)** includes sixteen federal agencies that can be called on for their individual expertise as needed. The NRT participates in national contingency planning and assists with regional planning. The EPA is the lead agency of the NRT.

  National Response Team (NRT)
  A team of sixteen federal agencies involved in spill planning and response

- **Regional Response Teams (RRTs)** (thirteen in number) consist of federal and state personnel. An RRT provides assistance as needed in response actions. It also maintains a Regional Contingency Plan and generally takes the lead in regional preparedness.

  Regional Response Teams (RRTs)
  Thirteen teams of federal and state members that participate in spill planning and response in their respective regions

- One individual, from the EPA or another agency, is designated as the federal on-scene coordinator (FOSC), to direct the entire response—all federal, state, and private response activities.

The National Contingency Plan promotes effective and coordinated response to releases by providing for

- Preparedness and planning

- Prompt reporting

- Unified command of personnel and resources

- Clear lines of communication

Further, the NCP establishes procedures and standards for assessing a release, criteria for response to the release, and provisions for informing the public and involving the affected community.

Responder Immunity

Although the federal government has authority and responsibility to conduct a response, the first people to reach a spill are more often state, local, or private responders. They are not required to wait for a federal official's go-ahead; to the contrary, the OPA is designed to encourage both early and ongoing response assistance from parties that have no obligation to get involved. To encourage such assistance, the OPA gives these responders certain legal protections.[7] They may not be held liable for removal costs or damages that result from any actions consistent with OPA objectives. There are, however, two exceptions. There is no immunity from liability if the responder was grossly negligent or guilty of willful misconduct, and there is no immunity in cases of personal injury or wrongful death.

This immunity provision does not apply to the spiller. The spiller cannot avoid liability by participating in the response.

LIABILITY AND PENALTIES

One way the OPA deters oil spills is to make the consequences very expensive for spillers. A spiller—that is, the owner or operator of the vessel or facility that discharged the oil—is officially referred to as the **responsible party (RP)**. The OPA imposes stringent liability and penalty provisions[8] on responsible parties.

responsible party (RP)
Under OPA, the facility or vessel responsible for a discharge

Strict Liability

The OPA imposes strict liability on responsible parties. This means spillers are subject to no-fault liability. They are held responsible even if they were not negligent or otherwise at fault for whatever caused the spill. This makes sense—the risk of such a discharge exists because of the vessel's or facility's operations, and they have profited from those risk-taking operations.

The OPA recognizes only three very narrow defenses to this strict liability: act of God, act of war, or act of third parties over whom the spiller had no control (such as terrorists). These defenses do not excuse a spiller from OPA's initial requirements. The spiller must still report the spill immediately, cooperate with authorities in the response, and pay the response costs and damage claims. But if a spiller qualifies for one of these special defenses, and if the spiller has complied with all these requirements, it may then seek reimbursement from the Oil Spill Liability Trust Fund (discussed later in the chapter).

What the Responsible Party Is Liable For

The responsible party is liable for the cost of all response activities. This encompasses not just the containment and removal of spilled oil, but also efforts to avert a threatened spill and the government's cost of directing and monitoring spill response. It includes actions necessary to protect fish, shellfish, wildlife, public and private property, shorelines, beaches, and natural resources (living and non-living). The responsible party is required to reimburse response costs, regardless of whether they were incurred by federal, state, or local authorities, or even by private parties.

In addition to response costs, the RP is liable for compensatory damages for losses caused by the spill. This includes compensation to governments or Indian tribes for damage to natural resources. RPs are also liable for damages for death and bodily injury, property damage, loss of revenues by all levels of government, and the loss of profits or earnings suffered by private individuals and businesses.

Joint and Several Liability

If there are multiple responsible parties, OPA imposes joint and several liability. This means that each is individually responsible to pay the full costs. If one RP pays more than its share, it can seek contribution (proportionate reimbursement) from other RPs. But the existence of others does not relieve a responsible party from paying in the first instance.[9]

Limitations on Liability

The potential liability of responsible parties is significant, but not unlimited.[10] Monetary limits on liability for response costs and damages were substantially increased by the OPA. For spills from vessels, the limit is based primarily on vessel tonnage, with the highest limit being $22,000,000 per incident. For spills from onshore facilities or at deep water ports, damages are limited to $350 million. For spills from offshore facilities (other than deep water ports), the limit on damages is $75 million. The limits do not apply if the spill resulted from the responsible party's gross negligence or willful misconduct. Finally, these are limitations only on the RP's obligation to pay, not on the rights of claimants to recover compensation for losses. If losses exceed liability limits, claimants can seek additional compensation from the Oil Spill Liability Trust Fund (see next section).

LIMITATIONS ON LIABILITY: *DEEPWATER HORIZON* CATASTROPHE

The explosion of the *Deepwater Horizon* oil drilling rig in the Gulf of Mexico in 2010 resulted in the largest oil spill in US history—over two hundred million gallons. Projected damages are unprecedented, amounting to billions of dollars. BP, the well operator, is one of the responsible parties. The usual liability limit for an offshore facility such as the *Deepwater Horizon* rig would be all removal costs plus $75 million, barring proof of gross negligence or willful misconduct. Although it denied any such misconduct, BP voluntarily waived the statutory limit for the Gulf spill. Following a meeting with President Barack Obama, BP created a special $20 billion trust fund to compensate victims of the spill. Litigation is still ongoing as to whether two main subcontractors also are financially liable: Halliburton for allegations that it provided a defective cement unable to meet the standards required to seal up the well, and Transocean for allegations that it failed to maintain appropriate standards in the construction and maintenance of the drilling rig. A federal court ruled, subject to appeal, that its contract with BP shields Halliburton from financial liability, but it still may be subject to punitive damages related to allegations that it knew that its cement slurry was faulty.

Penalties

The OPA provides severe civil and criminal penalties for discharges.[11] If there is any degree of fault, even simple negligence, a discharge can be prosecuted as a criminal offense. There is a graduated scale of criminal penalties, depending on the degree of fault:

- For negligently discharging oil: a fine of $2,500 to $25,000 per day, or up to one year in prison, or both;

- For knowingly discharging oil: a fine of $5,000 to $50,000 per day, or up to three years in prison, or both;

- For knowingly discharging *with the knowledge that it places someone in imminent danger of death or serious bodily harm*: a maximum fine of $250,000, or up to fifteen years in prison, or both. For an organization, the maximum fine is $1 million.

- For failure to notify federal authorities of a spill: a maximum fine of $250,000 and up to five years in prison. For an organization, the maximum fine is $500,000. (By contrast, the pre-OPA penalty was a maximum fine of $10,000 and up to one year in prison.)

OIL SPILL LIABILITY TRUST FUND

The **Oil Spill Liability Trust Fund** (OSLTF, or simply "the fund")[12] is essentially a financial safety net to promote the goals of the OPA. The fund is administered by the **National Pollution Funds Center (NPFC)**, which is part of the Coast Guard. The NPFC operates twenty-four hours per day, to enable federal on-scene coordinators to respond immediately to discharges.

Oil Spill Liability Trust Fund
A fund that can be used for spill response and payment of claims, subject to recovery from responsible parties

National Pollution Funds Center (NPFC)
A part of the US Coast Guard, it administers the Oil Spill Liability Trust Fund

Uses of the Fund

The fund can be used to pay for spill response, for example, if the spiller is unknown. More commonly, the fund is used to cover initial response costs, which will then be recovered from the spiller.

The fund may also be used to pay claims for compensation that cannot be collected from the spiller, for example, if the spiller successfully asserts a defense or if the total claims exceed the OPA limits of liability.

If a spiller has paid response costs as required by the OPA, and then is found to have a valid defense, the spiller is entitled to reimbursement. That reimbursement comes from the fund.

Where the Money Comes From

The major source of funding for the OSLTF is a tax on the oil industry for every barrel (forty-two gallons) of oil, whether imported or produced domestically. The idea is that the financial safety net for oil spills is paid for primarily by the industry, not by taxpayers. The tax was originally set at 5 cents per barrel, and it is

8 cents per barrel as of 2012. By law, the fund cannot exceed $2.7 billion. If it hits the statutory ceiling, as has happened at least once in the past, the barrel tax is suspended.

Responsible parties are another source of funding. Fines imposed on a spiller go into the fund. Additionally, when the fund gets reimbursed for response costs it has advanced, that reimbursement is deposited back into the fund.

CONCLUSION

There is a patchwork of federal environmental acts aimed at preventing releases of harmful substances into the environment, and providing for cleanup and liability when releases do occur. CERCLA and RCRA primarily address these matters on land. The OPA joins and greatly bolsters the Clean Water Act to deal with such threats on our navigable waters and shorelines. A major thrust of OPA is having federal and state government, as well as local communities and industry, work together to plan and prepare for spills. The intent is to enable a rapid, coordinated, and effective response when a spill occurs. Another major thrust is to deter carelessness or undue risk-taking by making spills very costly for the spiller.

No law can guarantee against all spills and disasters, such as the *Deepwater Horizon* catastrophe. But since OPA was enacted in 1990, it appears to have improved the protection of the country's navigable waters.

KEY TERMS

Facility	National Response Team (NRT)
Federal on-scene coordinator (FOSC)	Oil Spill Liability Trust Fund
National Contingency Plan	Regional Response Teams (RRTs)
National Pollution Funds Center (NPFC)	Responsible party (RP)

DISCUSSION QUESTIONS

1. Describe in your own words the difference between who is held liable under OPA versus CERCLA. Are the differences sensible? Why or why not?

2. Should there be limits on the amount a spiller is liable to pay for response costs and compensatory damages? Why or why not?

3. If you were Congress, what provisions would you put in the law to promote the best response to a spill?

NOTES

1. Major portions of the OPA are codified at 33 USC §§ 2701–2762; in addition, the OPA amended relevant provisions of the Clean Water Act (33 USC §§ 1251–1387), the Ports and Waterways Safety Act/Tanker Safety Act (PWSA) (46 USC §§ 3701–3718), and others; for a helpful exposition on OPA, see A. P. Olney, Oil Pollution Act, chapter 7, *Environmental Law Handbook*, 21st ed. (Lanham, MD: Government Institutes, 2011).

2. 33 USC § 2701(37) and (9).

3. See PWSA: regarding vessel construction standards, 46 USC § 3703a; drug and alcohol testing and other licensure matters, 46 USC Part E; manning of vessels, 46 USC Part F.

4. For example, 46 USC § 8502.

5. OPA's National Response System is codified at 33 USC § 1321(j); Oil or Hazardous Material Pollution Prevention Regulations for Vessels (Department of Homeland Security, Coast Guard) are at 33 CFR Part 155; regulations for Facilities Transferring Oil or Hazardous Material in Bulk (EPA) are at 33 CFR Part 154.

6. 40 CFR Part 300.

7. 33 USC § 1321(d)(3).

8. 33 USC § 2702.

9. 33 USC § 2709.

10. 33 USC § 2704.

11. 33 USC §§ 1319(c), 1321(b)(5); see also EPA, "Oil Pollution Act Overview," reference to § 4301(a) and (c), available at www.epa.gov/osweroe1/content/lawsregs/opaover.htm.

12. The various provisions related to the creation, use and source of the OSLTF are at 26 USC §§ 4611 and 9509(a)–(c); and 33 USC § 2712.

Chapter 9

Emergency Planning and Community Right-to-Know Act (EPCRA)

Key Concepts

- Preplanning for emergencies that could arise from the presence of chemicals in the community

- Cooperation and coordination between state and local officials, the facilities that have chemicals on site, and others

- The public's right to know about the presence of chemicals in the community, and releases of chemicals

In December 1984, a tank exploded at the Union Carbide pesticide plant in Bhopal, India. Hundreds of thousands of people in the surrounding community were exposed to methyl isocyanate gas and other chemicals that were released. Over two thousand people were killed immediately, and by the end of two weeks, the estimated total was eight thousand. In the years following the disaster, thousands more died of gas-related diseases. The government estimated that over half a million people were injured by the explosion and its aftermath.

The Bhopal catastrophe raised concerns around the world about the hazards presented by toxic chemicals to nearby populations. To reduce the risk of such a disaster in the United States, Congress enacted the Emergency Planning and Community Right-to-Know Act (EPCRA)[1] in 1986. Although officially part of the Superfund Act, EPCRA is commonly discussed as a stand-alone statute.

OVERVIEW

As its name suggests, the Emergency Planning and Community Right-to-Know Act seeks to empower communities to protect themselves with respect to hazardous chemicals in their midst. Whereas most federal environmental acts regulate activities that pollute or otherwise directly affect the environment, EPCRA works by fostering informed environmental involvement by many sectors of society.

Purpose

The act is intended to protect public health, safety, and the environment by

- Mandating public disclosure of information on storage, handling, and releases of toxic chemicals; and

- Improving emergency planning for, and response to, accidental releases of hazardous substances.

Substances Regulated

There are two categories of substances, subject to different requirements.

- An **extremely hazardous substance (EHS)** is defined by an official list that includes over 350 substances. The criteria EPA uses in designating an extremely hazardous substance are toxicity, reactivity, volatility, dispersability, combustibility, and flammability. The emergency planning and notification requirements of EPCRA apply only to extremely hazardous substances.[2]

  extremely hazardous substance (EHS)
  A listed substance subject to emergency planning and notification requirements under EPCRA

- **Hazardous chemicals** are a much broader group, consisting essentially of any chemical for which the Occupational Safety and Health Act (OSH Act) requires a safety data sheet. It encompasses all chemicals (including EHSs) which are physical hazards or health hazards. (The act carves out a few exceptions from this definition, including household products and products routinely used in agriculture.) The reporting requirements of EPCRA apply to all hazardous chemicals.[3]

  hazardous chemicals
  Under EPCRA, essentially all chemicals that are physical or health hazards

Implementation

EPCRA is implemented by the EPA, with the required participation of state and local governments. The act imposes requirements on facilities using or storing regulated substances to disclose information and to participate in contingency planning. EPCRA has four primary components:

- Emergency planning
- Data collection and reporting
- Release reporting
- Toxic Release Inventory

EPA offers assistance to state and local governments in emergency preparation and response, including educational resources and technological assistance.

threshold planning quantities
Under EPCRA, the amount of on-site extremely hazardous substances that triggers a facility's responsibility to participate in emergency planning

EMERGENCY PLANNING PROVISIONS

EPCRA imposes planning responsibilities on state and local governments. In addition, responsibilities are imposed on facilities with extremely hazardous substances on-site in excess of **threshold planning quantities** designated by EPA.[4]

State and Local Government Planning Responsibilities

State and local governments must have planning commissions and emergency planning processes. EPA regulations establish detailed requirements pertaining to the composition of commissions, contents of plans, and so forth.

State Emergency Response Commission

state emergency response commission (SERC)
State body with response expertise, involved in planning under EPCRA

Each state must appoint a **state emergency response commission (SERC)** to implement EPCRA. A SERC may incorporate preexisting emergency response organizations. It must be staffed with people who have technical expertise in the emergency response field.

Local Emergency Planning Committee

The SERC designates local emergency planning districts, which often consist of counties or other political subdivisions. For each district, the SERC appoints a local emergency planning committee (LEPC), which brings together government and industry personnel to help manage chemical emergencies. The LEPC includes representatives of many sectors of society:

- Elected state and local officials
- Police, fire, civil defense, and public health professionals
- Environment, transportation, and hospital officials
- Representatives of community groups and the media
- Owners and operators of regulated facilities

Local Emergency Plan

It is this broadly constituted LEPC that develops an emergency plan to respond to chemical emergencies within its district. Plans must be updated annually. Required planning includes

- Network
  - Coordination among regulated facilities, safety and emergency response agencies, media, and community groups
- Database
  - Transportation routes
  - Potential complications, such as other facilities with hazardous chemicals and natural gas facilities
- Resources and response methods
  - Location of hospitals and similar facilities
  - Response equipment available at regulated facilities and in the community
  - Evacuation plans
  - Alternate traffic routes
- Training
  - Program and practice exercises

Regional response teams established under the National Contingency Plan (see chapter 8) may review and advise on plans adopted under EPCRA. This helps with coordination of planning processes and gives access to federal expertise.

DATA REPORTING

Regulated facilities must provide detailed information to state and local planning commissions in order to facilitate emergency planning and response.[5] The local fire department also receives these reports, and has the authority to do an on-site inspection upon request to the facility owner-operator. The public has access to the reported information for a specified facility on request to the state or local commission.

Required reporting includes the identity and amounts of regulated chemicals on site. (EPA may set threshold amounts below which reporting of a chemical is not required.) In addition to identity and amount, the location of chemicals within the facility must be reported. Location can be crucial for effectively combating an emergency, and for the safety of emergency personnel.

Reporting requirements apply to all regulated substances, not just extremely hazardous substances.

TOXIC RELEASE INVENTORY

Toxic Release Inventory (TRI)
Publicly available database tracking releases of over 650 toxic substances by locality

The **Toxic Release Inventory (TRI)**[6] is a publicly available database that compiles annual reports of toxic releases by facilities. Over 650 toxic chemicals that pose a threat to health and the environment are tracked by the TRI. The TRI has heightened environmental awareness by letting people find out how much of which toxic chemicals are released in their own communities. The TRI also enables informed policy decisions by national, state, and local governments.

Release Reporting Requirements

EPCRA requires facilities to report annually on toxic substances released into the environment. This is the information that the EPA compiles to create the TRI. EPCRA and its regulations establish who must report and what they must report, under federal law. States have their own requirements for reporting releases, which may go beyond EPCRA requirements. Regulated facilities must inform themselves and make sure to comply with state requirements.

reportable quantity
The threshold amount that triggers the duty to report a release

Reporting Threshold EPA establishes **reportable quantity** thres-holds for hazardous substances and extremely hazardous substances. Any release of a regulated substance in excess of the reportable quantity must be immediately reported by the facility to the state and local commissions. This is what triggers the coordinated response detailed in the local emergency plan.

What Information Is Reported Facilities must report yearly to EPA the amounts of any of the 650 designated chemicals released into the environment. A *release to the environment* includes all releases, whether accidental or routine, whether to air, water, land, or underground injection.

In addition to releases into the environment, facilities must report the amount of each listed chemical:

- Transferred off site for treatment
- Recycled
- Used for energy recovery
- Disposed of
- Managed on site at the facility

All of this becomes public information on the TRI. The TRI database compiles and publicly discloses reported information by chemical, locality, and facility.

Who Must Report? Reporting requirements generally apply to facilities that have ten or more full-time employees, and that meet any the following thresholds for listed toxic chemicals:

- Manufactures or processes 25,000 pounds per year, or
- Uses 10,000 pounds per year

In addition to manufacturing facilities, other industries are required to report, including metal and coal mining facilities and electric generating facilities. Governmental as well as private facilities must report.

CONCLUSION

EPCRA carries on the theme of mitigating harm through planning and preparedness that we've seen in CERCLA and OPA. But even more important, EPCRA epitomizes the theme of transparency and citizen empowerment. Communities are integrally involved in EPCRA's emergency planning design. The public has access to information that is unheard of in most of the world. Are you wondering about potential hazards at a factory? Under EPCRA, you can find out what regulated substances are on site and how much. With a click of the mouse, you can find out what amounts of what toxic chemicals are being released into your local environment. EPCRA facilitates action by local environmental groups by, for example, providing information about the sources and amounts of chemicals being released in a metropolitan area, and enabling comparisons with other metropolitan areas. Nationally, the information provided by TRI was considered to be highly instrumental in Congress insisting on further control of hazardous air pollutants in the 1990 Clean Air Act Amendments.

KEY TERMS

Extremely hazardous substance

Hazardous chemicals

Reportable quantity

State emergency response commission (SERC)

Threshold planning quantities

Toxic Release Inventory (TRI)

DISCUSSION QUESTIONS

1. What are the concerns in your local community about actual or potential toxic releases? Have there been problematic releases to the air, land, or water? Are there industrial facilities that create concern?

2. Consult the TRI to find out what toxic chemicals were released in your locality in the past year. How do you compare with similar localities in your region or nationally? How could you or others in your community make use of this information?

3. Use the TRI to find out what trends or changes there have been in your community in the types or amounts of releases. Do you have any ideas about what caused any such changes?

4. Is there other information to which you would like public access, about things that affect the health and environment of your community? How could such public access be accomplished?

NOTES

1. 42 USC §§ 11001–11050.

2. 42 USC § 11002(a); the list of EHSs with their threshold quantities is at 40 CFR Part 355, App. A and B.

3. 42 USC §§ 11021(a), (e) and 11022(c).

4. 42 USC §§ 11001, 11003; EPA regulations on emergency planning are in 40 CFR 355, Subpart B.

5. 42 USC §§ 11021, 11022; 40 CFR 370, Subparts A–C.

6. 42 USC § 11023; 40 CFR Part 372; for chemicals covered, see § 372.65; for reporting thresholds, see § 372.25; the Toxic Release Inventory is available at www.epa.gov/tri/tridata /index.html; see also US National Library of Medicine (NLM) Toxicology Data Network (TOXNET) toxnet.nlm.nih.gov; view TRI-listed chemicals (by year) at www.epa.gov/tri /trichemicals/index.htm; for TRI-covered industries, see www.epa.gov/tri/coveredindustries /index.html.

Chapter 10

Occupational Safety and Health Act (OSH Act)

Key Concepts

- Employer has a duty to provide a safe workplace—not just to comply with specific safety standards.

- The act provides for highly protective toxic materials standards—but OSHA's rulemaking has been frustrated by a heavy burden of proof and other problems.

- Worker Right-to-Know: Thorough, understandable, and accessible information about chemical hazards must be provided to workers.

- Protection of whistleblowers against retaliation by employers.

During World War I, the US Radium Corporation of East Orange, New Jersey, produced luminous watches for the US Army for use by soldiers. The numerals were hand-painted on the watch dials by a factory of eighty young women and girls. This was a painstaking process. The workers used tiny camel-hair paintbrushes. They were taught to use their lips to keep a fine point on the brush. Unfortunately, the paint contained radium—that's what made it glow in the dark. As they "pointed" their brushes, the workers were exposed to radium, a carcinogen.

By the early 1920s, these young workers began developing bone cancer and radium necrosis (also called radium jaw) from their work exposures, and at least thirteen died. Their teeth ached, became loose, and fell out. Their jaws decayed. Their long bones rotted, so they could not raise their arms or support themselves on their legs. They had anemia, rheumatic pains, and more.

The company had never warned the dial painters of the risks of radium exposure, and in fact heightened that exposure by instructing them to put the brushes in their mouths. Meanwhile, the company bosses and scientists kept their distance and protected themselves with lead shields. Some of the sick and dying workers sued US Radium—something that was virtually unprecedented at that time. The case was dismissed on a technicality by an unsympathetic court. Later, some of the workers obtained a paltry settlement of about $1,000 each.

Despite their dismal failure in court, the workers' plight and their pioneering litigation effort roused press and public support. The shameful treatment of the Radium Girls, as they became known, helped raise public awareness of the need for laws protecting workers.

BACKGROUND

At first glance, you might not think of the Occupational Safety and Health Act[1] as an environmental law. But on-the-job exposures to hazardous chemicals and physical agents are greater than for any other subset of the American population—in terms of frequency, dose, and potential for harm.

Occupational safety and health laws came first at the state level. In 1934 the federal Department of Labor established a Bureau of Labor Standards to help state governments develop and administer protective workplace standards. But states varied greatly in the extent to which their laws protected workers, and to which these laws were enforced. Workers continued to be killed and injured at an alarming rate.

To make matters worse, scientific studies were revealing that on-the-job exposure to hazardous substances was causing lung diseases, cancers, and other chronic diseases among workers—a problem presaged by the experience of the Radium Girls. There are many diseases from work exposures, and some do not show up for decades—for example, asbestos exposure causes both lung cancer and asbestosis, a crippling lung disease; byssinosis is a lung disease of textile workers caused by inhaling fibers; benzene exposure causes leukemia; and silicosis (black lung disease) affects miners.

Congress enacted the Occupational Safety and Health Act (OSH Act) in 1970, and the federal government assumed responsibility for regulating workplace safety. Although there is still much to be done, on-the-job safety has improved immensely since passage of the act. For example, fatalities dropped 59 percent from 1970 to 2007, even though the number of workers almost doubled (see table 10.1). (After 2007, the format for these statistics changed somewhat, but the comparable fatality rate in 2010 was 3.6.)

TABLE 10.1   Workplace Fatalities: A Comparison of 1970 versus 2007[2]

Year	Fatalities	Total Workers (× 1,000)	Fatality Rate (deaths per 100,000 workers)
1970	13,800	77,000	18
2007	5657	147,215	3.8

Purpose of the Act

The stated purpose of the OSH Act is to assure, so far as possible, safe and healthful working conditions for every working man and woman in the United States.

Structure and Implementation

The Occupational Safety and Health Administration (OSHA), within the Department of Labor, is the federal agency chiefly responsible for implementing the OSH Act—specifically for the regulatory and enforcement functions. The scientific research function, however, is allocated to the National Institute of Occupational Safety and Health (NIOSH). NIOSH is a part of the Centers for Disease Control, which is a part the Department of Health and Human Services. By contrast, Congress structured the EPA to combine research and regulatory functions in the same agency.

The OSH Act permits and encourages states to participate in implementation. Twenty-five states have OSHA-approved state plans, authorizing them to implement the act.

Scope of the Act

The act covers all private sector employers and their employees. The act applies to employers as diverse as manufacturers, construction companies, agricultural concerns, law firms, hospitals, charities, and labor unions. Altogether, the act covers more than one hundred million employees in six million workplaces.

Who Is Not Regulated? Although the act's coverage is very broad, there are several noteworthy exemptions and limitations.[3]

- *Small employers*: There is an exemption—but only a partial exemption—for workplaces with up to ten employees. Even small employers are subject to certain protective provisions, including the worker right-to-know provisions discussed in this chapter (see Hazard Communication Standard).

- *Government*: Governments—federal, state, and political subdivisions of states—are not covered directly by the OSH Act. Instead, each federal department or agency has its own program covering its own employees. These programs must, however, be as protective as OSHA standards for private sector workers. Similarly, each state has its own program for state employees.

- *Employers covered by other laws*: Congress has established other laws and agencies that govern the activities of certain industries, including regulation of occupational safety and health. Examples are mining and railroads.

- *Self-Employed*: OSH Act protections do not cover a self-employed person. However, they do cover that person's employees.

- *Family farm*: If a farm is worked only by immediate family members and has no other employees, it is not covered.

- *Religious workers*: The act does not cover employees of a religious organization, provided their work is religious. But the act does cover the organization's secular employees.

- *Domestic household employees*.

Regulatory Approach

OSHA INSPECTIONS

Workplace inspections are an important enforcement tool. OSHA initiates inspections on its own, or in response to worker complaints. Although the OSH Act provides penalties, the priority is to correct or avoid workplace hazards. OSHA will work with an employer to improve safety and health conditions. NIOSH will evaluate health hazards in individual workplaces if requested by the employer or by an employee, employee representative, or government agency.

OSHA inspections are a controversial subject. Some people see the heavy hand of government interfering with American industry and costing jobs by driving up expenses. However, a 2012 study from the Harvard Business School suggests the opposite. The investigators reported that those businesses subjected to a California OSHA random inspection had a 9.4 percent decrease in injury rates and a corresponding 26 percent decrease in medical costs, averaging about $350,000 per company.[4]

The basic approach of the OSH Act is to make employers responsible for worker safety. OSHA sets standards designed to make workplaces and working conditions safe. But there can never be a specific standard for every possible hazard, so there is a general default rule: employers are required affirmatively to ensure the safety of their own workplaces.

The OSH Act addresses both mechanical and chemical hazards. In keeping with the goals of this book, this chapter will focus on the latter. The act uses two main tools to protect against chemical hazards: exposure limits and information. Both will be discussed in the following sections.

WHAT ARE EMPLOYERS' DUTIES?

The OSH Act imposes two duties on employers.[5]

Duty to Comply with Specific Standards

An employer must comply with all specific standards set by OSHA. There are many specific standards, aimed at a diverse array of hazards, including toxic substances, harmful physical agents (such as radiation), electrical hazards, fall hazards, hazardous waste, infectious disease, fire and explosion dangers, dangerous atmospheres, machine hazards, hazards associated with trenches and digging, and confined spaces.

General Duty to Provide a Safe Workplace

Every employer has a duty to maintain conditions and adopt practices reasonably necessary and appropriate to provide a safe workplace and protect workers on the job. This catch-all provision is very important. The number of potential workplace hazards is almost infinite. OSHA cannot realistically foresee and adopt specific standards for all of them. Recognizing this, the act requires employers to do more than comply with specific standards. Employers are responsible to find and correct hazards in their own workplaces.

OSHA AT YOUR DOCTOR'S OFFICE

OSHA's regulations also apply to physician's offices. One specific risk of concern is infection from contaminated needles, known as sharps, or from contact with potentially infectious body fluids. In 2000 Congress passed the Needlestick Safety and Prevention Act, which modified OSHA's Blood-Borne Pathogen Standard to make it more specific and detailed. Any physician's office with ten or more employees, and any hospital, must have a specific plan to minimize exposure to blood-borne pathogens.

Among other items, the law requires that the employer maintain a sharps injury log that contains the details of every occurrence of an employee being stuck by a needle, a scalpel, or other similar instrument while protecting the employee's identity. The law also requires that nonmanagerial health care workers at risk, such as physicians and nurses, be involved in identifying, evaluating, and choosing effective engineering and work practice controls. The act pushes the employer toward needleless systems and toward other effective means of eliminating the likelihood of a needlestick, including worker training. There are also requirements for the decontamination and safe disposal of waste, and for a hepatitis B vaccination program to protect against this common blood-borne disease. OSHA specifies that the sterilants and disinfectants to be used are those that are registered or cleared by the EPA or the FDA. The states and territories that operate OSHA-approved programs must adopt a blood-borne pathogen standard that is at least as effective as the federal standard.

HEALTH STANDARDS

Exposure to toxic and hazardous substances is one of the most serious threats facing American workers today. The most direct way OSHA seeks to protect workers from chemical hazards is by imposing standards[6] called **permissible exposure limits (PELs)**.

permissible exposure limits (PELs)
Standards limiting worker exposure to toxic substances in the workplace

Permissible Exposure Limits (PEL)

A PEL establishes the maximum amount or concentration of a toxic or hazardous substance that workers can be exposed to. Each PEL is tailored to the individual substance—what hazards it poses and how. Most commonly, PELs apply to air exposure, although some PELs also set maximum limits of skin exposure. PELs commonly set limits averaged over an eight-hour shift. Some set limits for other time periods as well, such as short term (fifteen minutes) or a forty-hour workweek. To illustrate, the benzene standard provides:

"**(1) Time-weighted average limit (TWA).** The employer shall assure that no employee is exposed to an airborne concentration of benzene in excess of one part of benzene per million parts of air (1 ppm) as an 8-hour time-weighted average.

(2) Short-term exposure limit (STEL). The employer shall assure that no employee is exposed to an airborne concentration of benzene in excess of five (5) ppm as averaged over any 15 minute period."[7]

Without this short-term exposure limit, it would be permissible to expose employees to as much as 32 ppm benzene for one 15-minute period each workday without violating the 8-hour TWA.

Monitoring and Other Requirements

Setting numeric limits is important, but how do you make sure they are met—that is, how do you give them teeth? In each standard, OSHA includes relevant requirements, which commonly include the following:

- Requirements—including methods—for monitoring and measuring of airborne levels.

- Medical surveillance of exposed workers, designed to detect signs of exposure. This typically consists of routine medical tests, such as blood counts or X-rays.

- Employee training and education, and the posting of warning signs, related to the hazards of the specific substance they are exposed to.

personal protective equipment (PPE)
Respirators and other protective devices for use by individual workers

- Requiring that employers implement engineering and work practice controls as the preferred means of complying with PELs, to the maximum amount feasible. Respirators or other **personal protective equipment (PPE)** are acceptable only as a supplementary means of compliance, and only to the extent the employer can establish that full compliance with the preferred controls is not feasible.

- Although not the preferred means for PEL compliance, personal protective equipment is still important. If OSHA deems PPE essential, OSHA standards make the employer responsible to pay for it, and to ensure that employees have it and use it.

SETTING HEALTH STANDARDS:
CONSENSUS, PERMANENT, EMERGENCY TEMPORARY

OSHA's task is to set and enforce standards to meet the act's goal of ensuring safe and healthful workplaces. The OSH Act provides for three types of PELs—national consensus standards, permanent standards, and emergency temporary standards.[8]

Consensus Standards

When OSHA was created in 1970, Congress did not make it start from scratch in developing PELs. Instead, the act allowed OSHA to borrow standards from other sources, on an expedited basis and without public hearing or comment. Some of these "startup" standards came from other government agencies, some from the American Conference of Government Industrial Hygienists (ACGIH), some from industry and elsewhere. These borrowed PELs are called **consensus standards**.

consensus standards
Workplace exposure limits borrowed from other sources by OSHA; intended to be temporary

Consensus standards filled a gap, but they had serious deficiencies. They covered approximately 425 hazardous chemicals—just a fraction of the hazardous materials workers are exposed to. Many were already outdated when borrowed, some even dating from the 1940s. Finally, most of them only provided threshold values. They made no distinction, for example, between what should be allowed as a peak exposure versus average exposure over an eight-hour shift. Consensus standards were intended to be an interim measure, until OSHA could adopt its own science-based PELs, called **permanent standards**.

permanent standards
Science-based permissible exposure limits adopted by OSHA pursuant to formal notice and comment procedures

Permanent Standards

The act gives OSHA broad authority to set specific standards regulating physical premises, processes, practices, and anything else that may involve a workplace hazard. Two important provision of the act are relevant here—a basic provision that applies to all occupational safety and health standards, and another provision applying only to toxic substances. Read together, these legislative provisions give OSHA its mandate and authority to set standards:

- *Basic OSH standards*: By definition, a safety or health standard means a standard that provides the degree of protection "reasonably necessary or appropriate to provide safe or healthful employment and places of employment."[9]

- *Toxic materials standards*: Where toxic materials or harmful physical agents are concerned, a standard must also provide the "highest degree of health and safety protection." The act goes on to say this must be the "standard which most adequately assures, to the extent feasible, . . . that no employee will suffer material impairment of health or functional capacity" even from regular exposure over an entire working life.[10]

Despite the protective language of these provisions, OSHA has largely been stymied in its efforts to promulgate new toxic substances standards. In its first eighteen years, OSHA managed to update standards for only 24 substances on a chemical-by-chemical basis. Dismayed by the slow pace, OSHA tried a new approach in 1988, setting generic standards for 428 chemicals at once. This approach was rejected in court (see text box on *AFL-CIO v. OSHA*). OSHA had to go back to setting standards on a chemical-by-chemical basis, and the effort has continued to lag.

AFL-CIO V. OSHA: COURT REJECTS GENERIC UPDATING OF PELS

In 1988, OSHA set permissible exposure levels (PELs) for 428 hazardous substances at once. OSHA explained that, if it continued to rely on a chemical-by-chemical approach, "it would take decades to review currently used chemicals and OSHA would never be able to keep up with the many chemicals which will be newly introduced in the future."[12]

Therefore, OSHA used an approach it called "generic" rulemaking. OSHA grouped the 428 substances into categories based on their primary health response, such as cancer, neuropathic effects, and sensory irritation. OSHA analyzed exposure, risk, and feasibility based on these categories rather than individual substance, and based on industry sector rather individual industry.

safety factor
Refers to making risk-based protective standards more protective than strictly indicated by study results to adjust for uncertainties such as the sensitivity of children or pregnant women

Recognizing that its generic approach might underestimate risk, OSHA determined the exposure level at which available scientific evidence found no significant risk, and then set the PEL even lower. In other words, OSHA reduced the standard by a **safety factor**. This is a common practice in setting protective risk-based standards, because science is not a perfect predictor of risk. In setting risk-based standards under the Clean Air Act and others, the EPA often applies safety factors for uncertainties—for example, those related to the need to extrapolate from animals to humans, or in order to protect sensitive populations such as children or pregnant women.

The US Court of Appeals for the Eleventh Circuit ruled in 1992 that OSHA's generic approach did not meet the requirements of the OSH Act. This landmark decision established that OSHA must assess exposure, risk and feasibility on a chemical-by chemical basis, and on an industry-by-industry basis. Further, OSHA cannot apply safety factors to offset the effect of scientific uncertainty, because OSHA has the burden of proof that a standard is necessary to protect workers.

Today, most PELs are still the decades-old consensus standards. Complaints are rampant about the inadequate protection these provide for workers. Why have they not been updated? Part of the reason may be OSHA's own priorities. Further, the act establishes relatively burdensome procedural requirements, which may also contribute to the slow pace. For example, OSHA is required to hold a formal hearing if requested, rather than using the simpler notice and comment procedures that the EPA uses under federal environmental laws.

But many attribute the PEL bottleneck mainly to the burden of proof placed on OSHA, which conducts risk assessments and feasibility studies, just as the EPA does in setting many health standards. But OSHA has a somewhat higher burden of proof than the EPA generally bears, making OSHA's regulations more vulnerable in court. This is partly because the statutory language is less precautionary and gives OSHA less discretion than the EPA has under environmental acts. For example, unlike the Clean Air Act, the OSH Act does not mandate health standards that provide a *margin of safety*. Further, OSHA must support its conclusions by **substantial evidence**—a less deferential standard of proof than the usual "arbitrary and capricious" standard applied to the EPA and many other agencies. But for these differences, the court in *AFL-CIO v. OSHA* might have approved generic standard-setting, or at least OSHA's use of safety factors (see text box, *AFL-CIO v. OSHA*). As things stand, new OSHA health standards have routinely been challenged in protracted litigation, and often rejected by courts, notably for failure to prove that a new health standard is *necessary*—a requirement derived from the basic OSH standard definitional language, quoted earlier.[11]

substantial evidence
A standard that requires the party with the burden of proof to present evidence that a reasonable person might find sufficient to support the decision

Emergency Temporary Standards

The act provides for a third type of PEL—**emergency temporary standards**. OSHA can issue such a standard to protect against immediate grave danger. An emergency standard is effective upon publication, with no advance notice and comment procedure required. But it is valid only up to six months. Therefore an emergency temporary standard is also treated as a proposed permanent standard, subject to the usual procedural requirements and judicial review. Theoretically, six months would allow time for adoption of a permanent standard, but in practice it takes many years, due to the problems referred to above.

emergency temporary standards
Permissible exposure limit adopted by OSHA, without advance notice and comment, to protect against immediate grave danger

HAZARD COMMUNICATION STANDARD (HCS)

One way OSHA addresses the threat of chemical hazards in the workplace is by regulations limiting exposures. Another major tool is to arm workers with knowledge that will enable them, so far as possible, to protect themselves.

Introduction

Hazard Communication Standard (HCS)
OSHA regulatory program for informing and educating workers about chemical hazards in their workplace

The **Hazard Communication Standard (HCS)**[13] is the name of a major OSHA regulatory program popularly known as the "Worker Right-to-Know Rule." Its goal is to promote safety by requiring that information about chemical hazards in their workplace be available and understandable to workers. OSHA estimates that HCS affects over five million workplaces in the United States that employ a total of about forty-three million workers. The major tools of this program are Safety Data Sheets, labeling, and training.

HCS was adopted by OSHA in 1983. Since then, there has been a major international effort to agree on hazard communication methods, in particular uniform warning symbols that would be recognizable worldwide. In 2012, OSHA revised HCS to incorporate some of these standardized warnings and other tools. These revisions will be phased in between 2012 and 2016.

What Chemicals Are Covered? HCS is intended to apply comprehensively to any chemical that poses a physical or health hazard to workers. The regulation incorporates by reference the chemicals from a number of master lists. More generally, it covers any chemical that has been shown, even by a single scientific study, to be toxic, carcinogenic, corrosive, flammable, or pose other dangers.

Safety Data Sheet (SDS)
Information sheet required for every chemical sold in the United States; data include health hazards, chemical characteristics, and so on

Safety Data Sheet (SDS)

For every hazardous chemical sold in the United States, the manufacturers (or importers) must create a **Safety Data Sheet (SDS)** and disseminate it to all downstream purchasers. This document was originally called a **Material Safety Data Sheet (MSDS)**. The name change is part of the 2012 revisions to align HCS with internationally agreed terminology.

Material Safety Data Sheet (MSDS)
Older term for Safety Data Sheet

Contents of SDS   The manufacturer must use the best available scientific information in developing a chemical Safety Data Sheet. Further, an SDS must be updated promptly to reflect new scientific evidence. The SDS is packed with important information. The new HCS revision will phase in a standardized box format for easier reference. The required contents include

- *Health hazards*: What are the signs and symptoms of exposure? What diseases is it associated with? In particular, is it listed as a carcinogen by authoritative sources? What are the primary routes of exposure (such as inhalation or skin absorption)?

- *The OSHA permissible exposure limit (PEL)*, if any.

- *Physical and chemical characteristics*: For example, vapor pressure and flash point.

- *Precautions for safe handling*: For example, hygienic practices and cleanup procedures.

- *Control measures*: For example, appropriate engineering controls or personal protective equipment.

- *Emergency first aid procedures.*

Availability   Manufacturers (and importers) must disseminate Safety Data Sheets to all purchasers. Most of those purchasers, of course, are employers.

Employers must have Safety Data Sheets for every hazardous chemical in the workplace. Failure to do so is a violation of the HCS. The employer cannot blame the manufacturer for not providing the SDS. If none is provided, the employer must procure it. The regulation requires SDSs in English, but the employer may voluntarily keep copies in other languages as well.

The employer must make the SDS available to employees. Safety data sheets cannot be stowed away in a file drawer in the manager's office; rather, they must be readily accessible to workers in each work area within the employer's premises.

Labels and Placards

An employer is responsible to ensure that all containers of hazardous substances in its workplace are properly labeled with health warnings and other required information. If a chemical is decanted into a different container, that new container must also be labeled unless it is intended only for the immediate use of the employee who performs the decanting. In some circumstances (such as bulk tank systems), OSHA allows the use of warning signs or placards in lieu of labels.

The employer must ensure that warnings are legible, in English, and prominently displayed on the container. The employer may voluntarily provide the warnings in other languages—for example, on signs and placards.

Some new elements and a standardized format will be phased in under the 2012 revisions. Of special interest, the new standardized requirements include

- *Pictograms*: There are nine internationally recognized hazard pictograms, a sampling of which is shown in figure 10.1. Eight of the nine pictograms warn of human health hazards, and they are mandatory where relevant—thus a chemical label may contain multiple pictograms. (The ninth pictogram warns of environmental hazard. OSHA made that one optional, since environmental hazards are not within its jurisdiction.) Manufacturers have until 2015 to phase in pictograms.

- *Signal word*: In a designated section for signal word, the label will say either "Warning" or "Danger." "Danger" is used for the more severe hazards, whereas "Warning" is used for less severe hazards.

- *Hazard statement*: One or more brief prescribed statements will be included to verbally describe the nature of the hazard(s). Examples of hazard statements: "Highly flammable liquid and vapor" and "May cause liver and kidney damage."

FIGURE 10.1   Sample HCS Pictograms

Health Hazard	Flame	Exclamation Mark
• Carcinogen • Mutagenicity • Reproductive Toxicity • Respiratory Sensitizer • Target Organ Toxicity • Aspiration Toxicity	• Flammables • Pyrophorics • Self-Heating • Emits Flammable Gas • Self-Reactives • Organic Peroxides	• Irritant (skin and eye) • Skin Sensitizer • Acute Toxicity • Narcotic Effects • Respiratory Tract Irritant • Hazardous to Ozone Layer (Non-Mandatory)

- *Precautionary statement*: This is a phrase that describes recommended measures to minimize or prevent adverse effects from exposure. Several statements may be required on a single label, as relevant. Examples of precautionary statements are

  - Do not breathe vapors.

  - Wear protective gloves.

  - Do not eat, drink, or smoke when using this product.

  - Wash hands thoroughly after handling.

Training of Workers

The Hazard Communication Standard requires employers to train and inform employees with respect to chemical hazards. Workers must be trained when newly hired, when assigned to a new workplace, and when any new chemical hazards are added to their work area. Workers must be educated, for example, concerning:

- What hazardous chemicals are present in their work area and which operations in the work area are those chemicals used in

- How to detect hazardous chemicals in the work area—for example, recognizing specific chemical odors and use of monitoring devices

- What are the physical and health hazards of each chemical in the work area, such as asphyxiation or lung cancer

- What protective measures are relevant to those chemicals, such as personal protective gear, work practices and precautions, and emergency procedures

- How to read and understand labels and Safety Data Sheets, and where the SDSs are located in the work area

- Their rights under HCS, including the right to know the hazards present and the right of access to Safety Data Sheets at any time

- The fact that their employer has its own written hazard communication program, their right to see it, and where it is kept in the work area

Employer's Written Hazard Communication Program

The Hazard Communication Standard requires each employer to have a written hazard communication program. As part of employee training, the employer must inform each worker of the existence, availability, and location of this written program. The written program must provide extensive information, including:

- The identity of all hazardous chemicals present in workplace or work area

- A detailed statement of the employer's training program and how the employer complies with other HCS requirements, such as those concerning labeling and Safety Data Sheets

- How the employer will warn employees of other hazards, such as chemicals in unlabeled pipes

- In multi-employer workplaces, how the employer will communicate hazards to other employers (such as subcontractors) and their employees

RECORDS AND REPORTING

The law imposes extensive documentary requirements on employers—reports that must be submitted and records that must be kept. This section focuses on occupational injuries and illnesses, but there are other requirements as well, including under the Hazard Communication Standard.

Records, of course, are only informative if people can see them. In addition to submitting required reports to OSHA, employers are generally required to make a broader array of documents available on request to OSHA or NIOSH. Employees and their representatives—such as unions—are also entitled to see many records on request. Among other things, a worker is entitled to see his or her personal medical file, as well as general workplace safety and health data.

Workplace Injuries

Employers must promptly report every work-related injury or illness to OSHA. In addition to documenting individual incidents, the employer must submit annual summaries, as well as maintain a log, so that the overall safety and health record can be seen at a glance. For ordinary injuries and illnesses, records must be kept for five years.

Where Hazardous Substances Are Involved

Stricter requirements apply when workers are exposed to hazardous chemicals or physical agents. Required records, including exposure and medical records, must be kept thirty years rather than just five. This makes sense. Such exposures can lead to chronic diseases that cannot be detected for a long time. For example, many cancers may take ten or twenty years to develop, or even longer.

These rules are stricter also in that they require the employer to provide more data and to categorize that data in ways that will help OSHA monitor specific hazards. The employer must separately categorize, for example, respiratory conditions due to toxic agents; dust diseases of the lungs; and skin diseases and disorders.

MONITORING AND ENFORCEMENT

The discovery and correction of occupational safety and health violations usually results from workplace inspections. Some inspections are prompted by complaints, but many more are part of OSHA's regular activities. There are over thirty thousand federal inspections each year, plus inspections by state authorities. OSHA inspections are usually unannounced. Anyone who gives advance notice of an inspection is subject to a fine up to $1,000, imprisonment for up to six months, or both.

Enforcement options include administrative citations, as well as judicial actions for civil or criminal penalties or injunctions. OSHA is more interested in eliminating dangers than punishing employers. For minor violations, an employer may be given guidance, the opportunity to correct the problem, and a relatively small fine, if any. The maximum civil penalty for most violations is $7,000. However, if the employer fails to correct it after receiving a citation, there can be an additional fine of up to $7,000 per day so long as the violation continues. Other penalties are prescribed as follows:

- Willful violations: maximum $70,000, minimum $5,000.

- Willful violation that causes a death: Under the OSH Act, a fine up to $10,000 ($20,000 for a second offense), imprisonment up to six months, or both. But under the more general federal statutes applicable to crimes, a court can impose a fine up to $250,000 for an individual or $500,000 for an organization, upon conviction of a misdemeanor resulting in death.[15]

- False statement on any report or other representation: fine up to $10,000, imprisonment up to six months, or both.[16]

WHISTLEBLOWER PROTECTION

A whistleblower is someone who reports a violation of law or other infraction. An employee who reports a dangerous condition in the workplace, for example, is a whistleblower. Not surprisingly, an angry employer might want to fire or otherwise penalize a whistleblower. The law tries to protect whistleblowers,[14] because they help alert authorities to the need for enforcement and remedial action.

Violations of OSH Act

The law prohibits retaliation against a worker for reporting dangerous conditions or other violations to OSHA. The prohibition extends to retaliation in any form. An employer cannot legally fire, demote, transfer, or reduce the pay of an employee for filing a complaint. Nor may an employer take any other adverse action, such as blacklisting, denying promotion, disciplining, or ostracizing an employee for whistleblowing.

An employee making a complaint to OSHA can request anonymity. But sometimes the employer can deduce or guess who made the complaint. Anonymous or not, the worker is entitled to whistleblower protection.

Violations of Other Laws

Over the years, Congress has expanded whistleblower protection. Now, employers are explicitly forbidden to retaliate against employees for reporting not just occupational violations, but violations of several other laws as well. This includes, for example, violations of the Clean Air Act, Clean Water Act, the Superfund Act, and Toxic Substances Control Act. OSHA's Whistleblower Protection Program enforces provisions contained in more than twenty federal statutes. Many states also have laws protecting whistleblowing. At both the federal and state level a, such protections are not universal but they are increasing.

Report to Whom?

Whether a whistleblower is protected may depend on whom the violation is reported to. The basic protection is for filing a report or complaint with the agency responsible for enforcement—be it OSHA or the EPA or a state agency.

What if you report a violation to your own employer? This seems eminently reasonable and gives the employer an opportunity to correct the problem itself. Some—but not all—laws protect against retaliation by the employer in this situation.

Reporting to a third party—such as the media—is less likely to be protected.

Remedies

The remedy for illegal retaliation depends on the nature of the retaliation. Common remedies include reinstatement and back pay.

Practical Problems

Was an employee fired in retaliation for whistleblowing, or was it for legitimate reasons? This is a frequently disputed issue in court cases. Commonly, an employer doesn't announce its intent to retaliate, so employee advocates must rely on circumstantial evidence to prove bad motive. Meeting that burden of proof can be an uphill battle. To counter this, some laws presume that disciplinary action taken within a certain time after a complaint is retaliation, shifting the burden to the employer to prove otherwise.

CONCLUSION

The OSH Act has helped greatly reduce work-related injuries and illnesses. The major concerns, in the authors' view, have been the slow pace of updating and adding new permissible exposure limits, and the need for additional resources for OSHA to perform its oversight function. Adequate protection of worker health requires additional budgetary support for this chronically underfunded agency, and may require new legislation to ease OSHA's burden of proof in updating safety and health standards. Congress and OSHA both need to consider how the standard-setting process can be improved and expedited.

The Worker Right-to-Know rules—officially, but less colorfully, known as the Hazard Communication Standard—constitute the act's second major thrust for health protection. This is a well-developed program that has empowered workers and provided effective protection.

The act has also empowered employees—and promoted compliance—through whistleblower protection. This provision was introduced in amendments to the OSH Act in 1977. Since then, Congress has added similar provisions to twenty other federal acts.

All of these protections have brought us a long way from the dismal working conditions and dangers that existed in the days of the Radium Girls.

KEY TERMS

Consensus standards	Permissible exposure limits (PELs)
Emergency temporary standard	Personal protective equipment (PPE)
Hazard Communication Standard (HCS)	Safety Data Sheet (SDS)
Material Safety Data Sheet (MSDS)	Safety factor
Permanent standards	Substantial evidence

DISCUSSION QUESTIONS

1. What are the implications of the landmark 1992 decision in *AFL-CIO v. OSHA*? Who benefits? Why do you think Congress has given OSHA a higher hurdle than the EPA has in setting protective standards?

2. What would you do if you became aware of a health or safety violation at work? Report it to OSHA? Anonymously? Bring it to your supervisor's attention? Would your approach depend on the type of violation? On anything else?

3. What purpose is served by requiring each employer to have its own written Hazard Communication Program? Is this a redundant requirement?

4. Is it really helpful to provide workers with information such as SDSs and access to employer reports and records? What information is helpful? What is not? Why?

NOTES

1. 29 USC §§ 651–678.

2. For a yearly chart from 1970 to 2007, see 2012 AFL-CIO report, "Death on the Job: The Toll of Neglect," 35, which can be downloaded at www.aflcio.org/Issues/Job-Safety/Death-on-the-Job-Report; see also Bureau of Labor Statistics at www.bls.gov/iif; OSHA, Workplace Injury, Illness and Fatality Statistics, available at www.osha.gov/oshstats/work.html.

3. 29 CFR §§ 1975.4–1975.6.

4. Levine, David I., Michael W. Toffel, and Matthew S. Johnson. "Randomized Government Safety Inspections Reduce Worker Injuries with No Detectable Job Loss." *Science (Weekly)* 336, no. 6083 (May 18, 2012): 907–911.

5. 29 USC § 654.

6. 29 CFR 1910, Subpart Z; an index of links to these standards is available at www.osha.gov/dsg/topics/pel/index.html.

7. 29 CFR § 1910.1028.

8. 29 USC § 655.

9. 29 USC § 652(8).

10. 29 USC § 655(b)(5).

11. See, for example, American Industrial Hygiene Association, "Top Public Policy Issues," (October 11, 2012), available at www.aiha.org/news-pubs/govtaffairs/Pages/Government AffairsNews.aspx; October 2011, Public Citizen, "OSHA Inaction: Onerous Requirements Imposed on OSHA Prevent the Agency from Issuing Lifesaving Rules," available at www.citizen.org/Page.aspx?pid=5127; National Safety Council, "Reaching the Limit on PELs: Calls Increase for OSHA to Update Decades-Old Regulations," available at www.nsc.org /safetyhealth/Pages/510PELs.aspx#.UUiqio7R38s.

12. *AFL-CIO v. OSHA*, 965 F.2d 962, 971 (C.A. 11, 1992).

13. 29 CFR § 1910.1200.

14. 29 USC § 660(c); 29 CFR Part 1977; OSHA maintains a site on its Whistleblower Protection Program at www.whistleblowers.gov.

15. For the larger fines, see 18 USC § 3571(b)(4) and (c)(4).

16. See 29 USC § 666 re: penalties.

Chapter 11

Toxic Substances Control Act (TSCA)

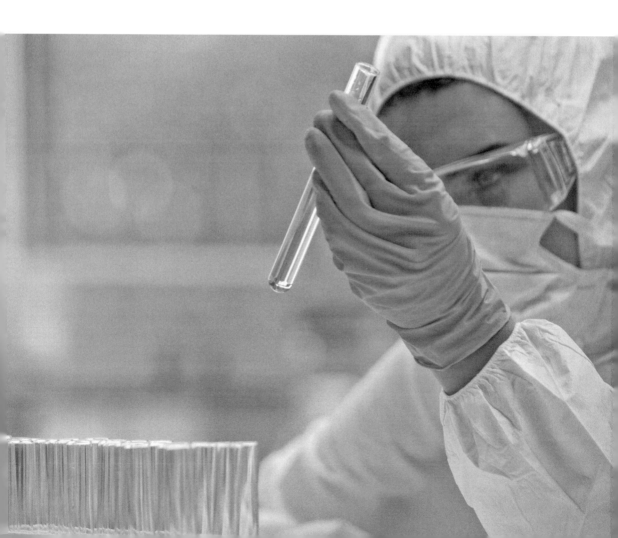

Key Concepts

- Review of new chemicals before they enter the stream of commerce, to determine whether they pose unreasonable risk.

- Whether a chemical poses *unreasonable* risks depends on balancing risks and benefits.

- Risk depends on both hazard and exposure; new uses that significantly increase exposure warrant the same scrutiny as new chemicals.

Making poisons and medicines using chemicals extracted from nature is an ancient art. But it was not until the nineteenth century that the science of chemistry developed. Modern chemicals have revolutionized and benefited society, but they still retain the ability to poison us. In fact, to a toxicologist, all chemicals are intrinsically hazardous—they all cause toxicity at a sufficiently high dose. Even water will drown us.

A chemical's toxicity may be easy to recognize at high doses. More recently, we have learned that the same chemical can have much more subtle effects at lower doses. For example, lead can cause convulsions, coma, and death at high doses; this is old knowledge. But only in recent decades have we become aware that even low doses of lead in consumer products, such as paint or gasoline, can cause subtle effects on the brains of children. Some chemicals that cause acute reactions at high doses can, at low doses, trigger a mutation in the body that causes eventual cancer—an effect than may not become visible for decades. At least theoretically, a single molecule of some chemicals is enough to trigger such a mutation.

The development of tests to predict which chemicals can cause mutations or other toxic effects, as well as whether a chemical will persist in the environment, provide the scientific tools to help regulators minimize risk, and manufacturers to limit liability.

SCOPE AND IMPLEMENTATION

The Toxic Substances Control Act (TSCA)[1] was enacted in 1976 to protect against unreasonable risk to health and the environment from chemicals. To accomplish this goal, TSCA provides for the evaluation and regulation of chemicals—both new and existing—by the EPA. TSCA is different from other acts we've studied so far, in that the substance regulated is a useful product, not a polluting waste. The act explicitly states that the EPA should exercise its authority in "such a manner as not to impede unduly or create unnecessary economic barriers to technological innovation," while at the same time fulfilling the primary purpose of assuring that chemical innovation and commerce "do not present an unreasonable risk of injury to health or the environment."[2] This is an appropriate but tricky balancing act.

Who Is Regulated?

TSCA regulates the chemical industry. The lion's share of requirements falls on those who introduce a chemical into the American market—namely, chemical manufacturers. That term is generally used to encompass importers of chemicals, since they perform the same function of placing chemicals in our midst.

The act also imposes certain requirements on chemical processors, distributors, commercial users, and disposers. In short, it touches the whole gamut of companies whose business involves—and who profit from—the proliferation of chemicals in our society.

What Chemicals Are Regulated?

TSCA covers all chemicals and chemical mixtures legally in commerce in the United States, with few exceptions.[3] It reaches both new and existing chemicals. Particular attention is paid to chemicals produced in very large quantities—over one million pounds per year—because of the greater potential for exposure. There are three to four thousand of these, called high production volume (HPV) chemicals. Special attention is also paid to certain categories of chemicals known or suspected of being highly persistent or highly destructive, such as polychlorinated biphenyls (PCBs) and chlorofluorocarbons (CFCs). As science and technology advance, the EPA is challenged to address new developments such as biotechnology and nanotechnology products.

TSCA does not cover (nor does the TSCA inventory include) chemical substances subject to other federal statutes, such as pesticides, foods, drugs, cosmetics, tobacco, nuclear material, or munitions. Nor does TSCA apply to by-products with no commercial purpose. Further TSCA does not apply to chemicals manufactured only for research and development purposes—and therefore not really in the stream of commerce.

TSCA Inventory

TSCA Inventory
A compilation by the EPA of all chemicals currently in commerce

The EPA maintains a compilation of all chemicals currently in commerce in the US, called the **TSCA Inventory**.[4] A substance on the list is, by definition, an *existing chemical*. There are over eighty-four thousand chemicals on the list, but the number constantly changes as the new chemicals are approved and added. The inventory includes information such as a chemical's production (or import) volume and any restrictions on manufacture or use.

New Chemicals

new chemical
Any chemical not on the TSCA Inventory

Any chemical not on the TSCA Inventory is, by definition, a **new chemical**.[5] It is therefore subject to the notice and other requirements pertaining to new chemicals.

NEW CHEMICALS PROGRAM

TSCA calls for the EPA to review new chemicals before they are manufactured and introduced into the stream of commerce. The EPA has established a New Chemicals Program (NCP)[6] to perform this gatekeeping function. The major tools are notice, testing, and regulation. The act is intended to protect against unreasonable chemical risks before the new product reaches the market. And Congress articulates a policy that the development of adequate data concerning the effect of a chemical on health and the environment should be the responsibility of the manufacturer.[7] But consistent with the coexisting policy not to hamper innovation, TSCA gives the EPA relatively limited regulatory authority.

TSCA gives the EPA authority to require testing and to impose restrictive regulations on new chemicals, but that authority is conditional. The EPA can require testing if it determines the substance *may present* an unreasonable risk of harm to health or the environment. The EPA can impose restrictions on sale only if it concludes from the tests that the substance *presents or will present* an unreasonable risk of harm. Both decisions require risk assessment.

Premanufacture Notice

Ninety days before a new chemical is manufactured and introduced into commerce, the manufacturer must submit a **Premanufacture Notice (PMN)**[8] to the EPA. The PMN provides basic information about the chemical and projections for it, such as chemical identity, production volume, by-products, use, disposal practices, anticipated human exposure, and anticipated volume of environmental releases.

Premanufacture Notice (PMN)
Formal notice from manufacturer to EPA, required before a new chemical is manufactured or sold

In addition, the manufacturer (or processor or distributor) must submit with the PMN any data on the health or environmental effects of the substance. But the manufacturer's legal responsibility is less than you might expect. The manufacturer must submit any "known" or "reasonably ascertainable" studies. This would encompass published studies in the professional literature. If the manufacturer has access to private, unpublished studies, those are also required. But what about its own research on the potential risks posed by its new product? *If* the manufacturer has conducted any studies, those must be submitted. But the manufacturer is *not required to conduct* any tests or studies at this stage. There is no protocol or standard for any health or safety prescreening by the manufacturer.

The EPA has just ninety days to review the chemical and make a decision on whether testing or regulation are needed. If so, the EPA has some hurdles to jump. Absent any action from the EPA, the manufacturer is free to manufacture and sell the chemical after ninety days. The manufacturer then submits to the EPA a Notice of Commencement of Manufacture or Import (NOC). On receipt of the NOC, the EPA adds the chemical to the TSCA inventory, making it officially an existing (no longer new) chemical. The EPA receives between five hundred and a thousand NOCs each year.[9]

Testing Triggers

The EPA can require testing if it determines the substance *may present* an unreasonable risk of harm to health or the environment. Before a substance is thoroughly tested, how does the EPA decide if it *may present* unreasonable risk? Risk is a function of hazard, which is an intrinsic property of the chemical, plus exposure. A decision by the EPA to require testing can be triggered by either the severity of the hazard *(hazard trigger)* or by the level of exposure *(exposure trigger)*, or both.[10] The EPA assesses the potential risks of new chemicals, based on information in the PMN. This is essentially a triage process, looking for testing triggers.

Hazard Trigger   Generally, the EPA looks for evidence a substance might cause such adverse effects as cancer, gene mutations, or birth defects. Evidence may come from the physical and chemical properties of a new substance. If a new chemical is structurally similar, for example, to a known carcinogen, that raises a red flag. Previous studies or anecdotal evidence may also raise red flags.

Exposure Trigger   Under TSCA, testing is triggered if production, release, or the number of people exposed is *substantial*. The EPA has published numerical guidelines it uses to help determine if exposure is substantial enough to trigger testing. These guidelines are not binding on the EPA—it can rely on other evidence of exposure in individual cases. But under EPA guidelines, any of the following is enough to qualify as *substantial* for purposes of the exposure trigger:

- Production of 1 million pounds per year, or

- Release of 1 million pounds per year, or

- Human exposure of:

  - 100,000 from the general population, or

  - 10,000 consumers, or

  - 1,000 workers

Relation of Hazard and Exposure Triggers   There is a noteworthy distinction between hazard and exposure as triggers, based on a commonsense public health principle. No matter how much evidence of toxicity, hazard alone can't trigger testing unless there is at least some evidence of exposure. By contrast, exposure alone justifies testing, regardless of hazard. Why does this make sense? Think about rattlesnakes, which are known to be highly toxic and can cause rapid death. They are not a concern in Alaska, because there are none; there is zero exposure and therefore zero risk. On the other hand, hazard is an intrinsic property of all chemicals, so the more people exposed, the more caution is indicated.

Test Rule

If the EPA determines, from its review of the PMN and any other information it can find, that the substance *may present* an unreasonable risk of harm to health or the environment, only then can the EPA look to the manufacturer to conduct tests. The EPA does not have authority simply to order testing. Rather, what is "triggered" is a **test rule**,[11] which is a proposed order from the EPA to the chemical manufacturer for testing of a specific substance. Calling it a *rule* underlines the fact that the EPA must go through the formal rulemaking process, with the usual requirements of notice and opportunity for objection, as well as the right to judicial review of the final order.

test rule
A proposed EPA order requiring testing of a new chemical under TSCA; so called because it is subject to formal rulemaking procedures

Application and Contents of Test Rule
A test rule applies to all manufacturers and processors of the chemical in question. In the rule, the EPA specifies required testing standards, as well as the risks to be tested for. Examples of common risks to be tested for are

- General toxicity
- Oncogenicity (ability to cause cancer)
- Teratogenicity (ability to cause birth defects)
- Mutagenicity (ability to induce or increase the frequency of mutation)
- Neurotoxicity
- Environmental effects

The EPA can choose from an arsenal of available tests, depending on the nature of the risks involved. For example, if the EPA expert panel reviewing the chemical structure of a proposed new chemical raises concerns about toxicity to the central nervous system, the EPA may require only a battery of tests specific to the nervous system. The extent of testing will depend upon the degree of suspicion and the likelihood of significant exposure—for a carcinogen, it can range from a battery of rapid and relatively cheap short-term test tube assays to two-year animal studies.

Implementation of Testing   The EPA favors a practical, informal approach where possible. Negotiation with manufacturers is preferred over a formal test rule. Commonly there are multiple manufacturers and processors, and the EPA encourages cooperation among them. Typically, this would consist of a joint venture of some or all of the companies to perform the testing, with a negotiated agreement for cost sharing. If an informal approach is unsuccessful, the EPA will designate one or more manufacturers to do the testing. In that case, the EPA will allocate costs among all of the responsible parties, for example, by market share.

Regulation

If the EPA finds there is a reasonable basis to conclude that the substance *presents or will present* an unreasonable risk to human health or the environment, the next step is to impose requirements or restrictions on manufacture and sale.[12] The unreasonable risk may arise from the manufacture, processing, distribution, use, or disposal of the chemical, or any combination of such activities.

What Is an "Unreasonable" Risk?   TSCA itself does not define "unreasonable risk." But in the EPA's interpretation, a chemical presents an *unreasonable risk* if its risks outweigh its benefits.[13] The factors that the EPA considers are

- What adverse effects does the chemical have on humans or the environment, or both, and how great is the exposure?
- What are the benefits of the chemical for various uses, and are there substitutes available?
- What economic consequences would follow from regulation? This includes economic consequences not just from the impact on business, but also the impact on the environment and public health.

Imposition of Regulation   TSCA requires that the EPA select the least burdensome restrictions needed to protect against the unreasonable risks of a chemical. Note this is less protective than antipollution statutes, and appropriately so. Pollution has no value to society, but chemicals do. So in TSCA, Congress directs the EPA to find a reasonable balance between protection and availability.

There are numerous regulatory options that can be tailored to the needs of the situation. The EPA can impose restrictions on production, including volume produced, concentration, and even an outright ban. The EPA can require the manufacturer to provide specific warnings, instructions, or other information on the product label and through other means. The EPA can impose restrictions on commercial users, for example, disallowing certain uses or regulating the method of use. TSCA also looks ahead to ultimate disposal: the EPA can regulate the method of disposal, even prohibiting certain methods.

As with any rulemaking, the EPA must provide public notice and opportunity for comment on the proposed regulation, and the final regulation is subject to judicial review.

EXISTING CHEMICALS

In 1976, when TSCA was enacted, there were about 62,000 chemicals on the market. These were essentially grandfathered in; they were listed on the TSCA inventory as *existing chemicals*, without the review given to new chemicals. Since then, about 22,000 additional new chemicals have been developed and, after review, been added to the TSCA inventory as existing chemicals. Now there are a total of about 84,000 existing chemicals on the inventory.[14]

TSCA gives the EPA authority over existing chemicals (whether pre- or post-1976). Specifically, the EPA can collect data, initiate testing, and regulate existing chemicals. But, just as for new chemicals, there are conditions on that authority. Moreover, the huge numbers of existing chemicals make their management a challenging task. The EPA's strategies have evolved over the years, but its general approach is to prioritize and focus its limited resources on chemicals of most concern—most notably **high production volume (HPV) chemicals**—those produced or imported in amounts over one million pounds per year—and substances whose chemical characteristics make them likely to pose significant risk.

high production volume (HPV) chemicals Chemicals produced in very large quantities (over one million pounds per year)

Given the vast number of existing chemicals, coupled with the high cost of performing comprehensive risk assessments and, if appropriate, risk management, the EPA has adopted a three-pronged approach intended to get the maximum progress from its finite resources. As the first prong, the EPA began risk assessments in 2012 of eighty-three chemicals selected on the basis of hazard and exposure. The criteria for selecting these chemicals were

- well-characterized concerns for human health or environmental toxicity;

- persistent and bioaccumulative;

- used in consumer or children's products;

- have dispersive uses; or

- have been detected in human or environmental biomonitoring.

The EPA expects it will take several years to complete the risk assessments on all eighty-three chemicals. If the risk assessments indicate significant risk, the EPA will pursue appropriate risk reduction action, either through formal rulemaking or by negotiated agreement with industry.

While risk assessments of the eighty-three target chemicals are ongoing, the EPA is also collecting data and screening other existing chemicals, to select the next candidates for priority risk assessments. This data collection and screening is the second prong of the EPA's current strategy.

The third prong is a greater emphasis on public involvement. The EPA has actively sought stakeholder input, including in developing the criteria by which it selected the group of eighty-three chemicals for current risk assessment. The EPA has also increased efforts since 2009 to improve public access to chemical information. The EPA has created the Chemical Data Access Tool (CDAT), online at http://java.epa.gov/oppt_chemical_search, to provide easy public access to health and safety data, on a chemical-by-chemical basis. Much of the data submitted by industry under TSCA have been classified pursuant to claims that they are confidential business information. As part of its increased push for public involvement since 2009, the EPA has been on a campaign to declassify as much of this data as possible. As of April 1, 2013, the EPA had declassified nearly nine hundred such cases, so the public could have access to that data.[15] The EPA provides extensive information online, including free online access to the TSCA inventory.[16]

SIGNIFICANT NEW USE

The **significant new use** of an existing chemical can raise the same concerns as the introduction of a brand new chemical. TSCA authorizes and directs the EPA to protect against unreasonable risk resulting from a significant new use.[17]

significant new use
A new use of a chemical that significantly increases risk, usually by increasing exposure

What Is a Significant New Use?

A new use is considered significant if it significantly increases risk to health and the environment, usually by increasing exposure. TSCA directs the EPA to determine whether a potential new use of a chemical substance rises to the level of a *significant* new use based on the following factors:

- The projected volume of manufacturing and processing

- The extent to which the use changes the type or form of exposure of humans or the environment

- The extent to which the use increases the magnitude and duration of exposure

- The reasonably anticipated manner and methods of manufacturing, processing, distribution in commerce, and disposal of the chemical substance

Significant New Use Rule

If the EPA makes the determination that a new use is significant, it can issue a **Significant New Use Rule (SNUR)**. A SNUR does not prohibit or restrict a new use. Essentially the EPA is saying, "If anyone is thinking of doing this, we want to take a look first." Before it can issue a SNUR, the EPA must go through a rulemaking process, including notice and opportunity for comment.

A SNUR requires that the EPA be given ninety days advance notice before commencement of the specified use(s). The notice is called a **Significant New Use Notice (SNUN)**, and it provides the same information as a premanufacture notice for a new chemical. A SNUR commonly applies to the company employing the specified new use, plus everyone in the chain of

Significant New Use Rule (SNUR)
A proposed order (subject to rulemaking procedural requirements) requiring advance notice before commencement of a significant new use

Significant New Use Notice (SNUN)
Formal notice to the EPA before commencement of a significant new use of a chemical

supply—manufacturers, distributors, and processors. All are jointly responsible for reporting. (For an example, see Mercury SNUR text box.)

On receipt of a SNUN, the EPA evaluates to determine whether to require testing and then whether to impose restrictions, with the same criteria and time limits as for new chemicals.

MERCURY SNUR

In 2003, American automakers voluntarily discontinued the use of elemental mercury in switches for convenience lights, antilock brake systems (ABS), and active ride control systems. In case anyone changed their mind about the voluntary discontinuance, the EPA later issued a significant new use rule (SNUR) requiring ninety days' notification prior to any manufacture, import, or processing of elemental mercury for any of these purposes.

The EPA's announcement explained that the notice before any resumption will provide the opportunity to evaluate risks and, if necessary, to prohibit or limit such use in order to prevent unreasonable risk to health or the environment. The announcement also gives a glimpse of the EPA's risk-benefit balancing. Making an exception for certain aftermarket replacement switches in pre-2003 vehicles, the EPA explained that it "believes that there currently are no suitable non-mercury substitutes for such replacement parts and that the remaining market for such products is limited and declining."[18]

CONCLUSION

TSCA is the only major federal environmental protection act that has not been significantly revised since it was first enacted in 1976. Compared to two other commodities—therapeutic drugs and pesticides—our regulation of chemicals is far less precautionary. (See later chapters on the Food, Drug, and Cosmetic Act [FDCA] and the Federal Insecticide, Fungicide, and Rodenticide Act [FIFRA].) Unfortunately, TSCA has not been fully effective in catching dangerous chemicals and protecting against their proliferation.

The EPA and many others advocate legislative reform to improve protection against chemical risks to health and the environment. Some of the proposed reforms would bring TSCA into line with comprehensive chemical regulation adopted in 2006 by the European Union, called the Registration, Evaluation, and Authorization of Chemicals (REACH). The EPA has articulated what it calls Essential Principles for Reform of Chemicals Management Legislation—its goals for TSCA reform:[19]

1. The EPA should have clear authority to establish standards based on scientific risk assessments that will protect health and the environment. This would empower the EPA to adopt regulations managing risk in the face of uncertainty. By contrast, TSCA now authorizes restrictive regulation only if the EPA finds the chemical *presents or will present* an unreasonable risk of harm.

2. Manufacturers should be required to provide sufficient hazard, exposure, and use data for a chemical (new or existing) to support a determination by the EPA that the substance meets the safety standard. This would shift the burden to the manufacturer to show that a chemical is safe, whereas TSCA now places the burden on the EPA to show that it is unsafe. Now, if there is not sufficient data to know whether a chemical is safe or unsafe, the uncertainty cuts against regulation.

3. The EPA should have clear authority to take into account a range of considerations when making risk management decisions, including the needs of sensitive subpopulations.

4. The EPA should have authority to set priorities and deadlines for itself *and industry* for conducting chemical reviews, particularly for chemicals that might impact sensitive subpopulations.

5. TSCA should encourage and support green chemistry—that is, the design of safer and more sustainable chemicals and processes. Further, TSCA reform should promote transparency and public access to chemical information. In particular, there should be stricter requirements for a manufacturer to claim that data must be classified as confidential business information.

6. The EPA should be given adequate and consistent funding to carry out its chemical safety mission. Chemical manufacturers should be required to provide funding for the costs of implementation.

The authors agree that such reforms are needed. Although TSCA has improved chemical safety, it does not adequately regulate either new or existing chemicals. In fact, one could argue that the most important impact of TSCA is unseen—namely, the chemicals that were never developed. It is extremely expensive for industry to develop a new chemical from conception to readiness for market. Having a new chemical banned due to unreasonable risk, after investing all that time and money, would be a significant financial blow. For that reason, companies usually take a hard look at potential environmental and human health risks before they sink their money into a potential loser.

There are an almost infinite number of possible chemical molecules that industry could develop. Companies typically work on many new molecules simultaneously. Most of these are gradually weeded out for various reasons, keeping only the most promising. Thanks to TSCA, the reasons for weeding out include health and environmental impacts—not just market potential. For example, manufacturers may subject new molecule candidates to the Ames test, a simple screen for mutagenicity. If the test is positive, the candidate is scratched. A company will not invest the large sums needed to develop the molecule, because of the likelihood that it would not pass EPA review. (And even if it does, the EPA's initial approval would not shield the industry from eventual toxic tort liability if it turns out that the chemical does cause an adverse effect.)

As with many preventive measures, we cannot accurately estimate how many cancers have not happened, or ecosystems not been destroyed, by chemicals that were not brought to market because of TSCA. But our society should not rely on the indirect influence of TSCA and the voluntary restraint of industry. TSCA needs to be strengthened to empower the EPA to protect directly against chemical risks.

KEY TERMS

High production volume (HPV) chemicals	Significant New Use Notice (SNUN)
New chemical	Significant New Use Rule (SNUR)
Premanufacture notice (PMN)	Test rule
Significant new use	TSCA Inventory

DISCUSSION QUESTIONS

1. How important is transparency in this context, compared to other acts you've studied? Is it appropriate that manufacturers be allowed to claim

confidentiality for business information—that is, claimed trade secrets? What types of information should or should not be confidential?

2. Manufacturers and others in the industry are already required to report certain information about existing chemicals they sell, such as any adverse reactions they become aware of. What, if any, other information should they be required to report?

3. Articulate in your own words the burden of proof under TSCA and its ramifications. Compare that to the changes the EPA proposes.

4. Is it beneficial to the United States to attempt to harmonize our rules for regulating chemicals with those of the rest of the world?

NOTES

1. 15 USC §§ 26012697.

2. 15 USC § 2601(b)(3).

3. 15 USC §§ 2602(2) and 2607(b); 40 CFR § 710.4; the EPA issues test rules for HPV chemicals pursuant to 15 USC § 2602(a)(1)(B) and 40 CFR Part 799; concerning HPV chemicals, see, e.g., the EPA's HPV Information System, available at www.epa .gov/hpvis/aboutrbd.htm.

4. 15 USC § 2607(b); also see, e.g., "EPA's TSCA Chemical Substance Inventory: Basic Information," available at www.epa.gov/opptintr/existingchemicals/pubs/tscainventory/basic .html, which has multiple links, including how to access the inventory.

5. 15 USC § 2602(9).

6. 15 USC § 2604; EPA's New Chemicals Program at www.epa.gov/oppt/newchems.

7. 15 USC § 2601(b)(1).

8. 15 USC § 2607(d); 40 CFR Part 720.

9. See EPA, *TSCA Chemical Substance Inventory: Basic Information*, available at www.epa .gov/oppt/existingchemicals/pubs/tscainventory/basic.html.

10. Re: testing: 15 USC § 2603, 40 CFR Part 790, and EPA's Chemical Testing & Data Collection index page at www.epa.gov/opptintr/chemtest/index.html.

11. See EPA, TSCA Section 4 Test Rules at www.epa.gov/opptintr/chemtest/pubs/sct4rule.html.

12. 15 USC § 2605.

13. "Making a Finding on Unreasonableness of Risk," www.epa.gov/oppt/newchems/pubs /unrerisk.htm.

14. 15 USC §§ 2601(b) and 2603; 40 CFR Part 712; see EPA, "Existing Chemicals," at www
.epa.govw/oppt/existingchemicals, including link to Existing Chemicals Strategy; see also
EPA's index page on Chemical Testing and Data Collection at www.epa.gov/oppt/chemtest
/index.html.

15. EPA, "Declassifying Confidentiality Claims to Increase Access to Chemical Information,"
www.epa.gov/oppt/existingchemicals/pubs/transparency-charts.html.

16. See EPA, "TSCA Chemical Substance Inventory," at www.epa.gov/oppt/existingchemicals
/pubs/tscainventory/index.html; EPA also includes critical chemical information on
Data.Gov, a federal website providing access to many public databases.

17. 15 USC §§ 2604 and 2607; 40 CFR Part 721; www.epa.gov/oppt/newchems/pubs/snun
.htm.

18. "Significant New Use Rule for Elemental Mercury in Certain Motor Vehicle Switches,"
www.epa.gov/mercury/snur.htm.

19. See EPA, "Essential Principles for Reform of Chemicals Management Legislation," at
www.epa.gov/opptintr/existingchemicals/pubs/principles.html; see also, for example, M. L.
Phillips, "Obstructing Authority: Does the EPA Have the Power to Ensure Commercial
Chemicals Are Safe?" *Environmental Health Perspectives*, 2006 December; 114(12): A706–
A709, available at www.ncbi.nlm.nih.gov/pmc/articles/PMC1764141/; for more informa-
tion on REACH, see, for example, John Applegate, "Synthesizing TSCA and REACH:
Practical Principles for Chemical Regulation Reform" *Ecology Law Quarterly*, 35, 2008
721.

Chapter 12

Federal Insecticide, Fungicide, and Rodenticide Act (FIFRA)

Key Concepts

- Manufacturer (or importer) has burden of proving safety and efficacy.

- "Safe" does not mean no-risk; it means the risk is not *unreasonable*, which depends on balancing of risks and benefits.

- Ongoing oversight through requirement of periodic reregistration, and mechanisms for cancellation and suspension.

There is a fundamental difference between pesticides and other toxic chemical products. Many chemical products have unwanted toxic side effects, but pesticides are meant to kill. It is their inherent poisonous nature that makes them valuable.

Pesticides provide tremendous benefits. They help protect us from vector-borne diseases, such as malaria and West Nile virus that are carried by mosquitoes. They help control vermin such as rats that are a danger to public health. They help protect crops from weeds, insects, and other pests, thus enabling America's farm productivity.

But a poison that kills one species is likely to pose dangers to other species as well, including humans. Hence, governmental regulation of pesticides is more stringent than for most chemicals.

BACKGROUND

The Federal Insecticide, Fungicide, and Rodenticide Act (FIFRA)[1] is an old law, first adopted in 1947 and administered originally by the Department of Agriculture. Its original concern was the efficacy of pesticides—to protect farmers from snake oil salesmen. It was rewritten in 1972, soon after the Environmental Protection Agency was formed, and after Rachel Carson's book *Silent Spring*[2] alerted the public to the adverse effects of pesticides. FIFRA is now an environmental statute administered by the EPA. While it still addresses effectiveness, its main purpose is to protect health and the environment from unreasonable adverse effects. The act has been amended numerous times, sometimes making it more protective and sometimes less, in a push-pull between environmentalists on the one hand and pesticide companies and agricultural interests on the other.

FIFRA is the main federal statute regulating pesticides. In addition, there are some provisions in the Food, Drug, and Cosmetic Act (FDCA) relating to pesticide residue on foods and in the Occupational Safety and Health Act relating to the safety of workers who apply pesticides.

Definitions

FIFRA regulates pesticides and pesticide devices. The act's concept of "pesticide" is broader than you would probably expect, so some definitions may be useful.[3]

Pesticide: FIFRA's primary definition of a pesticide is "any substance . . . intended for preventing, destroying, repelling, or mitigating any pest."[4] This is consistent with a commonsense understanding of the term, with a couple of exceptions. First, it is based on intent. If the manufacturer makes no claims that a product is a pesticide, FIFRA doesn't apply. For example, an effort by the EPA to regulate citronella candles was rejected in court because the manufacturer does not label or advertise them as a pesticide.[5] Second, the term "pest" is unusually broad.

Pest: Under FIFRA, a pest is "any insect, rodent, nematode, fungus, weed, or . . . other form of . . . plant or animal life or virus, bacteria, or other microorganism" that the EPA administrator determines is "injurious to health or the environment."[6] Lest these words be read too literally, Congress explicitly excludes humans from the definition of "pests."

Pest control device: With few exceptions, this term encompasses "any instrument or contrivance (other than a firearm) which is intended for trapping, destroying, repelling, or mitigating any pest or any other form of plant or animal life (other than man)." If a device incorporates a substance—either to attract or repel pests—it is treated as a pesticide rather than a device under FIFRA. For example, an ant trap that contains a chemical to attract ants to the physical container constitutes a pesticide, not a device.

> **pest control device**
> A device to trap, destroy or repel pests.

To avoid absurd extremes, EPA has designated two categories of instruments as exempt from FIFRA regulation as pest control devices. One is any device that depends mainly on the performance of the person using it, such as a flyswatter.

The other unregulated category is for devices that (without using glue or pesticides) entrap vertebrate animals, such as an old-fashioned mousetrap baited only with cheese.

Devices are subject only to limited regulation under FIFRA, consisting mainly of truth-in-labeling requirements, reporting, and registration of the manufacturer with EPA. But FIFRA's main provisions for product registration are not applicable. *Caveat*: Even though not regulated by FIFRA, state laws may impose requirements.

A BEAR SPRAY STORY

In bear country, some hikers carry firearms in case of a bear attack; others carry bear spray. Bear spray is a pepper spray with the same active ingredient as the purse-size spray can some people carry in case of attack by a human aggressor. The difference is that bear spray is intended to repel a bear rather than a human and the label has a picture of a grizzly bear instead of a mugger. In the mid-1990s, we stopped to buy some bear spray at a sporting goods store in Anchorage, Alaska, before setting out on a hike. We were surprised when the store clerk told us that he could no longer sell bear spray, because it had been banned by the EPA. But, he assured us, we could still buy the same product in the form of anti-mugger spray.

Bear spray, it appears, had been banned by the EPA because it had not been scientifically tested for efficacy and toxicity and registered under FIFRA. This was the source of some amusement in Alaska. True, bear spray qualifies as a "pesticide" under the act, because it's a substance intended to repel an animal, and animals are included in the definition of "pests." Mugger spray isn't a pesticide, because FIFRA expressly excludes humans from the definition of "pests." So the EPA's demand for testing was consistent with the law which is intended to prevent inappropriate use of pesticides. But no sane person was going to inappropriately initiate an attack on a grizzly bear with pepper spray. Alaskans also had a good laugh over which EPA official would volunteer to contribute to the efficacy study by testing the placebo on an attacking bear. Eventually, the EPA backed down and agreed to register the bear spray.

PESTICIDE REGISTRATION PROGRAM

The basic approach of FIFRA is to require that all new pesticides be registered by the EPA before they can be distributed and sold.[7] To obtain registration of a new pesticide, the burden is on the manufacturer to establish that the product will not pose unreasonable adverse risks to health and the environment. Typically, the manufacturer applying for registration must conduct extensive scientific testing to meet this burden.

Registration is essentially a license to sell a pesticide, but it is not a carte blanche license. The EPA can and does impose conditions on a product's registration, including labeling and packaging requirements and restrictions on use. Each registration is specific for intended use and dosage. If a pesticide is intended for use on multiple types of crops, for example, or if it has variable dosages, the manufacturer must go through a separate registration process for each. This is largely because the safety and efficacy data may vary for different uses and doses.

FIFRA also regulates existing pesticides. They must be reregistered every fifteen years, with the same burden on the manufacturer to show there is no unreasonable risk.[8] This avoids one of the major problems of the Toxic Substances Control Act (TSCA)—that is, older substances being grandfathered in without adequate review. Further, if evidence of unreasonable risk turns up at any time (not just during the reregistration process), the EPA can take a pesticide off the market.

Registration requirements mainly affect manufacturers (and importers). Regulations also apply to distributors and sellers, to the extent they cannot distribute or sell any pesticides that are not properly registered, or that have been ordered off the market by the EPA.

Criteria for Registration

The EPA will approve and register a pesticide only if it meets all of the following criteria[9] to the EPA's satisfaction:

- The product's chemical composition warrants its claimed purpose.

- The label and other required materials provide appropriate warnings and other information.

- When used as intended, it will not have unreasonable adverse effects on health or the environment.

- When used in accordance with widespread and commonly recognized practice (which is not always the same as the intended use stated on the label), it will not generally cause unreasonable adverse effects on health or the environment.

In short, the EPA scrutinizes the product for efficacy, safety, and proper labeling.

Efficacy   A pesticide must be effective for its advertised purpose. The manufacturer is responsible to test for efficacy before the product is marketed. But the EPA does not routinely require the manufacturer to submit this test data, so long as the chemical composition is consistent with its claimed purpose and there are no red flags.[10]

Safety   Health and environmental safety have long since surpassed efficacy as the main emphasis of FIFRA. Note that safety is evaluated not just for intended use, but also taking into account any customary and widely recognized practice. The relationship between labeling and safety are discussed more in the following.

Labeling

The label is a key part of pesticide regulation. The proposed label (including package inserts and other materials) must be submitted to the EPA for review, as part of the registration process. The EPA must be satisfied with the label before it will register the pesticide.[11] The EPA scrutinizes the format as well as the content of a label—for example, to make sure an important warning is not buried in fine print. The label must appear exactly as approved—nothing may be added, deleted, or modified without approval.

Originally, FIFRA's regulation of product labels was concerned primarily with making sure the claims were true—that the product was effective and buyers would get their money's worth. Efficacy is still relevant, but now the main emphasis is on safety—avoiding harm to health or the environment.

A major function of the label is to translate the scientific data required for the registration process into specific directions and precautions. The label specifies how the product may be used, who can use it, where, how much, and how often. These directions on the label are not mere suggestions—they are legally enforceable. As stated on every pesticide label, "It is a violation of Federal law to use this product in a manner inconsistent with its labeling."[12]

All required text on the label must appear in English. However, the EPA may require, or the applicant may propose, the addition of a second language, if the EPA considers it necessary to protect the public. For example, in recognition that many of the agricultural workers in the United States come from Spanish-speaking countries, the EPA's Worker Protection Standard for Agricultural Workers includes a requirement that certain parts of the label be written in Spanish as well as English. Under consideration is a petition by a farmworkers' organization to require all of the required agricultural pesticide labels be bilingual. When a label is translated, all required label contents must appear in both languages.[13]

Manufacturer's Burden of Proof

The burden of proof is on the manufacturer to satisfy the EPA that a new pesticide does not pose unreasonable risk for human health or the environment.[14] The EPA will not grant registration until the manufacturer meets that burden. Commonly, this requires scientific testing that can take years and cost the manufacturer millions of dollars.

Contrast this to the Toxic Substances Control Act, under which chemicals can be freely marketed if the EPA does not act within ninety days, and the EPA can require testing only if it makes a formal risk determination. The treatment of pesticides under FIFRA is more like the treatment of pharmaceuticals under the Food, Drug, and Cosmetic Act (see chapter 13) with respect to the burden of establishing safety and efficacy.

Balancing of Risks and Benefits

Pesticides are inherently risky. In deciding whether to register a pesticide, the question the EPA addresses is not whether the product will pose a risk, but whether it will pose an *unreasonable* risk to health or the environment. To answer this question, the EPA conducts a risk assessment, balancing the product's risks against its benefits. Specifically, FIFRA directs the EPA to take into account economic, social, environmental, and health costs and benefits.[15]

In General There are many factors that could weigh on the benefit side of the EPA's risk assessment. Avoiding loss of crops from insect damage enables American agriculture to provide ample and affordable food—an example of an economic benefit. For a completely different example, consider the health benefit of a product that provides an effective alternative to a more dangerous pesticide.

Based on its risk assessment, the EPA can refuse to register a pesticide, or impose restrictions. FIFRA directs the EPA to adopt the least restrictive measures that are consistent with protecting health and the environment. For example, limiting the use of a pesticide to trained applicators would be less restrictive, and therefore preferable, to denying registration entirely.[16]

The risk assessment is somewhat different for two categories—public health pesticides and pesticide residues on food.

Public Health Pesticides A **public health pesticide**[17] is one used primarily for public health programs. One example would be antibacterials. Another type is

public health pesticide
A pesticide used primarily in public health programs, such as against mosquitoes to control West Nile virus

pesticides intended to control "vector-spread" disease—such as Lyme disease that is spread by ticks or West Nile virus that is spread by mosquitoes. A public health pesticide is assessed somewhat differently than other pesticides, in that the risks of the product are weighed against the risks of the diseases it is intended to control.

Pesticide Residues on Food Pesticide residues on foods[18] are treated specially. Both the EPA and the Food and Drug Administration (FDA) are involved. The EPA sets the standards and the FDA handles enforcement.

The rules come jointly from FIFRA and the Food, Drug, and Cosmetic Act (FDCA)—specifically, a portion of FDCA known as the Food Quality Protection Act (FQPA). The FQPA directs the EPA to set "safe" standards for allowable pesticide residues, and FIFRA incorporates the FQPA standard in its own definition of unreasonable risk.

tolerance
The allowable level of pesticide residue on foods

The amount of pesticide residue allowable on food is called a **tolerance**. The EPA's task is to set tolerances at a safe level, meaning there is a reasonable certainty that no harm will result from aggregate exposure. "Aggregate exposure" here means all anticipated dietary exposures plus all other anticipated exposures to the pesticide, which presumably makes a challenging job for the EPA's risk assessors.

In addition to all other considerations, the Food Quality Protection Act of 1996 required the EPA to apply an additional safety factor of ten for the protection of children, whose growing bodies are often more susceptible to harmful effects than adults. This safety factor can be waived, but the language squarely puts the burden of proof on the manufacturer by stating: "Notwithstanding such requirement for an additional margin of safety, the Administrator may use a different margin of safety for the pesticide chemical residue only if, on the basis of reliable data, such margin will be safe for infants and children."[19]

FROM PINEAPPLES TO MILK[21]

In January 1982, the state health department in Hawaii discovered the pesticide heptachlor in milk from Oahu dairy farms, at levels much higher than the safety limit set by the EPA and the Food and Drug Administration—almost six times higher. Looking further, the state found exceptionally high levels of heptachlor in the breast milk of nursing mothers. Heptachlor is a known animal carcinogen and persists in the environment. The state routinely tested for heptachlor in milk every six months, but none had been detected previously. The dairy milk was recalled, but the mystery was how the heptachlor got into it.

Investigation found that pineapples were to blame. Pineapples—a major crop in Hawaii—were treated with heptachlor to ward off pests. Earlier testing had shown that this treatment did not contaminate the fruit itself, but heptachlor residue collected in the leaves and roots. Unfortunately, after harvesting, these leftovers were sold to dairies as cattle feed. Thus, heptachlor got into the food cycle—from pineapple greens to cow to dairy milk.

---

no observed adverse effect level (NOAEL)
The threshold dose below which a substance has not been found to cause harm

Specific chemicals cause specific health effects. For some chemicals, the scientific understanding is that there is a threshold dose below which they do not cause harm. For pesticides with such a threshold, the EPA sets the tolerance at the **no observed adverse effect level (NOAEL)**.

For carcinogens, there is generally no threshold. At least theoretically, a single molecule can trigger the cell mutation that eventually leads to a tumor, so there is no NOAEL. Instead, the EPA sets the tolerance so that the increased lifetime risk from residue is no more than one in a million.

There was a time, under a provision known as the Delaney Clause (since repealed), that federal law had a zero tolerance for residue of any carcinogen on food. This became unfeasible as scientists became able to detect smaller and smaller trace amounts of chemicals. The standards summarized above represent a change from a policy of zero risk to negligible risk.[20]

REMOVING PESTICIDES FROM THE MARKET

What happens if new information comes to light, indicating that an existing registered pesticide poses a greater risk than previously known? FIFRA gives the EPA authority to review an existing pesticide and, if warranted by findings, cancel a pesticide's registration (or modify the registration to impose restrictions).

Cancellation of Registration

cancellation
The regulatory process to remove a pesticide from the market due to unreasonable risk

The EPA cannot order **cancellation**[22] by fiat. Rather, the EPA must go through a formal process, which begins with a notice of intent to cancel a pesticide's registration.

What Precipitates Cancellation? Usually, the EPA initiates a cancellation process because it believes there is a highly probable threat to health or the environment. But the EPA does not have to wait until a threat rises to the "highly probable" level. If new information raises concerns, the EPA can initiate the process in order to learn more. In addition, if a citizen lawsuit challenges a product's safety, the EPA may initiate a cancellation process as a way to gather information and provide the opportunity for all sides to air their views.

The Cancellation Process The overall goal is the same as for registration itself—to determine whether the product poses an unreasonable risk to health or the environment. And the burden of proof is still on the manufacturer to satisfy the EPA that the risk is not unreasonable. Thus, the manufacturer must typically undertake more scientific studies to address the new risk concerns. The EPA conducts a risk assessment and risk-benefit balancing as for an initial registration.

As with any major administrative action, there are requirements for notice and an opportunity for comment from the public, and particularly from the registrant threatened with cancellation. In addition to written comments, the EPA may hold public hearings, where both industry and environmentalists can present their views. In addition to these usual procedural measures, a cancellation process commonly involves review by a scientific advisory committee. If the EPA ultimately issues an order cancelling the registration, the registrant is entitled to judicial review.

Effect of Cancellation   If registration is cancelled, the product may no longer be shipped and sold in the United States. But cancellation does not result in a ban on exports. This is because cancellation is based on balancing the product's risks and benefits in the United States. The balancing would not necessarily be the same elsewhere. For example, in tropical areas where malaria and dengue are severe problems, the benefits of DDT are deemed by some to outweigh its risks.

Although cancellation also results in a ban on use, the existing supplies are not necessarily recalled. Based on the risks and benefits of the specific situation, the EPA may decide that it's better to let existing supplies be used up. For example, the EPA did not recall cancelled mercury-based pesticides, because it concluded the remaining quantities were less harmful when spread over a wide area than if they were recalled and concentrated in one location. DDT was not immediately recalled after cancellation, in order to allow time for production of adequate supplies of alternative products.

Suspension of Registration

The cancellation process can take months or years to reach conclusion. During that time, there is ordinarily no requirement to suspend production and use. But if a product poses an imminent hazard to health or the environment, the EPA has authority to immediately ban production and distribution. This is called **suspension**.[23] The word may sound more innocuous, but it is a more stringent measure than cancellation.

suspension
The regulatory process to remove a pesticide from the market due to imminent hazard

Imminent Hazard   Whereas an unreasonable risk to health or environment is sufficient to justify cancellation, a suspension is only warranted by the more severe and urgent circumstance of imminent hazard. The term is self-explanatory with one proviso: it is not limited to effects that will occur immediately. Courts have interpreted FIFRA to allow suspension even if the adverse impact will not manifest for many years, such as cancers. Courts have also ruled that the imminent hazard need not be to human health—it can be a hazard to fish or wildlife.

Suspension Process   In most cases, the EPA is required to give the registrant five days' advance notice of a suspension order. This allows the registrant to seek an expedited hearing in court, if it wishes to challenge the suspension. If no hearing is requested, the order takes effect after five days, and there is no further right to judicial review.

Emergency Suspensions   In extreme situations, FIFRA authorizes the EPA to order *emergency suspension*. This immediately halts all uses, sales, and distribution of the product. The EPA is not required to give notice in advance, but the registrant is entitled to an expedited court hearing once the order is entered.

Emergency suspension, with its scant procedural protection for the registrant, is an extreme measure rarely utilized by the EPA. FIFRA allows it only if the administrator makes a determination that an emergency exists that does not allow time for a hearing before suspending use. Courts have outlined criteria the administrator should consider in making such a determination:

- Seriousness of the threatened harm

- Immediacy of the threatened harm

- Probability that the threatened harm will in fact occur

- What, if any, public benefits would derive from continued use during the cancellation process—that is, if the EPA did not suspend use on an emergency basis

- Nature and extent of the information available to the EPA administrator at time of making the determination

Duration of Suspension   A suspension of registration is not intended to be permanent. Although there is no set time limit, it is a temporary measure intended to allow time for the EPA to review the risks. Generally, it is expected that a cancellation process will be initiated, if one was not already underway.

Impact of Suspension The EPA's suspension order compels immediate cessation of production, distribution, and, if the EPA so designates, use of the product. But like cancellation, it does not necessarily lead to immediate recall. That depends on the circumstances. Also like cancellation, suspension does not prohibit export.

Compensation for Cancellation

For years, the EPA was required to indemnify manufacturers for economic losses due to cancellation or suspension of a product's registration.[24] Industry supporters insisted on this provision as a condition of passing the amendment that authorized cancellation and suspension. The stated purpose of the indemnity was economic fairness. But the obvious impact was to discourage the EPA from using its cancellation and suspension authority, since the funds came directly from its pesticide regulation budget.

Now, only end users get compensation—essentially farmers and applicators who cannot use the supplies they have already paid for. Moreover, the money comes from a special government fund, not from the EPA's budget.

REGULATION OF PESTICIDE USE

Use restrictions are part of the product's registration, and they are legally binding.[25] The restrictions basically fall into two categories—how the pesticide may be used and who may use it.

Restrictions on Allowable Use

When considering an application for registration, the EPA performs a risk assessment not just on each pesticide, but also on each proposed use. The risks and benefits may well differ for different uses and different doses. Therefore, the EPA may register a product for one use, but bar another proposed use. For example, a pesticide might be approved for use on apples but not on grapes, for use on a dry field but not a marshy area, for outdoor but not indoor use. Restrictions on what a product can be used for, where, how much, and how often are spelled out on the product label. See box on pesticides in birdseed.

Restrictions on Who Can Use

The EPA may classify a product, or a particular use of a product, as *restricted use*. A product (or use) thus classified may only be applied by, or under the supervision of, a certified pesticide applicator.

Certified Users The EPA has developed training programs and standards for the certification of applicators[26] of restricted use pesticides. Unfortunately, the certification program has built-in weaknesses. The biggest weakness is that FIFRA absolutely prohibits the EPA from requiring any test of competence as a condition of certification. Instead, FIFRA relies on the individual applicant's signature as assurance of training and competence.

Second, someone who is not personally certified, but who is working under the direct supervision of a certified applicator, can legally use a restricted use product. However, FIFRA's concept of *direct supervision* is looser than the term implies. As defined by FIFRA, it includes someone "acting under the instructions and control of a certified applicator who is available if and when needed, *even though such certified applicator is not physically present at the time and place the pesticide is applied*"[27] (emphasis added). In other words, absentee "direct supervision" is adequate for FIFRA.

private applicator
An applicator certified to use or supervise application of pesticides on his or her own property

commercial applicator
An applicator certified to use or supervise application of restricted-use pesticides to the property of others

You may hear the terms "private applicator" and "commercial applicator." **Private applicators** are certified to use or supervise application only on their own property. Most commonly, these are farmers using pesticides on their own farms. **Commercial applicators** are certified to use or supervise application of a restricted use pesticide on other people's property.

Certification of applicators is commonly handled by the states, but their certification programs must meet EPA standards and be approved by the EPA. In states without an approved program, the EPA handles certification.

Legally Binding

When a product is classified as restricted use, the restrictions are legally binding.[28] Not only the person who misuses the product, but also the supplier who makes it available for misuse, commits a violation.

PESTICIDES IN BIRDSEED

From 2005 to 2008, a company sold birdseed that had been treated with two broadly acting chemical pesticides to protect it from insects during storage. These two pesticides were approved by the EPA for grain storage; but they were prohibited for use on birdseed because of toxicity to birds. The company, which is said to have sold over seventy million packages of birdseed in one year, voluntarily recalled the birdseed in 2008 when it discovered the violation.

In enforcement proceedings by the EPA in 2012, the company acknowledged its negligence and agreed to pay a civil penalty of $6 million and spend another $2 million on environmental projects. The violation was exacerbated because an employee, apparently without anyone else's knowledge, falsified the pesticide registration documents. Although the company was reportedly unaware, it is responsible for its employee's acts and agreed to pay a criminal fine of $4 million. The employee—now a former employee—pleaded guilty and is awaiting sentencing.[29]

NEARLY EXCLUSIVE FEDERAL CONTROL

Most federal environmental statutes encourage the participation of states and the public. But in several respects, such participation is avoided by FIFRA.

Limited State Role

Most federal environmental acts provide for state implementation, upon EPA approval of the state's program. A state program can usually impose standards different from the federal act, provided they are at least as strict as federal standards. A state with an EPA-approved program can essentially step into the EPA's shoes and take charge.

FIFRA is different, particularly with respect to pesticide labeling. The EPA prescribes the contents of a pesticide label, and states are not allowed to impose any variance. Thus, for example, states cannot require any additional safety warnings on a product label. To some extent, this required uniformity was at the behest of the pesticide manufacturers, who argued it would be difficult to comply with a multiplicity of label requirements in different states. The restriction also serves to prevent nonessential labeling, which can dilute the impact of a warning.

States' main involvement with FIFRA involves product use. Commonly, states handle certification of pesticide applicators and prosecution of use violations. In addition, states have limited authority to register additional uses for a pesticide to meet special local needs. Such a registration is temporary, not to exceed ninety days. Further, it cannot conflict with any prior EPA decision, nor can it affect food residue tolerances.[30]

No Citizen Suits

Unlike most federal environmental acts, FIFRA does not provide for citizen enforcement actions. Citizens may, however, initiate court action to compel the EPA to perform some mandate of the act or to seek judicial review of an EPA action or regulation.

Tort Lawsuits

FIFRA arguably limits, to some extent, private tort actions by plaintiffs against pesticide companies for personal injury.[31] Most lawsuits seeking compensation for injuries caused by a commercial product are based on claims that the product was defective, or that there was inadequate warning of its dangers, or both. When the product involved is a pesticide, there is a major controversy over whether a plaintiff can sue the manufacturer for failure to warn of the product's dangers.

The argument against allowing failure-to-warn suits is based on the fact that tort law is state law, not federal law. If a state court can award damages on the theory that pesticide warnings are inadequate, doesn't that conflict with the EPA's sole authority to prescribe label requirements? In some jurisdictions, courts have been persuaded by this argument; in others they have not. To get a definitive answer may take an amendment of FIFRA, but no congressional action is presently anticipated.

CONCLUSION

FIFRA provides a reasonably effective approach to protect public health and the environment against unreasonable risks of pesticides. The act gives the EPA much more discretion than does TSCA to include precaution in risk assessments and imposing restrictions. This is appropriate because, though highly useful in our world, pesticides are uniformly and inherently more dangerous than the universe of chemicals as a whole. Relatively effective regulation under FIFRA can also be attributed in part to the fact that the number of substances regulated is far smaller than the eighty-four thousand chemicals covered by TSCA. Sheer size or volume can greatly complicate regulation of any sort, and FIFRA has an advantage in that regard.

KEY TERMS

Cancellation	Private applicator
Commercial applicator	Public health pesticide
No observed adverse effect level (NOAEL)	Suspension
Pest control device	Tolerance

DISCUSSION QUESTIONS

1. Compare the respective requirements of FIFRA and TSCA with respect to information the manufacturer must provide on a new product and criteria for approval before it can be marketed. Which, if any, of the more stringent FIFRA controls do you think should be incorporated into TSCA?

2. FIFRA imposes the burden on the manufacturer to establish that a pesticide will not cause unreasonable adverse effects, not only if used as intended, but also if used in accordance with common practice. Is it fair to place this extra burden on the manufacturer?

3. Do you agree with that part of the law that allows a pesticide that has been cancelled in the United States to continue to be exported to other countries? What about a pesticide that has been suspended under the more rigorous standard of "posing an imminent hazard to health or the environment"?

4. Why do you think that FIFRA affirmatively prohibits the EPA from requiring applicators to undergo any test of competency as a condition of certification?

5. Would Congress have to rewrite FIFRA to require that all agricultural pesticide labels be in both Spanish and English, or does the EPA have this

authority? What role would OSHA play? For a household pesticide, if the advertisement is at least partly in Spanish to attract Spanish-speaking customers, should the manufacturer be required to provide bilingual safety and warning labels?

6. The tolerance for pesticide residue on foods must be reduced by an additional safety factor of ten for the protection of children, unless there is adequate scientific evidence to show that children are not more sensitive than adults. Should pesticide manufacturers be allowed to expose children to chemicals in scientific studies for this purpose?

NOTES

1. 7 USC §§ 136–136y; see also EPA Summary of FIFRA at www.epa.gov/lawsregs/laws/fifra .html and other pages of interest at http://epa.gov/pesticides/regulating and www.epa .gov/oecaagct/lfra.html.

2. Carson, Rachel. (2002). *Silent Spring*. Boston: Mariner Books. [1st. pub. Houghton Mifflin, 1962].

3. Definitions are in 7 USC § 136.

4. 7 USC § 136(u).

5. *Gulf Oil Corp. v. EPA*, 548 F.2d 1228 (5th Cir. 1977).

6. 7 USC § 136(t) and 136(c)(1).

7. 7 USC § 136a; 40 CFR Part 152.

8. 7 USC § 136a(g).

9. 7 USC § 136a(c)(5).

10. See, for example, 40 CFR 158.400 and 158.2070.

11. 7 USC § 136a(c)(9); EPA's detailed regulations on pesticide labeling requirements are covered in 40 CFR 156.10; for EPA's pesticide *Label Review Manual*, see www.epa.gov /oppfead1/labeling/lrm, and for *Pesticide Label Review Training*, see www.epa.gov/pesticides /regulating/labels/pest-label-training.

12. 7 USC § 136j(g); the quoted language is required by 40 CFR 156.10(i)(C)(4)(ii).

13. 40 CFR 156.10(a)(3); www.epa.gov/pesticides/regulating/labels/bilingual-pesticide-labels .html.

14. See, for example, www.epa.gov/oecaagct/lfra.html#Summary%20of%20the%20Federal %20Insecticide,%20Fungicide,%20and%20Rodenticide%20Act.

15. 7 USC § 136(bb); see also EPA, Overview of Risk Assessment in the Pesticide Program at www.epa.gov/pesticides/about/overview_risk_assess.htm.

16. 7 USC §§ 136a(c)(3)(6) and 136a(d)(1).

17. Public health pesticide is defined at 7 USC § 136(nn). The statutory direction to assess its risks differently appears in the definition of "unreasonable adverse effects" at 7 USC § 136(bb).

18. EPA authority to set tolerances is at 21 USC § 346a, adopted by reference in FIFRA at 7 USC § 136(bb); individual tolerances and related regulations are at 40 CFR Part 180; for more information on the FQPA see, for example, www.epa.gov/agriculture/lqpa.html.

19. See, for example, www.epa.gov/oppfead1/trac/10xiss.htm (FQPA Safety Factor (10X); National Academies of Science, Pesticides in the Diets of Infants and Children, 1993, available at www.nap.edu/openbook.php?record_id=2126&page=1; Oleskey, C. et al. "Pesticides Testing in Humans: Ethics and Public Policy." *Environmental Health Perspectives* 112, 914–919 (2004).

20. For more information on the Delaney Clause see, for example, Charles H. Blank, "The Delaney Clause: Technical Naivete and Scientific Advocacy in the Formulation of Public Health Policies," *California Law Review* 62, 1084 (1974), available at http://scholarship .law.berkeley.edu/californialawreview/vol62/iss4/3.

21. See Matthew Rothschild, "Del Monte Accused of Contaminating Dairy Cattle Feed," *Multinational Monitor* 3, 5 (May 1982), available at www.multinationalmonitor.org/hyper/issues /1982/05/rothschild.html; Program on Breast Cancer and Environmental Risk Factors, "Pesticides and Breast Cancer Risk: Heptachlor," available at http://envirocancer.cornell.edu /factsheet/Pesticide/fs12.heptachlor.cfm; *Toledo Blade*, April 8, 1982, "Pesticide Found in Mothers' Milk," available at http://news.google.com/newspapers?nid=1350&dat=1982040 8&id=gU5PAAAAIBAJ&sjid=qQIEAAAAIBAJ&pg=5576,5296805; *Toxipedia*, "Heptachlor," available at http://toxipedia.org/display/toxipedia/Heptachlor; Gertraud Maskarinec, "Mortality and Cancer Incidence among Children and Adolescents in Hawaii 20 Years after a Heptachlor Contamination Episode," DOI: 10.1615/ *Journal of Environmental Pathology, Toxicology and Oncology* 24.i4.10, 235–250, available at www .dl.begellhouse.com/journals/0ff459a57a4c08d0,78109ddb2703bae7,4cd787c3134f5b38 .html; the decision in a class action in Hawaii state court, *Ahn v. Meadow Gold Dairies-Hawaii*, No. 76335 (1st Cir. 1986) was reported in *Association of Trial Lawyers of America Law Reports* 30, 234 (June 1987).

22. 7 USC § 136d(b); see also www.epa.gov/pesticides/regulating/cancellations.htm.

23. 7 USC § 136d(c); see also www.epa.gov/opp00001/regulating/registering/suspensions.htm.

24. 7 USC § 136m; see also *Environmental Law Handbook*, 21st ed. (Lanham, MD: Government Institutes, 2011), 829–830.

25. 7 USC § 136a(d)(1); *EPA Restricted Use Pesticide Report* (November 2012), available at www.epa.gov/opprd001/rup.

26. Definition of certified user is at 7 USC § 136(e); see also 7 USC §§ 136u and 136w-5 (states' participation); EPA, Certification and Training of Pesticide Applicators, available at www.epa.gov/oppfead1/safety/applicators/applicators.htm.

27. 7 USC § 136(e)(4).

28. 7 USC § 136j(a)(2)(E)—(G).

29. For more information see, for example, http://magblog.audubon.org/pesticides-bird-seed-scotts-miracle-gro-fined-125-million, and www.triplepundit.com/2012/09/scotts-miracle-gro-fine.

30. 7 USC §§ 136v and 136w-1.

31. For further information see, e.g., Miller, "Pesticides," *Environmental Law Handbook*, 21st ed. (Lanham, MD: Government Institutes, 2011), 838–840.

Chapter 13

Food, Drug, and Cosmetic Act (FDCA)

Key Concepts

- Regulation based on science, risk assessment, and balancing of risks and benefits

- Different levels of precaution for different categories of products, depending largely to whom the act allocates the burden of proof

- For drugs, focus on safety and efficacy for intended use

- Adulteration and misbranding—two types of product defects

In the nineteenth century, there were no legal protections for workers, consumers, or others who lacked wealth and power. "Survival of the fittest" and "Buyer beware" were the hallmarks of the day. Around 1900, a few investigative journalists and other reformers began to shine the spotlight on corruption and inequities in our society. They were known as "muckrakers."

One of those muckrakers was the novelist Upton Sinclair. He worked undercover in the Chicago stockyards, and then wrote an exposé called *The Jungle*. This book revealed terrible safety and sanitary conditions in the meatpacking industry, including incidents of workers falling into giant rendering vats and left to become part of the lard sold by the company. Sinclair cared mainly about the workers, but readers focused on his descriptions of filth and contamination. The public was alarmed about eating contaminated beef.

President Theodore Roosevelt sent trusted representatives to investigate, and they confirmed Sinclair's accusations (except they didn't observe any workers falling into rendering vats). Prompted by their report and a public outcry, Congress enacted the Meat Inspection Act and the Pure Food and Drug Act of 1906, which created the agency that would become, in 1930, the Food and Drug Administration.

PURPOSE AND PROGRAMS

The Food, Drug, and Cosmetic Act (FDCA)[1] is among our oldest federal public health laws. Its purpose is to protect consumers from health risks, misinformation, and other pitfalls with respect to food, drugs, dietary supplements, cosmetics, tobacco. Its roots date back to 1906, but the act in substantially its present form was enacted in 1988. Before and since then, there have been numerous additions and amendments, often in response to public health crises.[2]

The act regulates foods, medical products such as therapeutic drugs, dietary supplements, and cosmetics. Tobacco was added to this list in 2009. All of these, except for cosmetics, will be discussed in this chapter. The FDCA establishes separate and quite different programs for each regulated commodity group. In particular, the programs vary with respect to degree of precaution exercised by Congress and the powers granted to the Food and Drug Administration. But regulation of all these commodities is based on science and risk assessment, and decisions generally involve balancing risks and benefits.

Implementation

The act is implemented by the Food and Drug Administration (FDA), which is an agency within the Department of Health and Human Services (HHS). When the act refers to the administrator, it means the FDA administrator. When it refers to the secretary, it means the secretary of HHS.

Unlike many environmental acts, states do not jointly implement the federal law. However, the FDCA does not prohibit state regulation of the same matters, so long as state or local laws do not conflict with or undermine federal law.

FOODS

The FDCA is intended to protect public health by ensuring that the foods consumers buy are safe, wholesome, and properly labeled.[3] With regard to food, the act is moderately precautionary—though less so than for drugs. Regulation is science-based and relies on risk assessment and the balancing of risks and benefits. Regulation is directed primarily at those who introduce food products into commerce—manufacturers, processors, and importers. There are also regulations affecting sellers and others in the chain of supply. Farmers are affected by the provisions related to pesticide residues (see chapter 12, Federal Insecticide, Fungicide, and Rodenticide Act).

The act has two main approaches. First, it prohibits the sale of what it refers to as "adulterated" food. Second, it imposes certain label requirements, including a prohibition of what is called "misbranding."

What Is Food?

This part of the act covers articles for food or drink for humans or animals, or components of such articles.[4] The definition includes, for example, chewing gum, spices, coffee beans, and cooking oil. It does not include tobacco, which is now regulated by the act, but not as a food. Nor does it include wine.

Meat and poultry are major exceptions to foods regulated by the FDA—they are regulated by the Department of Agriculture (USDA). The borderline between these two agencies zigzags a bit. The FDA regulates eggs in the shell under its food program, but the Department of Agriculture regulates pasteurized egg products.[5] Foods prepared and served in restaurants are mainly regulated by local health departments, not by the FDA.

Food safety is just one of the many examples for which cooperation among different federal and state agencies is crucial. An outbreak of disease due to food contamination is usually first detected by a local or state health department. Depending upon state law, the health department will have the authority to take immediate measures, such as closing a restaurant or food supplier. Involvement of the federal Centers for Disease Control (CDC) is often requested, particularly if the state's own public health laboratory does not have sufficient expertise to readily identify the causative agent or if the outbreak affects multiple states. Federal regulatory agencies—most commonly the FDA, the EPA, or the Department of Agriculture's Food Safety and Inspection Service—may be brought in through their state counterparts or through the CDC, to help search for the origins of the contaminated foods, test for causative agents, and recall the foods. In addition to regulatory action, a food-borne disease outbreak subjects the responsible party to tort lawsuits by individuals who suffer harm.

Adulterated Foods

adulteration
A defect in a food, drug, or other product, usually resulting from an additive or from conditions of preparation that make it deleterious to health

The FDCA prohibits the sale of **adulterated** foods.[6] This term encompasses a wide variety of threats to public health. It refers not only to the actual content of food, but also the conditions to which the food is exposed before reaching the consumer.

In general, a food is deemed adulterated if it contains any "poisonous or deleterious substance which may render it injurious to health." Further, the term "adulterated" applies to any food that may be injurious to health because "it consists in whole or in part of any filthy, putrid, or decomposed substance, or if it is otherwise unfit for food." Note that the law does not require the FDA to show actual harm to a consumer, nor even actual toxicity; it's sufficient to show that the food *may* cause harm.

The act specifically mentions food additives and pesticide residues. Color and other food additives are allowed in foods only if approved in advance by the FDA. Pesticide residues on foods must be within **tolerances** (limits) prescribed in advance by the Environmental Protection Agency, working in cooperation with the FDA. Foods not meeting these restrictions are deemed adulterated.

tolerance
The allowable level of pesticide residue on foods

There are other criteria, besides actual content, that rise to the level of adulteration. If a food was prepared, packed, or held under unsanitary conditions whereby it may have become contaminated with filth or become injurious to health, it is adulterated. This means that if inspectors find a dirty food processing plant, they don't have to show that the plant's output is also dirty. The condition of the premises themselves is sufficient to violate the prohibition on adulteration.

Other criteria that constitute food adulteration include:

- The container is composed of any poisonous or deleterious substance which may render the contents injurious to health

- It is, in whole or in part, the product of a diseased animal or one that died other than by slaughter

- Any valuable constituent has been omitted

- It has been intentionally subjected to radiation, except as specifically allowed by law

Labeling and Misbranding

The law imposes strict labeling requirements for processed foods, for the safety and education of consumers. Omitting required label information is called **misbranding**. The FDCA prohibits the sale of misbranded foods.[7]

The FDA does not preapprove individual product labels, but it establishes certain requirements. Labeling requirements have evolved over time as society's health concerns have evolved. The traditional requirements are a list of basic ingredients, as well as

misbranding
Any of several acts that tend to misinform the consumer with regard to food, drugs, or other regulated products, such as misstatements on the label or omitting required information from the label

quantity or volume. As concern about chemicals increased, disclosure of additives was required—such as artificial flavoring, coloring, or chemical preservatives. Now, a label must also have a nutrition panel, in easy-to-read format, showing information such as calories, dietary fiber, fat, carbohydrate and certain vitamin and mineral content. Among the latest developments, the panel must disclose transfat content, as well as certain ingredients strongly associated with allergies such as peanuts, wheat, cow's milk, and shellfish.

The FDA regulates not just the contents, but also the format of food labels, including wording, size of type, and placement. This assures that important warning and educational information will not be hidden in the fine print.

The omission of required label information is not the only act that constitutes misbranding. The term also encompasses such wrongs as false and misleading statements or unauthorized claims of health benefits. Even certain nonverbal features constitute misbranding, such as containers that give the illusion of greater than actual volume, or a container designed to imitate another product.

Food Safety Modernization Act

In 2011 Congress enacted the Food Safety and Modernization Act (FSMA)[8] in response to a number of nationwide food-borne disease outbreaks. This new legislation amends the FDCA to broaden federal enforcement powers and increase food safety planning and testing. The FDA has adopted regulations under this new authority. But the Office of Management and Budget (OMB), a White House office that regularly reviews agency regulations, made changes that have weakened that intended protection.

DRUGS AND MEDICAL DEVICES

The FDCA is intended to protect public health by assuring that drugs, medical devices, and other medical products are safe and effective.[9] Like other parts of the act, drug regulation involves science-based risk assessment and balancing of risks and benefits. This part of the act is highly precautionary, much more so than the food provisions.

As with other parts of the act, this part includes labeling requirements and uses the concepts of misbranding and adulteration. But for drugs, FDCA also requires rigorous premarket testing and review.

This discussion will focus on drugs, but much the same approach applies to other medical products, which include medical devices, biologics such as vaccines, blood products, and biotechnology products.

What Are Drugs?

The term basically refers to therapeutic drugs, both prescription and over-the-counter. The definition essentially incorporates everything recognized in the official *US Pharmacopoeia* and other specified compendia (encyclopedic listings).

But there is a broader functional definition as well, that goes beyond the *Pharmacopeia*. The statutory definition of drugs includes:

- Articles intended for use in diagnosis, cure, mitigation, treatment, or prevention of disease in humans or animals

- Articles (other than food) intended to affect the structure or any function of the body of humans or animals[10]

Making advertising claims along these lines is tantamount to representing a product to be an FDA-approved drug. Thus it is a violation of the act to make such claims for any product not so approved. This is particularly relevant to dietary supplements, which are subject to far less stringent regulation than drugs.

Pre-approval of New Drugs

The FDA has responsibility for ensuring that therapeutic drugs and other medical products are safe and effective. One of the major tools for this purpose is the requirement that the FDA approve any new drug before it can be legally marketed in the United States.[11] Drug manufacturers, which must be registered with the FDA, must conduct testing and submit extensive information as part of the approval process.[12]

Determination of Safety and Efficacy   The FDA will approve a new drug only if it determines that the product is safe and effective for its intended use. That determination is based on scientific testing and risk assessment. Essentially all drugs have some risks. Therefore, "safe" does not mean risk-free. The FDA must balance a product's risks against its expected benefits.

Efficacy matters because, if a drug is not effective for its intended use, then its benefits are merely illusory and cannot outweigh even minimal risks. Indeed, an ineffective drug carries the extra risk that its user (or prescriber) will feel falsely secure and not seek a more effective treatment.

Scientific Basis The manufacturer applying for approval of a new drug is responsible for providing adequate scientific evidence to demonstrate safety and efficacy. This requires rigorous, well-controlled studies, including clinical trials, all of which can cost the manufacturer millions of dollars and take years to complete.

There is an unavoidable tension between the desire to make promising drugs available as soon as possible and the need to protect consumer safety. The act is highly precautionary with respect to drugs, choosing to err on the side of safety. Even if existing scientific data is very promising, the FDA cannot approve a new drug until it is satisfied the data is adequate to demonstrate safety and efficacy. Although patient advocates sometimes become understandably impatient, such precaution has often prevented tragic outcomes.

THALIDOMIDE

Thalidomide was developed in Europe in the 1950s. Pregnant women and their doctors welcomed it as an effective and apparently safe drug to aid sleep and combat morning sickness in early pregnancy. In 1960, the manufacturer applied for FDA approval to market Thalidomide in the United States. By then, the drug was sold in forty-six countries.

An earlier version of the FDCA was in effect in 1960, but it already required an FDA review of safety before a new drug could be sold here. Because the drug was so popular, everyone thought FDA approval would be easy. Everyone, that is, except Frances Kelsey, the FDA's newest medical reviewer, who was given the assignment. She was not convinced that safety was adequately demonstrated by existing science. Despite industry pressure, she refused to approve the sale of Thalidomide.

The following year, scientific evidence began to show that Thalidomide can cause terrible birth defects. Worldwide, ten thousand babies were born with shortened arms and legs, or with no limbs at all. Thanks to Kelsey's caution, only seventeen babies in the United States suffered such injuries (attributed mostly to Thalidomide obtained while traveling abroad or in clinical trials).

This tragedy, and the benefits of Kelsey's caution, catalyzed the beginnings of the rigorous drug approval and monitoring systems in place at the FDA today. Kelsey received the Gold Medal for Distinguished Civilian Service from President John F. Kennedy in 1962. The public and media praised her as a heroine.[13]

Comparison to Other Laws The regulation of drugs under FDCA is far more precautionary than the regulation of chemicals under the Toxic Substances Control Act (TSCA). Under TSCA, a new chemical can be freely marketed unless the EPA takes action within ninety days, and the EPA cannot require scientific testing without making a preliminary risk determination. By contrast, extensive testing is required for all new drugs, and they cannot be marketed without FDA approval.

The FDCA's approach to drugs is much more like the regulation of pesticides under the Federal Insecticide, Fungicide, and Rodenticide Act (FIFRA). The two are similar in that the burden is on the manufacturer to provide adequate scientific data to demonstrate safety and efficacy for intended use. But there is also an important difference between FIFRA and FDCA. Under FIFRA, an approved pesticide can be legally used only for the use(s) explicitly approved by the EPA. There is no such restriction on drug use under the FDCA. Once approved, drugs can be used for *any* therapeutic purpose, not just the use specified in the application. One justification for this difference is the supervisory role of the prescribing physician. Another justification is that drugs affect only the user, whereas pesticides can have an extensive effect on public health and the environment.

Within the FDCA, regulation of drugs is much more precautionary than regulation of dietary supplements, related largely to burden of proof. For drugs, the manufacturer has the burden of demonstrating that its product is safe, so scientific uncertainty cuts against approval. For dietary supplements, the FDA has the burden of proof that a product is *un*safe, so scientific uncertainty cuts against protection.

Misbranding of Drugs

FDCA prohibits sale of misbranded drugs.[14] The term *misbranding* covers a variety of violations, some related to labeling, some not. Generally, the term misbranding is used for violations that relate to information and distribution requirements.

The FDA closely controls labeling of drugs. Labeling generally refers not just to the container label itself, but also includes the package insert, advertising, and similar materials. Medical products that are not properly labeled are referred to as misbranded. A product is misbranded if, for example, its label:

- Contains false or misleading statements

- Lacks adequate directions for safe use

- Lacks warnings about contraindications and side effects

The concept of misbranding goes beyond labeling alone. Other reasons a drug will be deemed misbranded, and therefore illegal, include:

- It endangers health even when used as prescribed or recommended; or

- For prescription drugs,

  - It is dispensed without a prescription

  - Its label omits the required warning that "Federal law prohibits dispensing without a prescription"

  - The manufacturer is not registered, as required by the act.

Adulterated Drugs

The FDCA prohibits the sale of adulterated drugs.[15] Generally, this means violations concerning purity and quality of the product. For example, the act deems a drug to be adulterated, and therefore illegal, if

- It contains ingredients that are poisonous or unsanitary

- It is manufactured in unsanitary conditions that present undue risk of contamination

- Its strength, quality or purity are misrepresented or differ from the *Pharmacopoeia*

- The composition of its container is toxic or unsafe

- It contains unsafe color additives

DIETARY SUPPLEMENTS

Congress amended the FDCA in 1994 to add regulation of dietary supplements. The 1994 legislation was called the Dietary Supplement Health and Education Act (DSHEA). If you hear references to the DSHEA, be aware it's just another name for part of the FDCA, which is what we'll call it here.

For dietary supplements, as for drugs, the FDCA's stated purpose is to protect public health by regulating safety and efficacy. But unlike drugs, the act gives the FDA almost no power to enforce this goal. Instead, the act essentially relies on the honor system, allowing manufacturers to police themselves.

This state of affairs reflects, at least to some extent, effective public relations by the dietary supplement industry. It also reflects the popular misconception that all things "natural" or "herbal" are harmless. As the Food and Drug Administration warns consumers, just because a product is "natural" does not mean it is wholesome or safe. On the contrary, dietary supplements can pose serious adverse effects. For example, supplements containing natural estrogen have been found to cause men to develop enlarged breasts and blood clots.[16]

The Food and Drug Administration is clearly frustrated by its powerlessness to protect the public against these risks. The FDA warns consumers to seek medical advice before taking dietary supplements. More surprising, the FDA advises consumers to contact the manufacturer for information before taking a dietary supplement. It is unrealistic to think many people will do so, given the inconvenience. But merely suggesting it underlines the fact that FDA itself has no information about individual products.[17]

What Is Regulated

The term **dietary supplement** refers to a broad array of products (other than conventional food items) that are taken by mouth, and that include a dietary ingredient. Common examples are vitamins, minerals, amino acids, and herbal products. Dietary supplements

dietary supplement
Any of a broad array of products taken by mouth that include a dietary ingredient, such as vitamins and herbal products

come in many forms, such as pills, powders, energy bars, and liquids. Under the act, dietary supplements are classified as a subset of foods, not as drugs.[18]

Requirements for New Products

Before marketing a new dietary supplement, the manufacturer is required to develop adequate data to provide reasonable assurance of safety. However, once its testing is done, the manufacturer can just stick its data in a file drawer. The maker is not required routinely to submit the data to the FDA, nor to get approval from the FDA, nor even to notify the FDA before a new product is marketed. The manufacturer, not the FDA, is the judge of what is *adequate* to assure safety.[19]

Misbranding

As with other commodities regulated by the FDCA, the sale of *misbranded* dietary supplements is prohibited.[20] Again, the act is more lenient toward dietary supplements with respect to what constitutes misbranding. A supplement is deemed misbranded if the label (or advertising):

- Makes health claims that are untrue or misleading

- Makes health claims the manufacturer does not have data to substantiate

- A claim is made that the product can "diagnose, treat, cure or prevent" a specified disease, and the manufacturer fails to notify the FDA of this claim within thirty days after the product goes on the market

Note that notice to the FDA is required only for very specific health claims, and then not until after the supplement is already on the market. More general health claims—for example, that a product helps prevent a specified disease—are allowed unless untrue or unsubstantiated. But recall that the FDA has the burden of proving that a claim is untrue or misleading. Further, the burden has been set relatively high. The FDA's attempts to disallow health claims for dietary supplements have generally been overturned in court, in large part because the First Amendment free speech rights of the dietary supplement purveyor have trumped the weak language in the law.[21]

THE EDS STORY

Ephedrine alkaloid dietary supplements (EDS) are a class of chemical stimulants sold in the past for weight loss and enhancement of athletic performance. Unfortunately, they had severe side effects, including heart attacks, strokes, seizures, and death. The FDA banned EDS in 2004, but only after they had been in use for twenty years and spawned nineteen thousand Adverse Event Reports (AERs). Why was such a harmful product on the market for so long? The answer lies in the approach of the Food, Drug, and Cosmetic Act to regulation of dietary supplements.

Under the act, the FDA had no data or the authority to review product safety prior to marketing. Even once alerted it to a potential problem, the FDA had no authority to regulate EDS nor to require manufacturers to submit scientific data on their products. This is because the act gives the FDA the burden of proof that a dietary supplement is unsafe, rather than the manufacturer having to prove that the product is safe. The FDA essentially had to start from scratch, at taxpayer expense, to gather scientific evidence on EDS. This included hiring a pharmacologist to conduct research, commissioning a study by the National Institutes of Health, and much more.

The FDA abandoned its first regulatory effort in 1997, due to objections (including from the Government Accounting Office) that the evidence at that point was not sufficient to carry the FDA's burden of proof. Finally, in 2004, bolstered by additional research, the FDA banned EDS. The ban was immediately challenged in court. The FDA lost the first round. The US District Court threw out the ban, concluding that the FDA had not provided adequate scientific proof. The FDA appealed, and won its case before the US Court of Appeals in 2006. Thus, after twenty years of use and two years of litigation, EDS was banned.[22]

Postscript: If you do a web search on "ephedrine" today, you'll find numerous advertisements touting how to buy it legally, some with disdainful remarks about repressive laws.

Adulterated Dietary Supplements

The FDCA prohibits the sale of *adulterated* dietary supplements,[23] but these rules are less rigorous than the corresponding rules for drugs. A supplement is adulterated if, among other things,

- It poses a significant or unreasonable risk of illness or injury

- Good manufacturing practices (GMP) were not adhered to in its production, packaging, and so forth

The act explicitly imposes the burden of proof on the FDA to prove that a dietary supplement is adulterated, rather than on the manufacturer to prove it is not. With respect to the first bullet, the FDA has the burden of proving unreasonable risk by substantial scientific evidence. If the science is uncertain, the FDA cannot restrict sale of the product. As to the second bullet, the act authorizes the FDA to adopt mandatory GMP standards for dietary supplements. Pursuant to that authority, the FDA adopted GMP in 2007. But the FDA's authority is limited in that GMP must be based on generally available analytic methodology. If there is none, the FDA cannot impose GMP standards. Here again, uncertainty tends to defeat regulation of dietary supplements, rather than leading to protective restrictions.

FIRST MAJOR ENFORCEMENT OF GMP

In March 2012, a federal court entered a permanent injunction against ATF Fitness Products Inc. (ATF), a Pennsylvania manufacturer of more than four hundred dietary supplements. The FDA charged the company with substituting ingredients and products without noting the changes on the final product labels, in violation of the 2007 GMP. In addition to adulterating and misbranding their products, the FDA alleged the company failed to report serious adverse events, including one individual who reported a spike in blood pressure, hospitalization, and a subsequent mild heart attack.

The permanent injunction, entered pursuant to a consent decree, stops ATF from making and distributing dietary supplement products until the company has corrected deficiencies and complied with the law. The injunction requires ATF to hire an outside quality control expert until the FDA is satisfied that the company's manufacturing practices ensure product safety. ATF may not resume operations until it receives permission from the FDA.[24]

Incident Reports

The act requires manufacturers and distributors of dietary supplements to investigate and notify the FDA if they become aware of any serious adverse events related to use of their products.[25] The FDA also encourages health care providers and consumers to report adverse effects. This helps the FDA recognize early signals of potential safety risk, and may help provide the evidence the FDA needs to take regulatory action on those risks.

TOBACCO

Beginning in 2009, Congress gave the FDA authority to regulate tobacco products.[26] This is a unique challenge for the agency. Its mission is to protect public health against unreasonable risks; further, whether a risk is unreasonable depends on whether it is outweighed by the product's benefits. But tobacco is different from the other commodities regulated under the act. It has severe health risks and no benefits whatsoever. In fact, the US Supreme Court once said that the only regulatory measure consistent with the FDA's mission would be a total ban on tobacco products.[27]

The FDA cannot ban tobacco. Congress explicitly says so in the 2009 amendment that grants the agency authority to regulate tobacco. But the act does grant authority for the FDA to protect health by less extreme measures. Most notably, the FDA's efforts are aimed at tobacco marketing designed to induce children and teens to take up smoking.

Basics

Although it is part of FDCA, this 2009 legislation is often referred to as the Tobacco Control Act. You may also hear it called a longer name: the Family Smoking Prevention and Tobacco Control Act.

The Problem and the Goal Tobacco takes a severe toll on public health. Cigarette smoking causes many types of cancer, as well as heart disease and chronic lung diseases like emphysema. Smokeless tobacco causes gum disease and cancers of the mouth. Close to a half million Americans die prematurely each year due to smoking and exposure to secondhand smoke. The FDA reports that tobacco use causes more deaths each year than human immunodeficiency virus (HIV), illegal drug use, alcohol use, motor vehicle injuries, suicides, and murders combined.

The FDA can neither ban tobacco nor make it safe; thus, the FDA's goal is to reduce the impact of tobacco on public health.

What Is Regulated?   The act covers all tobacco products intended for human consumption, such as cigarettes, cigars, pipe tobacco, roll-your-own tobacco, and chewing tobacco.[28]

Approach   The FDA is authorized to regulate manufacturing, marketing, and distribution of tobacco products. Its most effective tools include its authority to set standards and requirements for product content, advertising, and labeling.

The FDA provides education and supportive programs to encourage tobacco users to quit. But the FDA's best hope of progress is to discourage new users from starting, especially young people. To achieve this goal, the FDA seeks to make tobacco products less enticing, through such strategies as education, labeling requirements, and control of ingredients.

The act uses its familiar terms—adulterated and misbranded—for the usual transgressions such as contamination, unsanitary factories, and poisonous packaging materials.[29] But this discussion will center mainly on the unique provisions related to tobacco.

Special Focus on Children and Teens   In the act, Congress recites disturbing facts about the impact of tobacco on young people. Virtually all new users are under age eighteen, the minimum legal age to buy tobacco. Many new users will become addicted before they are old enough to understand the risks, and many will die prematurely from tobacco-related diseases. Many of the tobacco provisions are intended specifically to protect children and teens.[30]

Product Standards

The act gives the FDA authority to regulate product ingredients for the protection of public health.

Flavored Cigarettes Prior to FDA regulation, tobacco companies sold flavored cigarettes[31] specially designed to attract young people to smoking. The FDA quotes internal industry memoranda referring to them as "candy-like," "youth cigarette[s]," and so forth.

Once it had authority to regulate tobacco, one of the FDA's first steps was to ban flavored cigarettes. The only flavor additive still allowed is traditional menthol. All other flavorings—strawberry, cinnamon, and so forth—are now prohibited. They are deemed adulterated products.

Other Standards The FDA also regulates other product ingredients, most notably nicotine levels. Nicotine is the ingredient that makes tobacco so addictive. In the past, tobacco companies added nicotine to their products, which made them more addictive. The FDA is now empowered to combat that practice.

Health Warning

Since 1965, the federal government has required that a health warning be printed on the side of each pack of cigarettes. The earliest warning simply said, "Caution: Cigarette Smoking May Be Hazardous to Your Health." Although the United States was the first country to require health warnings, it now has one of the least prominent warnings of any country. The warning on cigarettes sold in America today is slightly more detailed than in 1965, but it is still printed inconspicuously on the side of the pack.

Tobacco use is still widespread despite the warnings, and misperceptions persist. According to findings by Congress and the FDA, many people—especially minors—have no more than a vague idea of tobacco risks. They do not appreciate the severity or magnitude of those risks, nor what it's like to be addicted or to have cancer. They do not appreciate that it could really happen to them if they continue—or start—smoking.

In contrast to the limited effectiveness of health warnings, industry's advertising has been highly effective in popularizing and promoting tobacco. In the Tobacco Control Act, Congress noted that, in a single year, tobacco companies spent more than $13 billion "to attract new users, retain current users, increase current consumption, and generate favorable long-term attitudes toward smoking and tobacco use" and that they "often misleadingly portrayed the use of tobacco as socially acceptable and healthful to minors."[32]

Based on these and other findings, the Tobacco Control Act requires bigger, more prominent health warnings. On each pack of cigarettes, 50 percent of both the front and back panels must be devoted to prescribed warnings, both verbal and graphic. Otherwise, the product is deemed misbranded and cannot be sold. Similar requirements apply to smokeless tobacco labels.[33] The verbal messages for cigarettes include, for example, warnings that "smoking can kill you" and "cigarettes cause cancer." As to the graphic warnings, the act directs FDA to select color photos depicting the harmful consequences of smoking.

Industry mounted two major challenges with respect to health warnings on various constitutional grounds. One case challenged the color images selected by the FDA. For an infringement on commercial free speech, the FDA had the burden to provide substantial evidence that its images would effectively accomplish a legitimate governmental goal (reducing tobacco use) without being overly burdensome. The court ruled in favor of industry, saying the FDA had failed to provide such evidence. The decision was upheld by the Court of Appeals for the District of Columbia Circuit, and the FDA decided not to appeal further.[34]

The other case challenged the act itself. Industry argued, among other things, that such compelled speech was a violation of free speech rights, and that the compelled allocation of 50 percent of the label to government messages constituted a taking of private property without due process. The plaintiff companies filed this action in federal district court in Kentucky, presumably hoping a tobacco-producing state would be receptive to their arguments. The court, however, ruled that this and other provisions of the act were constitutional, and this decision was upheld by the Sixth Circuit Court of Appeal. The tobacco companies tried to appeal to the Supreme Court, but their petition was denied in 2013, opening the way for the FDA to select new graphic warnings.[35]

Reduced Risk Claims

The law restricts claims of modified risk—such as "low in tar" or "light." A manufacturer cannot make such a claim unless it has obtained a marketing order from the FDA in advance. To obtain an order, the manufacturer must submit sufficient data to satisfy the FDA that the claim is based on sound scientific evidence. In addition, the FDA must be satisfied that the claim will not mislead the public into thinking the product is benign. The overall labeling and advertising must help the public understand the overall risks of the product, or the claim will not be allowed. A product that makes a modified risk claim without a marketing order is misbranded and therefore illegal.

Restrictions on Sales

The major restrictions are designed to prevent sales to children.[36] Notably:

- Sales must be face-to-face. Thus, tobacco vending machines are prohibited. The only exceptions are for vending machines in adult-only facilities, where nobody under age eighteen is allowed.

- Sellers must require purchasers to show proof of age, to verify they are selling only to purchasers over age eighteen.

- It is illegal to break up packs and sell fewer than twenty cigarettes. This discourages underage use, because youngsters generally have less cash to buy a full pack.

Restrictions on Marketing

Past advertising campaigns by tobacco companies promoted tobacco use as fun or glamorous or "cool." Images of Joe Camel or the Marlboro Man were highly appealing, especially to youngsters. The new law seeks to thwart efforts to romanticize tobacco use, partly by restrictions on advertising. For example, tobacco advertising can only be textual and only in black and white—no more appealing color images. Industry has challenged these restrictions as violating the constitutional right to free speech. As of this writing the outcome is still uncertain, so the requirements are on hold.[37]

There are other marketing restrictions as well, including:

- Ban on free samples of tobacco products

- Ban on tobacco product sponsorship of sporting or entertainment events

- Ban on non-tobacco promotional items, such as baseball hats, with tobacco brand names and logos

- Ban on free gifts with tobacco purchases[38]

Disclosure, Administrative, and Other Requirements

The law imposes several other requirements, largely self-explanatory, that are worth noting:[39]

- Tobacco companies must report certain information to the FDA about each product, including all ingredients, with particular information about nicotine content, form, and delivery. Except for smokeless tobacco, the company must report on the harmful constituents of its product's smoke. A company must notify the FDA of any changes in ingredients.

- Industry must disclose to the FDA any research on health, toxicological, behavioral, or physiologic effects of tobacco use. This is not the same as saying that industry must *conduct* such research—there is no routine requirement. But the act empowers the FDA to require product research on an ad hoc basis, where it deems such research appropriate for protection of public health.

- Industry must disclose all marketing research. This reflects concern that industry marketing has historically targeted youth and enticed them to smoke.

- Before marketing a new product, the manufacturer must get a marketing order from the FDA. This requires submitting risk and other information for premarketing review. Without the order, the product is deemed adulterated.

- Tobacco companies must register annually with the FDA, and they are subject to FDA inspections every two years.

- Manufacturers and importers must pay user fees assessed by the FDA, based on their market share. Otherwise, the product is deemed adulterated. These funds are used to finance the FDA's tobacco-related activities.

Limits on FDA Authority

The act sets a few explicit limitations on what the FDA can do to accomplish its goal of reducing the public health impact of tobacco use.[40] The FDA cannot:

- Ban whole categories of products, such as cigarettes or cigars

- Reduce the standard for nicotine to zero for any product

- Require a prescription to purchase tobacco products
- Prohibit any particular type of retail establishment from selling tobacco products face-to-face

CONCLUSION

The Food, Drug, and Cosmetic Act is a complex act, and it might be easier to think of it as multiple acts. The provisions pertaining to food and drugs are appropriately protective, providing the FDA with the authority needed to keep our food and drugs reasonably safe. In the authors' view, the statutory provisions covering dietary supplements are not adequately protective. The FDA needs more authority to regulate these products for public protection. Natural chemicals are no less potentially harmful than synthetic chemicals.

Congress added tobacco regulation to the FDA's mission only a few years ago. This was a wise decision. The FDA has the expertise to tackle the threat to public health posed by tobacco products. Its efforts to reduce the number of young people who take up smoking tobacco. Some anti-tobacco actions—particularly labeling requirements and marketing restrictions—will undoubtedly continue to be an area of controversy and litigation. Stay tuned.

KEY TERMS

Adulteration

Dietary supplement

Misbranding

Tolerance

DISCUSSION QUESTIONS

1. Given that tobacco serves absolutely no useful purpose and takes a severe toll on public health, why do you think Congress restricted the FDA's authority to ban it? Do you agree with Congress?

2. If upheld by the courts, FDA regulations will require that half of a cigarette package be used for verbal warnings and disturbing graphics obviously designed to deter sale and use of the product. Do you support or oppose these requirements?

3. Do you agree or disagree with the FDCA's approach of regulating dietary supplements as foods rather than drugs? Should there be any sort of premarketing disclosure and review introduced for dietary supplements? Should manufacturers have the burden of proof that their products are safe? Effective?

4. Should regulatory control of drug labels shield a manufacturer against a tort lawsuit that a consumer was harmed due to inadequate warnings?

NOTES

1. 21 USC §§ 301–399f.

2. For more background, see FDA, Milestones in US Food and Drug Law History at www.fda .gov/AboutFDA/WhatWeDo/History/Milestones/default.htm, with links to History and to Significant Dates.

3. 21 USC §§ 341–350*l*-1.

4. Statutory definition is at 21 USC § 321(f) .

5. For a table summarizing FDA vs. UDSA jurisdiction, see exhibit 3–1 of FDA, Investigations Operations Manual 2012, available at www.fda.gov/iceci/inspections/iom/default.htm.

6. 21 USC § 342(a)-(e) defines adulterated food; 21 USC § 331(a)-(c) prohibits adulterated foods in interstate commerce.

7. 21 USC § 343 (a)–(r) defines misbranded food; 21 USC § 331(a)-(c) prohibits misbranded foods in interstate commerce.

8. See www.fda.gov/Food/GuidanceRegulation/FSMA/ucm247548.htm (re FSMA); see also http://grist.org/food/oh-rot-the-white-house-just-gutted-the-new-food-safety-rules and www.foodsafetynews.com/2013/03/documents-show-omb-weakened-fdas-food-safety-rules/#.UWgt8XDR38s (public advocacy reaction to OMB revisions).

9. 21 USC §§ 351–360ddd2.

10. 21 USC § 321(g)(1).

11. 21 USC § 355(a) (approval required); § 355 (b)(1) and (d) (application requirements, grounds for disapproval) .

12. Registration requirement for manufacturers and others is at 21 USC § 360 and 21 CFR 207.20.

13. For more information on thalidomide see, for example, National Institutes of Health Office of Science Education, http://science.education.nih.gov/home2.nsf/Educational+Resources /Resource+Formats/Online+Resources/+High+School/544E6D04B78B8E9E85256CC D0063E875; Fintel et al., *The Thalidomide Tragedy: Lessons for Drug Safety and Regulation,* at http://scienceinsociety.northwestern.edu/content/articles/2009/research-digest /thalidomide/title-tba.

14. 21 USC § 352.

15. 21 USC § 351.

16. DiPaola et al., Clinical and biologic activity of an estrogenic herbal combination (PC-SPES) in prostate cancer. *New England Journal of Medicine*, 1998 September 17;339(12):785–791, available at www.ncbi.nlm.nih.gov/pubmed/9738085.

17. See, for example, FDA Consumer Update: FDA 101: Dietary Supplements at www.fda .gov/forconsumers/consumerupdates/ucm050803.htm.

18. 21 USC § 321(ff) (definition of dietary supplement.

19. See, for example, FDA, Q&A on Dietary Supplements at www.fda.gov/Food/Dietary Supplements/QADietarySupplements/default.htm.

20. 21 USC § 343(r)(6) and (s) .

21. See, e.g., *Alliance for Natural Health US v. Sebelius*, 714 F. Supp. 2d 48 (D.D.C. 2010) and Walsh, "The First Amendment and FDA's Regulation of Dietary Supplements," presented to ABA Section of Litigation, Food & Supplements, Second Annual Workshop, June 12, 2012.

22. The US Court of Appeals case is *Nutraceutical Corp v. von Eschenbach*, 459 F.3d 1033 (10th Cir. 2006) (Cert. Den. 5/14/07); see also www.fda.gov/NewsEvents/Newsroom/Press Announcements/2004/ucm108379.htm (FDA's November 23, 2004, news release about removing EDS from the market).

23. 21 USC § 343(f) and (g).

24. See www.fda.gov/NewsEvents/Newsroom/PressAnnouncements/ucm281017.htm.

25. 21 USC § 379aa-1.

26. 15 USC §§ 1331–1341; 21 USC §§ 387–387u; 21 CFR Subchapter K.

27. *FDA v. Brown & Williamson Tobacco*, 529 US 120, 143 (USSC 2000).

28. 21 USC § 387a(a) .

29. 21 USC § 387b (adulteration) and 387c (misbranding).

30. See, for example, FDA, Youth & Tobacco at www.fda.gov/TobaccoProducts/ProtectingKids fromTobacco/default.htm.

31. The FDCA expressly prohibits flavored cigarettes, 21 USC § 387b(5) and 387g.

32. 21 USC 387 note sec2(16) and (17); re: industry marketing strategy, see, for example, FDA, Flavored Tobacco Product Fact Sheet at www.fda.gov/TobaccoProducts/ProtectingKidsfrom Tobacco/FlavoredTobacco/ucm183198.htm.

33. 15 USC § 1333.

34. *R.J. Reynolds Tobacco Co. v. FDA*, 696 F.3D 1205 (USD.C.) decided August 24, 2012.

35. *Discount Tobacco City & Lottery v. USA*, 674 F.3d 509 (6th Cir.) decided March 19, 2012; cert. den., *American Snuff Co. v. United States*, 133 S. Ct. 1996 (April 22, 2013).

36. 21 CFR 1140.14.

37. 21 CFR 1140.16, 1140.32 and 1140.34.

38. 21 USC §§ 387d (submission of information), 387j (new products) 387e (company registration and inspection), 387s (user fees).

39. *Discount Tobacco City & Lottery, Inc v USA*, United States Supreme Court, Case No. 12A102.

40. 21 USC §§ 387f and 387g.

Chapter 14

Common Law

Toxic Torts

Key Concepts

- Common law consists of judicial precedents accumulated over time—not a single authoritative statute.

- The tort system provides a means for injured parties to be compensated by whoever is responsible, primarily through the award of monetary damages.

- The most difficult issue in toxic torts is causation—general causation (is the substance capable of causing the disease?) and specific causation (did the particular exposure cause the particular case of the disease?). There is usually scientific uncertainty, and scientific experts are essential.

tort
A civil wrong that the law recognizes as deserving a remedy

A **tort** is a civil wrong for which a court will provide a remedy. Toxic torts do not constitute a separate category of law; rather, the term denotes any tort that involves a toxic exposure. Toxic tort litigation is a challenge for the judicial system. For one thing, the volume of toxic tort lawsuits has mushroomed in recent decades. In addition, some exposures can affect huge numbers of people—think of oil spills and defective pharmaceuticals among others. Sheer volume creates a burden on the judicial system. For another, the causation issues in toxic torts are highly complex.

TORT LAW: AN OVERVIEW

common law
A body of law developed from the accumulation of judicial decisions

Common law consists of principles that have evolved over time from the accumulation of court precedents. The evolution is usually gradual, but it means that there are variations in the law over time. Common law is mostly state law. There are variations from state to state, but the major principles tend to be similar across jurisdictional boundaries. The major areas of common law are contract law, property law, and tort law.

Federal common law is limited but highly relevant to the environmental context. It is limited to subjects of national concern, such as air and interstate waters. For example, courts have allowed a common law suit brought by one state to abate pollution emanating from another state.[1]

Tort law developed largely from common law, although now there are some statutes that support or limit tort actions. If the two are in conflict, statutory law supersedes common law. This section introduces principles and concepts of tort law in general. Later in the chapter we turn to the issues of toxic torts in particular.

What Is a Tort?

The word "tort" literally means "wrong" in French. In legal terms, a tort is a civil wrong—an invasion of one's rights—that the law recognizes as worthy of redress. The three basic requirements of a tort claim are (1) a tortious (wrongful) act by the defendant, (2) an injury (bodily or otherwise) to the plaintiff, and (3) causation, meaning that the tortious act caused the injury.

A tort is a *civil* wrong, as distinguished from a criminal wrong (or violation). For a criminal violation, the government prosecutes the wrongdoer who, if found guilty, is subject to a criminal penalty such as a fine or imprisonment. For a tort, the injured plaintiff sues the "tortfeasor" (wrongdoer) who, if found liable, is ordered to pay damages (compensation) to the plaintiff. Notwithstanding this distinction, the same conduct can constitute both a tort and a crime. For example, someone who commits assault and battery can be sued in tort by the injured victim as well as prosecuted for a crime.

Purposes of the Tort System

The purposes of the tort system are justice for the injured person and deterrence of harmful conduct by tortfeasors. When someone is injured due to the wrongful acts of another, our sense of fairness dictates that the burden of the harm should be shifted, to the extent possible, to the person at fault. The tort system is the means of achieving this in our society—through a lawsuit decided on the basis of evidence by an impartial court and jury. The tort system is imperfect and vulnerable to abuse, but it is better than the days when such disputes were resolved by force, or the injured person was left with no remedy at all.

The second purpose of tort law is to deter behaviors contrary to the public interest. Careless driving is an undesirable behavior. Making a defendant pay for the consequences helps deter that defendant and other drivers from such undesirable conduct.

Burden of Proof

preponderance of the evidence
A standard of proof requiring the party with the burden to prove that its version of the facts is at least slightly more likely to be true than the other party's version

As with most civil actions, the plaintiff has the burden of proving all necessary facts by a **preponderance of the evidence**, also called the *more-likely-than-not* standard. This means the jury must find the plaintiff's evidence more convincing than the defendant's—at least enough to tip the scales slightly in plaintiff's direction. If the evidence is of equal weight on both sides, the plaintiff loses.

Remedies

In awarding a remedy to a plaintiff, the tort system's goal is to "make the plaintiff whole"—that is, to return the plaintiff as closely as possible to the status quo that existed before the injury. Of course, a plaintiff who has lost an arm cannot be made whole in a literal sense. All the system can do is award monetary damages.

compensatory damages
A monetary award to compensate a plaintiff for losses associated with physical injury or other harm

Compensatory Damages **Compensatory damages** are intended to compensate the plaintiff for the losses associated with the injury. This is the most common tort remedy. The amount is determined by the jury (or judge, if there is no jury), based on the evidence of losses.

In a bodily injury case, damages are awarded for past and future medical expenses and lost earnings. Damages can also be awarded for less tangible losses, such as pain and suffering. There is no objective way to measure such losses; the jury must simply use its judgment and common sense in assigning a dollar amount. If the victim dies, the injury is called "wrongful death" (rather than "homicide," which is the language of the criminal law system). Damages can be awarded, among other things, for lost earnings that would have supported a dependent spouse and children, and also for the emotional distress of the surviving family.

If the injury is property damage, compensatory damages are usually based on cost of repair, but can also be based on loss of value due to the tort. Damages are also awarded for economic losses, for example, loss of use of a car until it's repaired, or lost profits while a damaged factory is shut down.

Punitive Damages **Punitive damages** are intended to punish the defendant, not compensate the plaintiff. They can be awarded only if the defendant's conduct was willful, grossly negligent, or otherwise egregious. Punitive damages are awarded in addition to compensatory damage. They are also called **exemplary damages**, because the intent is to make an example of the defendant, in order to deter others from similar conduct.

Punitive damages
A monetary award excess to a plaintiff's losses, intended to punish a defendant's egregious conduct

exemplary damages
Another term for punitive damages

There is a great deal of controversy about punitive damages. One concern is that "runaway" juries will award huge amounts based on passion—anger at the defendant or sympathy for the plaintiff—rather than on a reasonable consideration of the facts. Some jurisdictions have adopted or discussed various ways to curb excessive awards, either through the courts or legislation.

Although punitive damages are not intended to compensate the plaintiff, it is nonetheless the plaintiff who receives them. The award of punitive damages can be viewed as a windfall for the plaintiff, whose losses have already been covered by compensatory damages. There is some sentiment that punitive damages, when awarded, should not go to the individual plaintiff. This is especially so in cases such as the asbestos litigation, where huge numbers of people were exposed. Large punitive damage awards to the plaintiffs who get to court first can bankrupt a corporate defendant, leaving nothing for those plaintiffs whose diseases develop later. In mass cases where the disease is slow to develop, and nobody knows how many people will ultimately get sick and deserve compensation, there is some support for putting punitive damages in a fund for all plaintiffs.[2]

Injunction A tort plaintiff can also seek an injunction—a court order requiring the defendant to do some designated act or to stop doing some designated act (see text box on Injunctive Relief, chapter 4). Injunctive relief is granted sparingly. A court will usually grant an injunction only if monetary damages are an inadequate remedy and an injunction will make a significant difference. For example, say a bar opens in a residential neighborhood, and a family sues because the loud music keeps them awake late at night. Monetary damages would be useless. If the court finds the claim meritorious, it could enjoin the operation of the noisy bar. Similarly, if a drilling rig erected and operated in a residential neighborhood causes noise, air pollution, dangerous truck traffic, and other harmful effects, a neighbor could sue to seek an injunction.

Contributory Negligence: What If the Plaintiff Is Partly at Fault?

Sometimes the plaintiff is partly at fault. For example, if a pedestrian was hit while jaywalking, a jury might decide that the pedestrian's own negligence contributed to the accident. What happens then?

contributory negligence
Negligence of a plaintiff that is a partial cause of his or her own injury

comparative negligence
The concept or rule that a tort plaintiff's recovery will be reduced based on his or her contributory negligence

The old rule was absolute: any **contributory negligence** on the part of the plaintiff, no matter how slight, completely barred recovery. Over many years this all-or-nothing rule was increasingly seen as unfair, and society made a correction. Now, most jurisdictions recognize some form of **comparative negligence,** whereby the jury determines the percentage of fault attributable to the plaintiff, and the compensation awarded the plaintiff is adjusted accordingly. In some jurisdictions, the newer rule comes from the evolution of common law, and in some jurisdictions it comes from legislation.

COMPARATIVE NEGLIGENCE: *GATES V. TEXACO*

Gordon Gates[3] was a millwright who worked for an independent contractor at a Texaco refinery for many years. He contracted and ultimately died from leukemia. The jury found that Texaco had negligently exposed him to unreasonably high levels of benzene, which was the major cause of his leukemia. The jury also found that the disease was partly attributable to the benzene he was exposed to from smoking cigarettes, which constituted contributory negligence. The jury awarded $3.4 million. This was reduced by 17 percent to account for the extent the jury found that smoking contributed to his disease and death.

Joint and Several Liability: What If There Are Multiple Defendants?

joint and several liability
A legal rule that allows a plaintiff to collect 100 percent of the liability from any one of multiple defendants

In some cases, there are two or more defendants whose tortious conduct contributed to the plaintiff's injury. When multiple defendants are found liable, who pays? The traditional rule called **joint and several liability.** This means that the defendants are jointly liable for the full damage award, but also that each defendant is separately ("severally") liable for the full amount. The purpose behind this rule was to fully compensate the plaintiff, even if one of the defendants could not pay. Under a rule of joint and several liability, the plaintiff can collect the full amount from any defendant; that defendant then has the right to proportional reimbursement from other defendants found liable.

Many jurisdictions, either by court decision or legislation, have modified this rule. In those jurisdictions, the jury assigns a percentage share of fault attributed to each defendant. Some jurisdictions now follow a pure *several liability* rule, whereby a defendant is liable only for its percentage share of the total judgment. Other jurisdictions have variations, for example, that a defendant cannot be required to pay more than double its percentage share of the total judgment. These modifications of a pure several liability rule provide the defendants some protection from overpaying, but at the same time give the plaintiff some protection in case some of the defendants are bankrupt or otherwise unable to pay their share.

What If the Injury Occurred on the Job?

Many toxic tort cases arise from work-related injuries. This is not surprising, because the workplace is where a large proportion of toxic exposures occur. What might surprise you is that the employer is not a defendant in these lawsuits.

Under state laws, employers are required to provide workers' compensation insurance coverage to almost all employees. This insurance provides benefits to workers injured on the job for medical expenses and loss of earnings. Historically, an injured and perhaps disabled worker would commonly be fired and become destitute. Workers' compensation laws arose to protect relatively powerless workers from these ills. Although there are variances from state to state, presumptions are in the worker's favor, and payment is assured and usually automatic, with any disputes handled by a worker-friendly administrative system.

Workers' compensation benefits are payable for any on-the-job injury—not just when the employer is at fault. Benefits are paid even if the injury was the worker's own fault. There is a trade-off for assured, no-fault coverage: the employee is barred from filing a tort lawsuit against the employer. This is called the *exclusive remedy rule*, meaning that workers' compensation benefits are the injured worker's exclusive remedy against the employer. The rule does not, however, bar the injured worker from suing others. For example, an employee of a contractor can sue the owner of the premises for unsafe conditions (see text box on *Gates v. Texaco*). Or a worker might sue a chemical manufacturer for failure to give adequate warnings.

Sovereign Immunity: Can You Sue the Government?

sovereign immunity
Refers to the rule that the state is not subject to lawsuit involuntarily

The old saying "You can't sue city hall" reflects the much older concept of **sovereign immunity**. Historically, the king, as the sovereign, was immune from claims by his subjects, no matter how egregious his conduct nor how severe their injuries. Today, in the United States, the rule of sovereign immunity still exists, although with important modifications. The key factor is whether or not the government is acting in its unique governmental capacity.

Federal Tort Claims Act
A federal statute that allows some tort lawsuits against the government

A statute called the **Federal Tort Claims Act**[4] carves out exceptions to the rule of sovereign immunity. It allows a tort lawsuit against the federal government if the actions complained of consist of "ministerial" rather than governmental acts. An act is "governmental" if it involves exercising governmental powers or discretion. An act is "ministerial" if it is something that could be done by a private person. For example, the decision to issue permits required for operation of a nuclear power plant is an exercise of a governmental power. Neither the government nor its employees can be sued in tort for approving the permit. But if the government itself operates a nuclear power plant, it is doing something a private company could do. So if negligent maintenance by the government results in a radiation leak, people injured by the leak could sue the government for damages, the same as they could sue a private operator.

People who are unhappy with the government's policy decisions can seek judicial review under statutory law (see chapter 2) or they can seek relief through political channels, such as the ballot box, but not through tort litigation. Don't be confused by all the court cases you see where environmental groups or industry are suing the EPA. Those suits seek judicial review of agency actions or decisions—they are not tort actions for damages.

State tort claims acts, analogous to the federal act, partially waive the sovereign immunity of state and local governments. Sovereign immunity is waived only to the extent explicitly stated in the language of a tort claims act. These acts typically do not waive immunity with respect to no-fault liability or to punitive damages.

TOXIC TORTS

The term **toxic tort** is used to describe any tort involving a toxic exposure. Toxic torts encompass a broad spectrum of toxic exposures. The injury might arise from an accidental release of a toxic substance into the environment, such as an oil spill. It might be an intended release with unintended consequences, such as the exposure of American soldiers to Agent Orange in Vietnam. It might be a worker's exposure to chemicals routinely used in the workplace. It might be the exposure of neighbors to pollution levels routinely emitted from a factory. It might be a resident's exposure to formaldehyde from home construction materials and furnishings. It might be a side effect from a therapeutic drug. These are just a few examples.

toxic tort
A tort where the wrongful act consists of a toxic exposure

In some toxic tort cases, the injury consists of property damage, such as contamination of a well. Some toxic tort cases involve acute bodily injuries, such as chemical burns or asphyxiation from chemical fumes, which is analogous to the immediate and obvious injury of a pedestrian hit by a car. But most toxic tort cases involve diseases for which causation involves a great deal of scientific uncertainty. This creates special problems in toxic tort litigation, which will be discussed later in the chapter.

CAUSES OF ACTION

A tort is a breach of duty or invasion of someone else's rights that the law deems deserving of a remedy. The common law recognizes numerous different tort theories—essentially invasions it deems compensable. This section will introduce some of the tort theories that are frequently used in toxic tort cases: negligence, strict liability for abnormally dangerous activities, public nuisance, strict products liability, trespass, and nuisance. Each of these tort theories (also called *causes of action* or *claims*) has its own criteria that, if met, will support a recovery by the injured plaintiff. The facts of a lawsuit may meet the criteria of more than one tort theory, and it is common for plaintiffs to assert multiple causes of action.

Negligence

Negligence is the most common of all torts. A common definition for negligence is a breach of the duty to use reasonable (ordinary) care not to cause harm to others. Using more familiar language, it is a mistake, carelessness, but not egregious misconduct nor intentional harm. Most of us commit negligent acts every day, but usually with no untoward consequences. If you're daydreaming and run a stop sign, the critical factor is whether you hit anyone.

The basic rule is that someone who acts negligently is liable to anyone who is injured as a result. The injury must be reasonably foreseeable—it cannot be such a remote occurrence that a reasonable person would not anticipate it. This is usually not a high hurdle. It is not necessary that the plaintiff's specific injury be foreseen—simply that it be a type of harm that may naturally

proximate cause
Refers to the requirement that an injury must be reasonably foreseeable to be compensable under tort law

and foreseeably flow from the defendant's conduct. The legal term for this is **proximate cause**—the word *proximate* reflecting that the relationship of cause and injury cannot be excessively remote.

For simple negligence, a court will award compensatory damages, but not punitive damages.

Strict Liability for Abnormally Dangerous Activities

strict liability
Liability imposed regardless of fault

abnormally dangerous activities
Activities that create a high risk of harm to others, despite the exercise of great care

In certain circumstances, the common law imposes liability for harm resulting from one's actions, regardless of fault. In these special areas, the defendant will be held liable even if there was no negligence or other breach of duty. This no-fault liability is called **strict liability** (or sometimes "absolute liability"). This section discusses one area in which the common law imposes strict liability—**abnormally dangerous activities**. As with all common law, there are variations among jurisdictions. But these are the general principles.

What Is an Abnormally Dangerous Activity?   An activity is abnormally dangerous if, even with the exercise of great care, it creates a foreseeable, high risk of physical harm to others. The rule is that a defendant who engages in abnormally dangerous activities is strictly liable for resulting physical harm (bodily injury or property damage) to others. A frequently cited example of an abnormally dangerous activity is the storage and use of blasting caps and other explosives. No matter how careful the handler, blasting caps are inherently unstable and can explode other than when and where intended.

In many lawsuits, the parties hotly dispute whether the defendant's activity was in fact an abnormally dangerous activity. Although the rule of strict liability is widely accepted, the criteria for deciding whether an activity is abnormally dangerous vary from state to state. Some states place weight on whether the activity is common or uncommon, whether it is appropriate or inappropriate to the place where it occurred, and whether its danger outweighs its value to the community.

Why Strict Liability?   The rationale for strict liability involves both fairness and risk spreading. It is fair that the risk of harm be borne by the one who (even though not negligent) created the risk and probably profits from it, rather than the injured bystander. As for risk spreading, the one who chooses to engage in abnormally dangerous activities can buy insurance. Moreover, a business can adjust its prices to spread the risk among its customers.

Remedy   The successful plaintiff is awarded compensatory damages, but not punitive damages. A court will not award punitive damages solely on the basis of a no-fault claim. A lawsuit may, however, combine a no-fault claim with other claims for which punitive damages can be recovered, such as a claim for intentional harm.

Public Nuisance

public nuisance
The tort of unreasonably interfering with a right common to the public

Public nuisance is an important tort theory with a strange, archaic name; just accept the name and focus on the theory. There is a separate tort theory called *nuisance* (see the following). The similarity of names can be confusing, but they are unrelated to each other.

Definition   A public nuisance is the unreasonable interference with a right common to the general public. This concept is perhaps best understood by example. Rights common to the general public include the right to clean air, clean water, the use of public parks, the use of public streets, and so forth. Although I have the right to use the public park, it is not a private right exclusive to me. Rather, it is a common right I share with the whole community—a public right.

Whether an action rises to the level of unreasonable interference is not always clear-cut, but can be considered by weighing the utility of the conduct against the burden or cost imposed on the public. Consider a moving van that partially blocks the street for a few hours while a new resident's belongings are unloaded. The interference is relatively brief, not particularly onerous, and serves a necessary purpose; probably nobody would call it a public nuisance. But if a mineral company's slag heap completely blocks a public road for an extended period, most courts would probably recognize that as a public nuisance. In recent years, the tort theory of public nuisance has increasingly been asserted in environmental contexts.

Standing   As with any lawsuit, a plaintiff must have "standing" to be eligible to sue (see text box on Standing to Sue, chapter 2). Public authorities, such as a city or state, have standing to bring a public nuisance suit by virtue of their responsibility to protect the public interest. What might surprise you is that a private individual may also sue on behalf of the public. There is one prerequisite: in addition to sharing the general harm suffered by the public at large, the individual must demonstrate some injury to a private interest of his or her own. Say, for example, that ash from a lime kiln has contaminated a public lake, and it has also damaged my garden. I could assert a trespass claim against the kiln owner for the damage to my garden, and that injury would also give me standing to assert a public nuisance claim for contamination of the lake.

This special standing rule was the forerunner of citizen enforcement actions, which are authorized under most federal environmental acts. The fact that ordinary people are empowered to protect the public interest in the courts reflects the high value we place on public participation. It's a pretty amazing concept, not available in the rest of the world.

Remedies   If a plaintiff succeeds in proving the public nuisance, the defendant is liable for the resulting harm, both public and private. Damages for harm to the public interest—for example, the cost of cleaning up the ash-contaminated lake—go to the public treasury. Damages for private injury—for example, the cost to clean my property and replant my garden—go to me as the injured individual.

In addition to damages, a court can award injunctive relief.

Liability for Defective Product

Caveat emptor (let the buyer beware) was historically the rule of commerce. You, as the purchaser, were on your own to inspect goods before buying and satisfy yourself of their fitness and safety. Starting in the early 1960s, there was a relatively rapid turnaround, as tort law caught up to the reality that modern products are too complex for the lay consumer to evaluate. Today, the general rule is that the provider of a dangerously defective product is liable—and usually strictly liable—for harm to persons or property caused by the defect. By becoming familiar with the issues discussed here, the reader will be positioned to grasp variations that may arise in varying circumstances or among different jurisdictions.

Who Is a Provider?   Providers include not just the manufacturer, but also downstream providers such as distributors, wholesalers, and retailers. Basically, the term encompasses anyone in the chain of commerce that brought the defective product to the plaintiff. The rule only applies to someone in the business; selling your used car does not make you a provider.

Commonly, the consumer sues the manufacturer directly. But if the manufacturer is bankrupt or otherwise unavailable, allowing suit against downstream providers (who can insure or spread the risk) is the only way to protect the consumer. A downstream provider who did nothing but pass on the product is entitled to reimbursement from the manufacturer.

Strict Liability   The rationale for strict liability is based on fairness, risk spreading, and the goal of influencing conduct. On the one hand, the consumer is powerless to detect the defect or protect against it. By contrast, the defendant is a commercial provider who is profiting from the sale of the product, including defective units. The provider can anticipate there will be some defects and some injuries, and insure against the cost. Moreover, the seller can adjust the price to absorb the risk. Finally, the prospect of strict liability may influence a seller to improve quality control and other safety precautions.

What Makes a Product Defective?   A product is defective if it is unreasonably dangerous due to design, manufacture, or inadequacy of warnings.

- *Design defect*: A product is defective if its design creates a foreseeable risk of injury, and the danger could have been avoided or reduced by adoption of a reasonable alternative design. The fact that a product is dangerous does not automatically mean it has a design defect. Automobiles, guns, power mowers, and vaccines are all inherently dangerous. In deciding whether they are defectively designed, a court will weigh their utility against their risks. But even a highly useful product is deemed defective in design if the plaintiff can show there is a reasonable alternative design that could have eliminated or reduced the danger.

- *Manufacturing defect*: A product contains a manufacturing defect if it deviates from the product's intended design specifications. An example would be a nutritional supplement that has a safe formulation (design), but which contains a contaminated ingredient.

- *Inadequate instructions or warnings*: A product is defective if foreseeable risks of harm could have been avoided or reduced by reasonable instructions or warnings, and such instructions or warnings were not provided. The adequacy of instructions and warnings can also depend on whether there is an intermediary who can be relied on to warn the ultimate user, such as a prescribing physician. Whether the commercial provider can rely on an employer to pass on warnings, or must warn the employees directly, is an issue in some cases. The answer depends on reasonableness in the circumstances, considering factors such as how serious the potential injury, whether the danger is obvious or widely known, and how likely the employer is to convey warnings. Warnings are not a legitimate substitute for a reasonable design. If a product is defectively designed, the provider cannot simply add warnings instead of adopting a reasonable alternative design that would make it safer.

The Effect of a Safety Standard   There are statutes and regulations that set safety standards for some products. If the defendant's product does not comply with a specific safety standard, and the product causes the type of injury the standard is intended to protect against, the product is defective per se. That means the plaintiff does not have to prove the existence of a defect.

On the other side of the coin, compliance with a safety regulation does *not* automatically prove a product is *not* defective. Thus, compliance does not shield the defendant from liability. One potential exception is federally prescribed labels, such as those for tobacco and pesticides. Depending on the circumstances and jurisdiction, a federal labeling regulation may be deemed to preempt state tort law, effectively shielding the provider against a failure-to-warn claim.[5]

VACCINES: SPECIAL TREATMENT

In deciding what products to make and sell, pharmaceutical manufacturers take into consideration potential tort liability as compared to potential profit. Many vaccines do not fare well in this balancing process, which makes drug companies reluctant to manufacture and sell them. Yet vaccines are essential to protection of public health.

In 1988, Congress enacted the National Vaccine Injury Compensation Program (VICP) to ensure an adequate supply of vaccines, to stabilize vaccine costs, and to establish an accessible and efficient forum for vaccine-related claims. The VICP is a no-fault system and applies to numerous (but not all) vaccines. A person injured by a listed vaccine can be compensated for reasonable non-reimbursable medical expenses, lost earnings, and up to $350,000 for pain and suffering. The program also provides a death benefit up to $250,000. Compensation is paid from the Vaccine Injury Compensation Trust Fund, which is funded by an excise tax on vaccines routinely recommended for children.

Special Rules for Prescription Drugs   The product liability rules discussed above apply to most products. But for prescription drugs, the rules are somewhat different. Medical devices requiring a prescription, such as a prosthetic knee, are treated the same as prescription drugs. For convenience, this discussion will just refer to drugs.

- *Failure to warn*: As a general rule, a prescription drug will not be deemed defective based on inadequate warnings simply because the warnings are communicated to the doctor rather than the patient. There are a few exceptions, such as birth control pills, for which the law explicitly requires package inserts; mass immunization programs where there can be little doctor-patient interaction; and direct media advertising which some courts have said must include risk warnings.

- *Design defects*: All prescription drugs can have unwanted side effects—the risk of harm is inherent. The rule that has developed in the common law leaves it to physicians to balance risks and benefits of prescribing a drug for an individual patient. So long as there are some patients for whom physicians judge that the potential benefits justify the risks, the common law will not impose liability for a design defect. A prescription drug will only be deemed defective in design if its risks are so great that health care providers would not prescribe it for any class of patients.

- *Strict liability*: As with other products, the manufacturer is strictly liable for defects. But downstream providers of prescription drugs are strictly liable only for manufacturing defects. For design or warning defects, downstream providers are liable only if they failed to exercise due care.

Disclaimers and Waivers   Providers of products, in an effort to limit liability, often make disclaimers or require purchasers to sign waivers. But disclaimers and waivers do not shield a commercial provider from tort liability for bodily injury or property damage caused by a defective product.

Trespass and Nuisance

One of the oldest and most entrenched concerns of common law is the protection of property rights. This section deals with *real property* (real estate), which includes land and buildings. An owner (or legitimate occupant) of real property has recognized rights, and interference with those rights constitutes a tort.

trespass
The tort of interfering with an owner's right to exclusive possession of property

Trespass is a word most people recognize. It is an unauthorized invasion of an owner's right to exclusive possession of property. The invading entity need not be a person or animal—it can be anything—which makes this legal theory useful in a toxic tort context. If ash from a nearby lime kiln settles on my home and kills my lawn, that's trespass. If gasoline from a neighbor's leaky underground storage tank leaches into my well water, that's trespass.

nuisance
The tort of interfering with an owner's right to quiet enjoyment of property

The tort of **nuisance** also involves invasion of real property rights, such as by an offensive odor. The invasion is to the right of *quiet enjoyment* of one's property—a legal term most readers will have no need to decipher or remember. Nuisance is somewhat similar to, and sometimes overlaps with, the tort of trespass. For purposes of this book, there is no point in trying to unravel the details of nuisance versus trespass. As a rough rule of thumb, a trespass is an invasion of property by something tangible, whereas a nuisance is an invasion of property by something intangible—such as odors, noise, or vibrations. Sometimes nuisance is referred to as *private nuisance* to distinguish it from public nuisance. The two tort theories are unrelated except for the confusing similarity of their names.

The basic rule is that if you cause a trespass or nuisance, you are liable for resulting harm both to the real property itself and to persons. For example, the leaky underground storage tank referred to earlier caused property damage—namely the contamination of my well water—for which the defendant is liable. Further, if my child develops leukemia from the contamination, the defendant is liable for that bodily injury as well.

In a trespass or nuisance case, there is no requirement of negligence or other fault on the part of the defendant. The plaintiff only has to show that the invasion occurred and that it caused the harm in order for the defendant to be liable. Remedies include both injunctive relief and damages. Injunctive relief in the leaky tank example might include requiring the tank owner to remove the tank, clean up the contaminated soil, and even to provide an alternative drinking water supply until the contamination is eliminated. Damages in that example could include compensation for my child's medical expenses, for the property damage to my well, and for economic loss if the value of my home is adversely affected. If the defendant knew or recklessly ignored warnings of the leak, that conduct might be sufficiently egregious to warrant punitive damages. But trespass or nuisance alone, without a showing of fault, will not justify punitive damages.

CAUSATION PROBLEMS IN TOXIC TORT LITIGATION

Establishing causation is the biggest challenge in toxic tort litigation. There are inherent reasons for this, including scientific uncertainty and the long latency of many of the diseases involved. The plaintiff has the burden of proving all required elements of the case, including causation. So these inherent problems work to the plaintiff's disadvantage.

Toxic tort litigation can be quite acrimonious, inside the courtroom and out. The more extreme defense lawyers characterize plaintiffs as fakers relying on junk science. The more extreme plaintiff's lawyers characterize defendants as evil industry purveying poisons and distorting science. Even without that adversarial background noise, the issues are hard—sometimes impossible—to resolve.

General Causation versus Specific Causation

As in any tort case, the plaintiff must prove that the defendant's tortious act was the cause of the injury. In toxic tort cases, this raises two separate questions, called general causation and specific causation. To illustrate, say John Doe develops liver cancer, which he attributes to exposure to vinyl chloride emitted from defendant's factory. The two questions are

- *General causation*: Is the substance capable of causing the disease? In this case, does vinyl chloride cause liver cancer?

- *Specific causation*: Did the particular exposure cause the particular disease? Did exposure to the defendant's emissions of vinyl chloride cause the plaintiff's case of liver cancer?

Complicating Factors

There are a number of problems that can make it hard, if not impossible, to establish causation.

Scientific Uncertainty   Our knowledge of chemical causation of disease comes mainly from toxicological and epidemiological studies. Individual studies typically provide a piece of a puzzle; scientists prefer to have multiple studies before they will draw inferences. But scientific studies are expensive and time-consuming, and research funding is finite. Many potential exposure-disease pairings have not been studied enough to support an inference of a cause-effect relationship.

The basic question is whether exposure to a substance can cause a disease. But other questions are contained in that inquiry, notably: how much of a dose does it take? Does it matter how the substance gets into the body (for example, inhalation or dermal absorption)? How long does it take for the disease to develop?

Latency   Lung cancer develops slowly. From the first cell mutation, it can take decades before the disease is detectable to doctors. That time lag is called the *latency period*. Many diseases caused by toxic exposures are latent diseases. For example, leukemia usually takes five to fifteen years to develop; many other types of cancer often take from twenty to forty years. It is inherently difficult to link a specific case of disease to a suspected cause that occurred so long ago.

Pinning Down the Suspect Exposure   One impact of a long latency period is that the facts about a long-ago exposure become obscured. Was it actually vinyl chloride that John Doe was exposed to, or some other chemical such as carbon tetrachloride? How much of a vinyl chloride dose did he get? For how long?

In a work setting, some of this information should be available from records required by the Occupational Safety and Health Administration's Hazard Communication Standard (see chapter 10). But in practice, records are often imprecise or nonexistent. In contexts other than the workplace, reconstructing the facts of an exposure can be even harder.

Multiple Causes, Indistinguishable Cases   There are many causes of lung cancer. Some day, advances in molecular biology may enable experts to distinguish a tumor initiated by radiation exposure from a tumor caused by tobacco use, for example. But for now, that isn't possible. For a specific type of cancer, one case tends to look just like every other case, usually giving little or no clue of its cause. The same is true for almost all diseases involved in toxic tort cases. Major exceptions include two diseases caused by asbestos: mesothelioma and asbestosis. They are called *signature diseases*, meaning a disease that definitively comes from just one cause.

Other Possible Causes   In trying to pinpoint specific causation, one question is whether other possible causes of the disease can be ruled out. This is made more difficult if there is a long latency period. During the fifteen years after his exposure to the defendant's vinyl chloride, John Doe may have been exposed many times to other substances that can cause liver cancer. He may even have had other exposures to vinyl chloride that the defendant had no involvement with. Moreover, not every case of liver cancer results from a substance exposure. They can be related to alcohol use or diet or viral hepatitis, for example. There may be a genetic predisposition. For almost all diseases, there is a **background level** of cases of unknown origin.

> **background level**
> The incidence of a disease that exists in a population in the absence of a particular factor of inquiry, such as a chemical exposure

SCIENTIFIC EVIDENCE

Knowledge of causal relationships between substances and diseases comes mainly from the sciences of toxicology and epidemiology. Scientists seek this information for goals such as prevention and public health, not for the convenience of toxic tort litigation. There's not always a close fit between the needs of the litigation system and this research, but it's the best information available. In recent years there have been an increasing number of publications in the scientific literature aimed at specific toxic tort issues. While the fit might be better, impartiality is at risk when research is undertaken for litigation purposes.[6]

Toxicology

Toxicology is the study of adverse effects of chemicals and physical agents (such as radiation) on living organisms. Toxicologists study the effects of such agents on animals and cells, with the ultimate goal of learning about the effects on humans. Studies also are performed directly in humans under carefully controlled conditions, such as the investigation of a new drug. There are established protocols and standards that must be followed for such research to be accepted as reliable within the profession.[7]

The weaknesses of toxicology are that study results must be extrapolated from animals to humans and from high doses (necessary for study) to low doses (ordinarily experienced by humans). Toxicologists are trained to deal with these challenges. Laboratory animals are carefully bred, and part of designing a study is the selection of the proper animals. In a study of birth defects, for example, a species reflective of birth defects in humans will be used. Study design includes carefully controlling the exposure, with different exposure amounts for separate groups of study animals (including one group with no exposure). This provides important information about how an effect is related to dose level—what toxicologists call the "dose-response relationship."

The strengths of toxicology are that studies can be carefully controlled for precise results. The study animals are identical in genetic makeup, health, age, and in just about every other way. They are exposed only to the substance under study and in carefully controlled doses. Thus, if a study shows a higher rate of disease in the exposed group than the unexposed group, and if it shows that the rate of disease goes up as the dose is increased, those findings strongly support a relationship between the substance and the disease.

By demonstrating an association between exposure and risk of disease, toxicology can address the toxic tort issue of general causation—namely, can substance X cause disease Y, and at what dose? Toxicology can also shed light on the issue of specific causation—namely, whether the particular exposure more likely than not caused this plaintiff's disease.

An expert in toxicology who offers an opinion about specific causation in litigation should address a number of considerations, such as, was the plaintiff in fact exposed to the substance? Did the exposure happen in a way (inhalation, ingestion, or skin absorption) that the substance could affect the body? Was the dose sufficient to cause the effect? What is known about the distribution, metabolism, and excretion of the compound, both generally and concerning the plaintiff specifically? Was the time lapse between exposure and the onset of the plaintiff's disease consistent with known latency periods? These are all questions within the expertise of a toxicologist.

Some courts are leery of toxicological evidence, because the concept of extrapolating from animals to humans and from high dose to low dose is foreign to them. But extrapolation done by an expert with careful adherence to appropriate protocols produces valuable and reliable information about causation of disease in humans.

Epidemiology

Epidemiology is the study of disease in human populations, with the goal of understanding what causes a disease and how to prevent it. Epidemiologists cannot intentionally expose human subjects to toxic substances, so they cannot have direct, carefully controlled studies as toxicologists can with animals. Instead, epidemiologists must find indirect opportunities to study exposure-disease relationships. For example, an epidemiologist might study children living in an urban area with heavy traffic and high levels of automobile exhaust, to see whether they have higher rates of asthma than children in an area less congested with traffic. Or an epidemiologist might design a study to see if more women with breast cancer than without breast cancer are smokers. These epidemiological studies look for an *association*—that is, a relationship—between an exposure and a disease.[8]

Finding an *association* in an epidemiological study does not necessarily indicate a *causal relationship*. There can be other explanations. For example, a study may find a higher risk of colon cancer among smokers; but perhaps people who tend to smoke also tend to eat a high-fat diet. Because humans are so variable, unlike lab mice, it can be difficult to interpret the results of an epidemiological study.

Bradford Hill Criteria Epidemiologists look at a number of factors in trying to evaluate whether an association reflects a true causal relationship, commonly called Bradford Hill criteria, for the epidemiologist who first cogently expressed them. The Bradford Hill criteria are also regarded as important in the context of toxic tort litigation, in evaluating epidemiology results as courtroom evidence. There are eight criteria:

1. *Temporal relationship*: The exposure must precede the disease.

2. *Strength of association*: The stronger the association, as measured by statistical tests, between a risk factor and a disease, the more likely the relationship is causal.

3. *Dose-response relationship*: If the incidence of disease increases as exposure increases, that supports the inference that the relationship is causal. However, the absence of a dose-response relationship does not rule out causality. For some substance-disease pairings, the effect occurs only above some threshold exposure.

4. *Consistency*: Have the results been replicated in different studies using different study designs?

5. *Plausibility*: Is there a biologically plausible mechanism by which the exposure could cause the disease? For instance, the fact that benzene, like radiation, damages the chromosomes and destroys human bone marrow cells made it more plausible that, like radiation, it caused human leukemia—a cancer of bone marrow cells.

6. *Specificity*: Most (but not all) substances have a specific effect (or effects). For example, aspirin will sooth a headache but not relieve constipation. The more specifically an exposure affects one organ or body system, the more likely the effect is causal. However, a lack of specificity does not rule out causality.

7. *Coherence*: Is the association compatible with existing knowledge, especially from other sciences?

8. *Experiment*: If the exposure is stopped or decreased or increased, does the incidence of disease change accordingly? For example, if FDA bans a food additive and the incidence of an associated disease decreases, that tends to support that the association is causal. This type of data can only be collected when the opportunity arises. Scientists cannot ethically conduct such an experiment by intentionally exposing humans to harmful substances.[9]

Bradford Hill offered these criteria as helpful in the determination of causation, but he stressed that none except temporal relationship is an absolute requirement. However some courts have created an absolute requirement from Bradford Hill's second criterion, the strength of association. Some courts insist that a determination of causation requires one or more epidemiological studies showing more than a doubling of risk of disease associated with exposure to the substance—what epidemiologists would term a relative risk greater than two (RR>2.0). In epidemiological studies, a *relative risk* is the quantitative relationship between the number of cases observed in a population and the number expected.

As an example, assume ten cases of a particular disease would ordinarily be expected in a worker population of a given size, but when exposed to a certain chemical, that population was instead found to have twenty cases.

$$20 \text{ cases observed} \div 10 \text{ cases expected} = 2.0$$

This indicates a relative risk of two (RR=2.0)—equivalent to a doubling of the risk. Some courts have reasoned that *more than doubling* of the relative risk (RR>2.0) sounds beguilingly like the "more-likely-than-not" standard of proof in tort cases, and provides a quick and easy answer to confusing scientific questions. In the authors' view, a rigid rule of this type is not the best way to evaluate complex evidence.[10]

SCIENTIFIC EVIDENCE IN THE COURTROOM

In an auto accident case, a jury may have no trouble determining that the impact of defendant's car was the cause of my broken leg. But in a toxic tort case, a jury is not equipped to figure out causation on its own. Scientific evidence is essential, and it must be interpreted and explained by expert witnesses. Unfortunately, expert testimony may just serve to heighten confusion, because the jury gets two conflicting opinions. The plaintiff's expert says the exposure was the cause of disease; the defense expert says the opposite.

Why this conflict? From the litigation viewpoint, conflicting evidence is inevitable. This is an adversarial system, and if there were not evidence on both sides, the case wouldn't be in court. But from the scientific viewpoint, why don't the scientists agree? Some experts are willing to overstate their case, whether for pay or from an excess of zeal. But most scientific expert witnesses are reputable and honest. They may have different opinions because they are interpreting scientific studies that are often cutting edge and cannot give absolute and certain results.

The Debate

The plaintiff has the burden of proving causation by a preponderance of the evidence. That burden could be met if plaintiff's expert testified that, *based on generally accepted scientific principles*, it is *more likely than not* the plaintiff's disease was caused by the particular exposure. The jury doesn't have to accept the plaintiff expert's testimony over conflicting testimony from the defendant's expert. But if the jury is persuaded by plaintiff's expert, that more-likely-than-not opinion is sufficient to support and uphold a finding of causation.

So long as the expert had adequate professional credentials, courts traditionally permitted the opinion testimony, taking the witness's own word on general acceptance. As tort litigation increased, sometimes with huge monetary awards, the defense bar urged the courts to impose restrictions on what testimony could reach the jury. They contended that, in many cases, the plaintiff's expert resorted to "junk science," not supported by reliable data and accepted scientific principles. (Plaintiffs sometimes made similar criticisms of defense experts, but this was primarily a defense mantra.) Although there is valid concern about the quality of some expert testimony, this campaign clearly served the strategic interests of the defense bar and its clients. If the plaintiff's expert was not allowed to testify, the plaintiff could not meet the burden of proof on causation and the case would be dismissed without trial.

The *Daubert* Decision

In 1993, the US Supreme Court issued a decision in the landmark *Daubert* case.[11] Existing evidence rules already required that, to be admissible as evidence, expert testimony must be both relevant and reliable. The Court in *Daubert* imposed a new requirement that judges screen scientific testimony before trial to ensure it was relevant and reliable. As to reliability, the judge must ascertain whether the testimony is "ground[ed] in the methods and procedures of science." The Court emphasized that this inquiry is a flexible one. The decision articulated a nonexclusive list of four factors that bear on whether offered scientific evidence is properly grounded: (1) Is it empirical? Can it be tested? (2) Is it peer reviewed or published? (3) Are there known or potential error rates and standards? (4) Is the methodology generally accepted within the scientific community?

Daubert obligated federal judges to become gatekeepers—to bar the door to expert evidence they did not find reliable. Some states have adopted their own versions of gatekeeper roles. Unfortunately, judges are not, on the whole, any better qualified than juries to evaluate complex scientific evidence, and the results have been mixed. Some courts have adopted hard and fast rules, which are easier to apply but not particularly suitable for judging complex science. In a dubious application of *stare decisis*, some courts have cited judicial precedents rather than scientific sources as authority for declaring a scientific opinion invalid. Some judges have astonished and outraged the scientific community by rejecting the testimony of highly respected scientists. In toxic tort litigation, the controversy continues over how to evaluate expert scientific evidence.

Help from Nonpartisan Experts

Federal judges have the authority to appoint impartial experts to advise them in a case, but they seldom choose to do so. Scientists have shown themselves willing to work with courts. For example, the American Association for the Advancement of Science (AAAS) has a program to assist federal and state judges, administrative law judges, and arbitrators in identifying highly qualified scientists, engineers, and health care professionals to serve as scientific experts.[12]

One other way that scientists have helped is by educating judges about science. After the *Daubert* decision, the Federal Judicial Center enlisted experts from several relevant scientific fields to teach seminars for federal judges. These experts have also written reference guides laying out the basics on their respective specialties, which are published as the Federal Judicial Center's *Reference Manual on Scientific Evidence*.[13] The seminars and *Reference Manual* are specifically designed to help federal judges perform their gatekeeping obligations.

MASS LITIGATION

In some toxic tort litigation, there are hundreds or even thousands of plaintiffs claiming disease caused by the same exposure or related exposures. Examples are soldiers exposed to Agent Orange in the Vietnam War or emergency response personnel who responded to the destruction of the World Trade Center on September 11, 2001. Litigation such as this may be combined into one or a few "class action" lawsuits—rather than each case being tried separately—if the court approves. In making that decision, the court looks at whether joining the multiple cases into a class action would serve judicial economy. This depends largely on whether the cases share common issues of law or fact. If the answer is yes, proceeding as a class action could eliminate the need for the same evidence to be heard by juries at multiple trials, and for the same disputed points of law to be decided many times over.

Sometimes there are multiple class actions filed in multiple jurisdictions, such as with the Agent Orange litigation. One tool the federal court system has developed is to assign all the related class actions to the same court—either for the entire case or for particular issues. This can be more efficient for the judicial system, and it gives the one judge more opportunity to study and understand the scientific issues involved.

As a practical matter, proceeding as a class action is advantageous to plaintiffs, and requiring each plaintiff to sue separately is advantageous to defendants. As a result, the issue of whether to proceed as a class action is often hard fought.

Class actions occur in other types of cases too. But toxic tort litigation accounts for a large proportion of class actions—especially for massive class actions.

PUSHING THE ENVELOPE

Plaintiffs' lawyers have tried new theories over the years for toxic tort litigation. One such argument is that when a person is exposed to a toxic substance, the *increased risk* of disease is itself an injury that should be compensated, even if the plaintiff does not actually have a disease. A similar argument is that exposure to a toxic substance which increases risk causes *fear of getting the disease*, and that such emotional distress is itself an injury that should be compensated. Critics sometimes refer to this theory as *cancerphobia*. Courts have generally not accepted these theories. There is precedent for awarding damages for emotional distress in cases of bodily injury or death. But a claim for emotional distress alone, without physical injury or disease, is seen as too vague and subject to abuse.

An argument that has met with some success is that an individual exposed to a toxic substance—especially a carcinogen—needs medical monitoring to allow early detection and treatment of disease. Plaintiffs argue that the need for medical monitoring is itself an injury, and the cost is a loss that should be compensated by the defendant who caused the exposure. At first blush medical monitoring is appealing, but there are pitfalls. Some courts have wisely established three minimum conditions for a medical monitoring award. First, there must be an effective test to detect the disease early. Second, there must be effective treatment, so that early detection is beneficial. Third, a trust or other mechanism must be established so that the award is used only for the intended monitoring, not simply paid in a lump sum as damages usually are.

Even if these conditions are met, questions remain as to whether the benefit justifies the cost of medical monitoring. The potential for huge awards poses a great temptation for people who are not sick to file lawsuits, especially in jurisdictions where they can hope to collect a lump sum, and for lawyers who receive a percentage of the award.

CONCLUSION

The American tort system is flawed and subject to abuse, but it is nonetheless a valuable instrument for justice and corrective action—including in environmental matters. Even though federal and state legislation and regulations are now the main sources of environmental protection, the tort system remains a forceful means of accomplishing such goals.

KEY TERMS

Abnormally dangerous activities	Preponderance of the evidence
Background level	Proximate cause
Common law	Public nuisance
Comparative negligence	Punitive damages
Compensatory damages	Sovereign immunity
Contributory negligence	Strict liability
Exemplary damages	Tort
Federal Tort Claims Act	Toxic tort
Joint and several liability	Trespass

DISCUSSION QUESTIONS

1. In the last several decades, there have been many lawsuits against tobacco companies seeking compensation for death and disease caused by their products. Do you think a smoker should ever be awarded compensation for the harm incurred from smoking? Should the dependent family of a smoker be able to recover compensation? What about states that have paid for the medical care of patients with tobacco-related diseases?

2. Does requiring an epidemiological study reporting a relative risk of more than 2.0 for the plaintiff to get into court seem fair to you? What if an epidemiological study showed nineteen cases observed and ten cases expected. This would mean that despite the chemical being responsible for nine of the nineteen cases, any individual case would more likely than not be due to background causes. Would it be fair to let the chemical manufacturer cause a 90 percent increase in a disease without being liable for compensation? On the other hand, if the epidemiological study showed twenty-one cases instead of the expected ten cases, a relative risk of 2.1, would it be fair to the manufacturer to be forced to compensate all twenty-one of these individuals, including the ten who would have had the disease irrespective of exposure?

3. Most toxic tort cases settle out of court. Often the defendant insists that the settlement amount and other details be kept confidential, as a condition of agreeing to the settlement. The plaintiff is motivated to agree, in order to receive a favorable settlement. However, secrecy about the potential adverse effects of a drug or environmental chemical is not in the public interest. Are the litigants and lawyers in such a case acting ethically? Can there be conflicts of interest between legal ethics and public health?

NOTES

1. See, for example, *Missouri v. Illinois*, 180 US 208, 241–243.

2. See, for example, Behrens and Silverman, "Punitive Damages in Asbestos Personal Injury Litigation: The Basis for Deferral Remains Sound," *Rutgers Journal of Law & Public Policy* 8:1 (Fall 2011).

3. Gates v. Texaco, C.A. No. 05C-05–043 RRC, Superior Court of the State of Delaware (2008).

4. 28 USC §§ 2671–2680.

5. See discussion in *Bates v. Dow Agrosciences LLC*, 544 US 431, 446 et seq. (US Supreme Court 2005).

6. Wagner and McGarity, *Bending Science: How Special Interests Corrupt Public Health Research* (Cambridge, MA: Harvard University Press, 2008).

7. Goldstein and Henifin, "Reference Guide on Toxicology," *Reference Manual on Scientific Evidence*, 3rd ed. (National Academies Press, 2011), 633–686; Goldstein, "Toxic Torts: The Devil Is in the Dose," *Journal of Law and Policy* 16 (2007): 551.

8. Green, Freedman, and Gordis, "Reference Guide on Epidemiology," *Reference Manual on Scientific Evidence*, 3rd ed. (National Academies Press, 2011), 549–632.

9. Bradford Hill, "The Environment and Disease: Association or Causation," *Proceedings of the Royal Society of Medicine* 58 (5) (1965): 295–300.

10. Carruth and Goldstein. "Relative Risk Greater Than Two in Proof of Causation in Toxic Tort Litigation," *Jurimetrics* 41 (2000): 195.

11. *Daubert v. Merrell Dow Pharmaceuticals, Inc.*, 509 US 579 (USSC 1993); for a good discussion of *Daubert* and the Supreme Court's follow-up decisions see Berger, "The Supreme Court's Trilogy on the Admissibility of Expert Testimony," *Reference Manual on Scientific Evidence*, 2nd ed. (Washington, DC: Federal Judicial Center, 2000).

12. See www.aaas.org/spp/case/case.htm.

13. *Reference Manual on Scientific Evidence*, now in its third edition (2011), can be accessed and downloaded from www.fjc.gov/library/fjc_catalog.nsf.

Glossary

404 permit A dredge and fill permit.

Abatement order Under CERCLA, an order to a responsible party to undertake response action.

Abnormally dangerous activity An activity that creates a high risk of harm to others, despite the exercise of great care.

Administrative Procedures Act A legislative act that establishes procedural requirements for agency rulemaking and other actions.

Adulteration Under the FDCA, a defect in a food, drug, or other product, usually resulting from an additive or from conditions of preparation that make it deleterious to health.

Agency for Toxic Substances and Disease Registry A federal agency within the Public Health Service whose responsibilities include the health component of CERCLA.

Air toxics Another name for hazardous air pollutants.

ARAR Stands for any legally Applicable or Relevant and Appropriate Rule, state or federal; one of the Nine Criteria under CERCLA for selecting remediation measures.

Arbitrary and capricious A standard of review applicable, for example, to judicial review of some agency actions. Under this standard, the agency decision will be upheld unless there is no reasonable basis to justify it.

Background level The incidence of a disease that exists in a population in the absence of a particular factor of inquiry, such as a chemical exposure; can also refer to the background level of a chemical in air, water, or soil.

Balance of powers Refers to the allocation of governmental powers among multiple bodies, to avoid abuse of power by any single body.

Best adequately demonstrated technology Uniform technology-based emission standard; the basis for new source standards for criteria pollutants in the Clean Air Act.

Best available control technology Ad hoc technology-based emission standard applicable to emissions of criteria pollutants by new major sources under the Prevention of Significant Deterioration program of the Clean Air Act.

Best available demonstrated technology Under CWA, technology-based effluent standards applicable to new direct dischargers.

Best available technology Under CWA, technology-based effluent standards applicable to existing direct dischargers of nonconventional pollutants.

Best conventional technology Under CWA, technology-based effluent standards applicable to existing direct dischargers of conventional pollutants.

Best practical technology First technology-based standard for effluent reduction under CWA.

Beyond-the-floor limits Emission standards lower than otherwise indicated by EPA's assessment of technological feasibility, used if an entire industry is lagging in emissions control.

Brownfields Contaminated sites from past industrial activity that nobody will buy due to clean-up liability, that have therefore been left idle and unproductive.

Cancellation (of registration) Under FIFRA, a process to remove a pesticide from the market due to unreasonable risk.

Cap-and-trade system A market-based approach to emission control, which sets maximum total emissions allowed and permits facilities that emit less than their share to sell their "allowances" to other facilities.

Categorical standards National effluent standards issued under the CWA, so called because separate standards apply to different industrial categories.

Characteristic waste Under RCRA, a waste deemed hazardous, even if not listed as such by EPA, due to characteristics of corrosivity, ignitability, reactivity, or toxicity.

Checks and balances Strategy to limit exercise of excessive governmental power by any one individual or group; a hallmark of the US Constitution.

CIRT wastes Shorthand for characteristic wastes.

Citizen action An action in court by a private person or entity to enforce the law against a violator; allowed by most environmental acts.

Commerce Clause A clause of the US Constitution, it gives Congress the power to regulate interstate and foreign commerce.

Commercial Applicator Under FIFRA, an applicator certified to use or supervise application of restricted-use pesticides to the property of others.

Common law Principles of law that develop from the accumulation of judicial decisions.

Community water system A public water system that serves a fixed customer base year-round.

Comparative negligence The concept or rule that a tort plaintiff's recovery will be reduced based on his or her contributory negligence.

Compensatory damages A monetary award to compensate a tort plaintiff for losses associated with physical injury or other harm.

Consensus standards Workplace exposure limits borrowed from other sources by OSHA, intended to be temporary.

Consumer Confidence Report A detailed water quality report and disclosure statement that the SDWA requires a PWS to provide annually to each customer.

Contaminant Candidate List List of contaminants not regulated under SDWA, but identified by EPA as potential additions to the Contaminant List.

Contaminant List Official list of contaminants subject to regulation under SDWA.

Contribution Partial reimbursement paid by one defendant to another defendant who, under the principle of joint and several liability, has paid more than its share of a judgment.

Contributory negligence Negligence of a plaintiff that is a partial cause of his or her own injury.

Conventional pollutant Water pollutants, such as microbial agents and suspended solids, that are the traditional targets of public sanitation and water pollution control.

Criteria pollutants A short list of pollutants that are pervasive in the ambient air and harmful at ambient levels.

Dietary supplement Any of a broad array of products taken by mouth that include a dietary ingredient, such as vitamins and herbal products.

Direct discharger Under CWA, a point-source that discharges effluent directly to surface waters.

Discharge prohibition The default control measure of CWA that prohibits discharge of any pollutant not expressly allowed by a facility's permit, or in excess of the amount allowed in the permit.

Dredge and fill permit A permit issued by the Corps of Engineers and required for the deposit of fill or dredged material into surface waters.

Effluent standard Under CWA, a standard limiting the allowable concentration of a pollutant in discharges to surface waters.

Emergency temporary standard Permissible exposure limit adopted by OSHA, without advance notice and comment, to protect against immediate grave danger.

Emission floor The stringent default setting for MACT standards, based on the performance of the best-controlled 12 percent for existing sources and the single best-controlled for new sources.

Emission standard A restriction on how much of a pollutant an industrial source may emit into the air; the particular standard that applies depends on the type of pollutant and other circumstances.

Endangerment finding Formal determination by EPA administrator under the Clean Air Act that a pollutant's emissions may reasonably be anticipated to endanger public health or welfare.

Enumerated powers Powers explicitly conferred on the federal government by the US Constitution.

Environmental assessment Initial screening to decide whether a proposed federal action involves sufficient environmental impact to require an Environmental Impact Statement.

Environmental Impact Statement Formal statement documenting that a federal agency has conducted an in-depth inquiry to ascertain and consider potential environmental impacts before undertaking a major federal action, as required by the National Environmental Policy Act.

Environmental justice Refers to the disproportionate burden of adverse environmental impacts on minority and other disadvantaged communities.

Environmental Protection Agency Cabinet-level executive agency of the federal government, the EPA is the agency charged with implementing most federal environmental acts.

Exemplary damages Another term for punitive damages.

Exhaustion of administrative remedies Refers to the requirement that an aggrieved party try all avenues for relief at the administrative level before a court will hear a complaint against an agency.

Extremely hazardous substance A listed substance subject to emergency planning and notification requirements under EPCRA.

Facility Under CERCLA, almost any place hazardous substances are released from or end up; under OPA, any structure, equipment or device (other than a vessel) used in handling or other activities involving oil.

Federal on-scene coordinator The federal official designated to direct all response operations at a particular cleanup site.

Federal preemption See *Supremacy Clause*.

Federal Register Official daily record where federal announcements, required reports, and other matters are published.

Federal supremacy See *Supremacy Clause*.

Final action; finality For purposes of judicial review, refers to a formal, completed executive action, such as the issuance of final regulations. A court will review only final actions, not proposals or interim measures.

Finding of no significant impact (FONSI) Under NEPA, a finding that no Environmental Impact Statement is required.

Fracking See *Hydrofracturing*.

Greenhouse gases Pollutants that cause global warming.

Hard look doctrine A doctrine requiring serious scrutiny of a matter. Under the National Environmental Policy Act, a federal agency must take a hard look at whether a proposed action involves significant environmental impacts.

Hazard Communication Standard OSHA regulatory program for informing and educating workers about chemical hazards in their workplace.

Hazard ranking system Scoring system for hazardous waste sites, which helps focus responses where most needed.

Hazardous air pollutant Under the CAA, any chemical on the HAP list; typically pollutants creating risk of cancer, birth defects, and other specified health consequences.

Hazardous substance Definition varies from act to act, with much overlap. Generally defined by toxicity and other characteristics.

Hazardous waste Definitions vary under different statutes.

High production volume chemicals Under TSCA, chemicals produced in very large quantities (over one million pounds per year).

Hydrofracturing A technology to obtain fossil fuels bound in rock strata deep underground by injection of pressurized fluids.

Indirect discharger Under CWA, a point-source that discharges to a water treatment facility (POTW) rather than directly to surface waters.

Industrial category Refers to the classification system established by the *Standard Industrial Classification Manual* published by the federal Bureau of the Budget.

Industrial user An industrial point source that discharges effluent waste to a POTW.

Injunction A court order requiring someone to do—or refrain from doing—a designated act.

Integrated Risk Information System EPA database of scientific information pertaining to risk from environmental agents.

Interference Under the CWA, an industrial discharge to a POTW that disrupts or inhibits the POTW's treatment operations.

Interstate Commerce Clause See *Commerce Clause*.

Joint and several liability A legal rule that allows a plaintiff to collect 100 percent of the liability from any one of multiple defendants.

Judicial deference Customary practice of courts to give great weight to an agency's opinion on matters within its expertise.

Judicial review Review by a court of a challenged governmental regulation or other action.

Land ban Common term for stringent restrictions on land disposal of hazardous wastes.

Listed waste Under RCRA, a substance on EPA's list of hazardous wastes.

Local emergency planning committee Body that develops emergency response plan under EPCRA, it consists of local officials and representatives of industry, emergency services, public health, and other sectors.

Lowest achievable emission rate Ad hoc technology-based emission standard applicable to emission of criteria pollutants by new major sources in nonattainment areas.

LULU Locally undesirable land use, such as a hazardous waste disposal facility.

Major sources Under the CAA, a source whose emissions meet a threshold volume that varies depending on various factors but most commonly are set at either 100 or 250 tons per year.

Material Safety Data Sheet See *Safety Data Sheet*.

Maximum Achievable Control Technology Uniform technology-based emission standards applicable to emissions of Hazardous Air Pollutants under the CAA.

Maximum contaminant level Allowable level of a contaminant in drinking water, under SDWA.

Maximum contaminant level goal The level of a contaminant in drinking water that would lead to no adverse health effects.

Maximum individual risk A risk assessment concept that assumes lifetime continuous exposure; used in the CAA's Hazardous Air Pollution Program.

Misbranding Under FDCA, any of several acts that tend to misinform the consumer with regard to food, drugs, or other regulated products, such as misstatements on the label or omitting required information from the label.

National Ambient Air Quality Standards A program of the CAA that sets allowable concentrations of criteria pollutants in the ambient air.

National Contingency Plan A framework for response to spills and other contingencies, addressing the roles of federal, state, and local officials.

National Disease Registry A registry of serious diseases and illnesses maintained by ATSDR.

National Emission Standards for Hazardous Air Pollutants Under the CAA, uniform national standards for Hazardous Air Pollutants.

National Pollutant Discharge Elimination System Centerpiece program of CWA that regulates discharge of pollutants to surface waters, including the requirement of a permit for any discharge.

National Pollution Funds Center A part of the US Coast Guard, it administers the Oil Spill Liability Trust Fund.

National Priorities List A list of the hazardous waste sites posing the greatest danger to human health or the environment, and therefore priority cleanup sites.

National Response Center A clearinghouse for reports of pollution events under multiple environmental laws.

National Response Team A team of sixteen federal agencies involved in spill planning and response.

National Toxicology Program An interagency program, headed by NIEHS, whose mission is to evaluate agents of public health concern.

Navigable waters See *Waters of the United States*.

New chemical Under TSCA, any chemical not on the TSCA Inventory.

New chemical review EPA review under TSCA to decide whether to seek testing before the product can be sold.

New source A source that was constructed or modified after an applicable standard was initially proposed.

New Source Performance Standards Uniform standards for emissions of criteria pollutants by new sources under the CAA or for discharges by a new source under the CWA.

New Source Review Under the CAA, a program requiring review and issuance of a permit before construction of a new emission source is begun.

NIMBY "Not in my back yard"—the common response to the question of where to put a LULU.

Nine Criteria Under CERCLA, the criteria considered in selecting remediation measures for a hazardous waste site.

No Observed Adverse Effect Level The threshold dose below which a substance has not been found to cause harm.

Nonattainment Under the CAA, the failure of an area to meet national ambient air quality standards.

Nonattainment new source review A special version of New Source Review; the requirements for review and issuance of a construction permit are stricter in a nonattainment area.

Nonconventional pollutant Under CWA, a pollutant that is neither a conventional nor toxic pollutant; a catch-all category defined by an EPA list and including, for example, ammonia and chlorine.

Nontransient noncommunity water system A public water system that serves a fixed group of people at least sixty days per year, but not year-round.

Notice and comment Refers to procedural requirements for rulemaking by executive agencies, which include the requirement of public notice and opportunity for comment by interested persons.

Nuisance The tort of interfering with an owner's right to quiet enjoyment of property.

Oil Spill Liability Trust Fund A fund that can be used for spill response and payment of claims, subject to recovery from responsible parties.

Orphan site (or share) Under CERCLA, a hazardous waste site for which no legally responsible party is available or able to pay cleanup costs.

Pass through Under the CWA, the discharge by an industrial user to a POTW of any contaminant the POTW cannot effectively treat, which therefore passes through the POTW and contaminates the receiving waters.

Permanent standards Science-based permissible exposure limits adopted by OSHA pursuant to formal notice and comment procedures.

Permissible exposure limits Standards limiting worker exposure to toxic substances in the workplace.

Personal protective equipment Respirators and other protective devices for use by individual workers.

Pest control device Under FIFRA, a device that incorporates a substance to attract or repel pests.

Piece-mealing See *Segmentation*.

Pollutant Under CWA, almost anything placed in surface waters for purposes of disposal; definition varies among acts, but is usually broad.

Postclosure Refers to a thirty-year period following closure of a hazardous waste disposal facility; RCRA imposes physical and financial responsibilities for this period that must be secured by a bond or similar means.

Potentially responsible parties The universal term for parties liable under CERCLA for response costs and other harm from hazardous releases.

Preempt(ion) See *Supremacy Clause*.

Preliminary injunction An injunction based on summary presentations, intended to preserve the status quo until there can be a full hearing before the court.

Premanufacture notice Formal notice from manufacturer to EPA, required by TSCA before a new chemical is manufactured or sold.

Preponderance of the evidence A standard of proof requiring the party with the burden to prove that its version of the facts is at least slightly more likely to be true than the other party's version; also called the more-likely-than-not standard.

Pretreatment program Clean Water Act program requiring pretreatment of waste before discharge to a POTW, if the waste would otherwise cause the POTW to exceed effluent limits.

Prevention of significant deterioration A program of the CAA intended to avoid excessive degradation of air quality in an attainment area.

Primacy Primary responsibility for enforcement; SDWA gives primacy to states with approved programs.

Primary Drinking Water Regulations Regulations under SDWA for the protection of human health.

Primary standards In some acts, "primary" designates standards to protect human health, as opposed to secondary standards for the environment or public welfare.

Private applicator Under FIFRA, an applicator certified to use or supervise application of pesticides on his or her own property.

Proximate cause Refers to the requirement that an injury must be reasonably foreseeable to be compensable under tort law.

Public health pesticide A pesticide used primarily in public health programs, such as against mosquitoes to control West Nile virus.

Public interest review Inquiry conducted by the Corps of Engineers to determine whether to issue a 404 permit

Public nuisance The tort of unreasonably interfering with a right common to the public.

Public water system A water utility (whether publicly or privately owned) that has at least fifteen connections or serves at least twenty-five individual customers.

Publicly owned treatment work Water treatment facility owned by a local or other governmental entity.

Punitive damages A monetary award excess to a plaintiff's losses, intended to punish a defendant's egregious conduct.

Race to the bottom In the absence of national standards, refers to the economic incentive for states to be lax in environmental regulation, for the purpose of attracting new industry.

Reasonably available control technology Under the CAA, technology-based standards for emission of criteria pollutants by existing major sources in a nonattainment area.

Recovery action Under CERCLA, an action against responsible parties to recover response costs advanced from the Superfund.

Reference dose The maximum daily exposure, lifetime, shown not to cause adverse health effects.

Regional Response Teams Thirteen teams of federal and state members that participate in spill planning and response in their respective regions.

Regulatory taking Depriving a person of the benefit of their private property by operation of a regulation, such as restrictions on the development of wetlands.

Remedial Investigation and Feasibility Study Under CERCLA, steps in determining the appropriate response plan for a hazardous waste site.

Remediation Under CERCLA, a long-term and relatively thorough cleanup of a hazardous waste site.

Removal action Under CERCLA, a limited and typically temporary response, intended to quickly protect against acute danger from a hazardous release.

Reopener Refers to CERCLA provision for reopening a settled case and imposing further liability if future circumstances necessitate further cleanup of a hazardous waste site.

Reportable quantity Under CERCLA and EPCRA, the threshold amount that triggers the duty to report a release.

Residual risk standard Under CAA, ad hoc risk-based standard imposed on emissions of HAPs if technology-based MACT standards prove inadequate to protect public health with an ample margin of safety or, for carcinogens, to reduce lifetime excess cancer risk to less than one in a million.

Responsible party Under OPA, the facility or vessel responsible for a discharge.

Risk-based standard Sometimes called a health-based standard; a standard based on desired outcome, as opposed to a technology-based standard.

Safety Data Sheet Information sheet required for every chemical sold in the United States; data includes health hazards, chemical characteristics, and so on.

Safety factor Refers to making risk-based protective standards more protective than strictly indicated by study results, to adjust for uncertainties such as the sensitivity of children or pregnant women.

Scoping Defining the scope and limits of a proposed federal project, for purposes of assessing environmental impacts under NEPA.

Secondary Drinking Water Regulations Regulations under SDWA for protection of public welfare and the environment.

Secondary standards Under some acts, refers to standards intended to protect the environment or public welfare, as opposed to primary standards to protect human health.

Segmentation Under NEPA, the approach of looking at parts of a project in isolation, which tends to understate the potential adverse impacts of the whole.

Separation of powers Refers to the division of governmental powers among the branches of government, or between federal and state government, so that no one body has too much concentrated power.

Significant new use A new use of a chemical that significantly increases risk, usually by increasing exposure.

Significant New Use Notice Formal notice to the EPA before commencement of a significant new use of a chemical.

Significant New Use Rule A proposed order (subject to rulemaking procedural requirements) requiring advance notice to the EPA before commencement of a significant new use.

Sole source aquifer Designation for a water source that is the sole or principal (at least 50 percent) supplier of water to a community.

Source water assessment Assessment by each state of surface and groundwater sources serving public water systems.

Sovereign immunity Refers to the rule that the state is not subject to lawsuit involuntarily.

Stakeholders Individuals or organizations that have a stake—a valid interest—in a particular matter.

Standard of review The degree of scrutiny a court applies to a matter under review. The level varies, depending on the type of case.

Standing Eligibility to file a lawsuit that depends on one's having a sufficient stake in or connection to the matter.

Stare decisis Latin for "stand by the decision." The judicial tradition of deciding a case based on precedents in previous cases, to promote fairness and predictability.

State emergency response commission State body with response expertise, involved in planning under EPCRA.

State Implementation Plan A state program that meets requirements of the CAA and, with EPA approval, empowers the state to largely take over implementation of the federal act.

States' rights Refers to the powers reserved to states by the US Constitution; often a rallying cry for those who feel the federal government is encroaching on state authority.

Statutory law Law enacted by Congress or a state legislature. The terms *statute, legislation,* and (legislative) *act* are used interchangeably.

Strict liability Liability imposed regardless of fault.

Substance Priority List A list of substances at National Priorities List sites posing the greatest risk to health.

Substantial evidence standard A standard of review applicable, for example, to judicial review of some agency actions. For the court to uphold under this standard does not require a preponderance of the evidence, but there must be evidence that a reasonable person might find sufficient to support the decision.

Sulfur allowance The commodity traded in the CAA's acid rain cap-and-trade system—each allowance authorizes emission of one ton of sulfur dioxide in a designated year.

Superfund A trust fund the EPA can use as bridge funding for cleanups under CERCLA. The term is also used to refer to CERCLA as a whole.

Superfund tax A tax (no longer in effect at the time of this writing) on oil and chemical companies that was originally the source of some funding for the Superfund.

Supremacy Clause A clause of the US Constitution providing that, within the limits of the enumerated federal powers, federal law is supreme over contrary state law. Within its enumerated powers, federal law is said to "preempt" state law.

Suspension (of registration) Under FIFRA, a process to remove a pesticide from the market due to imminent hazard.

Technology-based standard A standard based on technological feasibility, as opposed to desired health outcome.

Technology-forcing Refers to risk-based standards that are not achievable by existing technology, which therefore force industry to develop new technology to comply.

Temporary restraining order A form of injunctive relief intended to preserve the status quo for a very brief period until the parties can make initial presentations of their cases to the court.

Test rule A proposed EPA order requiring testing of a new chemical under TSCA; so called because it is subject to formal rulemaking procedures.

Threshold planning quantities Under EPCRA, the amount of on-site extremely hazardous substances that triggers a facility's responsibility to participate in emergency planning.

Tolerance Under FIFRA and FDCA, the allowable level of pesticide residue on foods.

Tort A civil wrong for which courts will provide a remedy.

Tort claims act A federal or state statute that partially waives sovereign immunity to allow some tort lawsuits against the government.

Total Maximum Daily Load A written, quantitative assessment of water quality problems in a water body.

Toxic pollutant Under CWA, a pollutant that can cause death, disease, behavioral abnormalities, cancer, genetic mutations, reproductive malfunctions, and other severe effects in humans or other organisms; defined more specifically by a list of toxic pollutants.

Toxic Release Inventory Publicly available database tracking releases of over 650 toxic substances by locality.

Toxic tort A tort where the wrongful act consists of a toxic exposure.

Toxicological profile An evaluation and compilation of information by ATSDR on each hazardous substance on the substance priority list.

Transient noncommunity water system A public water system that serves transient visitors at least 180 days per year.

Transparency Conduct of government openly and readily visible to the public; the opposite of secrecy.

Treatment technique Under SDWA, an enforceable standard that the EPA may issue, if a numeric standard is deemed unfeasible.

Trespass The tort of interfering with an owner's right to exclusive possession of property.

TSCA Inventory A compilation by the EPA of all chemicals currently in commerce.

Underground Injection Control Program SDWA program to protect source waters from contamination by regulating the placement of fluids deep underground.

Uniform national standards Federal standards that apply uniformly across the country.

Waters of the United States Surface waters subject to regulation under CWA, including interstate waters, waters subject to the tides, waters that have some connection with interstate commerce; also called "navigable waters" even if they are not really navigable.

Acronyms

ARAR	Applicable or Relevant and Appropriate Rule
ATSDR	Agency for Toxic Substances and Disease Registry
BACT	Best Available Control Technology
BADT	Best Adequately Demonstrated Technology (CAA) or Best Available Demonstrated Technology (CWA)
BAT	Best Available Technology
BCT	Best Conventional Technology
BPT	Best Practical Technology
CAA	Clean Air Act
CCL	Contaminant Candidate List
CDC	Centers for Disease Control and Prevention
CEH	Center for Environmental Health
CERCLA	Comprehensive Environmental Response, Compensation, and Liability Act
CIRT	Corrosive, Ignitable, Reactive, Toxic
CWA	Clean Water Act
DHS	Department of Homeland Security
DOE	Department of Energy
EA	Environmental assessment
EHS	Extremely hazardous substance
EIS	Environmental Impact Statement
EPA	Environmental Protection Agency
EPCRA	Emergency Planning and Community Right-to-Know Act
FDA	Food and Drug Administration
FDCA	Food, Drug, and Cosmetic Act
FEMA	Federal Emergency Management Agency

FIFRA	Federal Insecticide, Fungicide, and Rodenticide Act
FONSI	Finding of no significant impact
FOSC	Federal On-Scene Coordinator
GHG	Greenhouse gases
GMP	Good Manufacturing Practices
HAP	Hazardous air pollutant
HCS	Hazard Communication Standard
HHS	Department of Health and Human Services
HPV	High production volume
HRS	Hazard Ranking System
IRIS	Integrated Risk Information System
IU	Industrial User (of a POTW)
LAER	Lowest achievable Emission Rate
LEPC	Local emergency Planning Committee
LULU	Locally undesirable land use
MACT	Maximum available control technology
MCL	Maximum Contaminant Level
MCLG	Maximum Contaminant Level Goal
MIR	Maximum individual risk
MSDS	Material Safety Data Sheet
NAAQS	National Ambient Air Quality Standards
NCP	National Contingency Plan
NEPA	National Environmental Policy Act
NESHAPs	National Emission Standards for Hazardous Air Pollutants
NIEHS	National Institute of Environmental Health Sciences
NIMBY	Not in my back yard
NIOSH	National Institute of Occupational Safety and Health
NNSR	Nonattainment New Source Review
NOAEL	No Observed Adverse Effect Level
NPDES	National Pollutant Discharge Elimination System
NPFC	National Pollution Funds Center
NPL	National Priorities List
NRC	National Response Center
NRT	National Response Team
NSPS	New Source Performance Standards

NSR	New Source Review
NTP	National Toxicology Program
OPA	Oil Pollution Act
OSH Act	Occupational Safety and Health Act
OSHA	Occupational Safety and Health Administration
OSLTF	Oil Spill Liability Trust Fund
PEL	Permissible exposure limit
PMN	Premanufacture notice
POTW	Publicly Owned Treatment Work
PPE	Personal protective equipment
PRP	Potentially responsible party
PSD	Prevention of significant deterioration
PWS	Public Water System
RACT	Reasonably Available Control Technology
RCRA	Resource Conservation and Recovery Act
RfD	Reference Dose
RI/FS	Remedial Investigation/Feasibility Study
RP	Responsible party
RRT	Regional Response Team
SDS	Safety Data Sheet
SDWA	Safe Drinking Water Act
SERC	State emergency response commission
SIP	State Implementation Plan
SNUN	Significant New Use Notice
SNUR	Significant New Use Rule
SPL	Substance Priority List
TMDL	Total Maximum Daily Load
TRI	Toxic Release Inventory
TRO	Temporary restraining order
TSCA	Toxic Substances Control Act
UIC	Underground Injection Control
USDA	US Department of Agriculture

Resources and Additional Reading

BOOKS AND ARTICLES

Applegate, John S., and Laitos, Jan G., *Environmental Law: RCRA, CERCLA, and the Management of Hazardous Waste* (New York: Foundation Press, 2006).

Applegate, John, and Wagner, Wendy (Eds.), *Risk Analysis in the Courts: A Roadmap for Risk Analysts* (McLean, VA: Society for Risk Analysis Risk Science & Law Specialty Group, 1998, updated 2000). Online casebook available at www.riskworld.com/Profsoci/SRA/RiskScience LawGroup/casebook.htm.

Carruth, Russellyn S., and Goldstein, Bernard D., "Overview of Environmental Public Health Laws and Their Relation to Risk," in Mark G. Robson and William A. Toscano (Eds.), *Risk Assessment for Environmental Health* (San Francisco: Wiley, 2007).

Carson, Rachel, *Silent Spring* (New York: Mariner Books, 2002).

Eggen, Jean Macchiaroli, *Toxic Torts in a Nutshell,* 4th ed. (St. Paul, MN: West, 2010).

Federal Judicial Center, *Reference Manual on Scientific Evidence*, 3rd ed. (Washington, DC: National Academies Press, 2011). Chapters on Exposure Science, Epidemiology and Toxicology.

Findley, Roger W., and Farber, Daniel A., *Environmental Law in a Nutshell*, 8th ed. (St. Paul, MN: West, 2010).

Firestone, David B., and Reed, Frank C., *Environmental Law for Non-Lawyers,* 4th ed. (Royalton, VT; SoRo Press, 2008).

Gaba, Jeffrey M., *Environmental Law*, 3rd ed. (St. Paul, MN: West, 2005).

Goldstein, Bernard D., "Toxic Torts: The Devil Is in the Dose," *Journal of Law and Policy*, 2008 16(2), 551–587.

Gostin, Lawrence O., *Public Health Law: Power, Duty, Restraint,* 2d ed. (Berkeley: University of California Press, 2008).

Gostin, Lawrence O. (Ed.), *Public Health Law and Ethics*, 2d ed. (Berkeley: University of California Press, 2010).

Guruswamy, Lakshman, *International Environmental Law in a Nutshell*, 4th ed. (St. Paul, MN: West, 2011).

Hoover, Alex, "Understanding California's Cap-and-Trade Regulations," Association of Corporate Counsel. Available at www.acc.com/legalresources/quickcounsel/UCCTR.cfm#Overview.

Laitos, Jan G., and Tomain, Joseph P., *Energy and Natural Resources Law in a Nutshell* (St. Paul, MN: West, 1992).

Lazarus, Richard J., & Houck, Oliver A. (Eds.), *Environmental Law Stories* (New York: Foundation Press, 2005).

Markowitz, Gerald, and Rosner, David, *Deceit and Denial: The Deadly Politics of Industrial Pollution* (Berkeley: University of California Press, 2013).

Markowitz, Gerald, and Rosner, David, *Lead Wars: The Politics of Science and the Fate of America's Children* (Berkeley: University of California Press, 2013).

McGarity, Thomas O., and Wagner, Wendy E., *Bending Science: How Special Interests Corrupt Public Health Research* (Cambridge, MA: Harvard University Press, 2008).

National Research Council, *Risk Assessment in the Federal Government: Managing the Process* [known as "the Red Book"] (Washington, DC: National Academies Press, 1983).

National Research Council, *Sustainability and the U.S. EPA; Committee on Incorporating Sustainability in the U.S. Environmental Protection Agency* [known as the "Green Book"] (Washington, DC: National Academies Press, 2011).

Powell, Mark R., *Science at EPA* (Washington, DC: Resources for the Future, 1999).

Sprankling, John G., and Weber, Gregory S. *The Law of Hazardous Wastes and Toxic Substances in a Nutshell,* 2nd ed. (St. Paul, MN: West, 2007).

State Environmental Law Handbook Series (catalog at https://rowman.com/Action/SERIES/GIN/SEL).

Sullivan, Thomas F. P. (Editor Emeritus), *Environmental Law Handbook*, 21st ed. (Lanham, MD: Rowman and Littlefield, 2011).

West, Bernadette M., et al., *The Reporter's Environmental Handbook,* 3rd ed. (Piscataway, NJ: Rutgers University Press, 2003).

WEBSITES

American Chemistry Council
    American Chemistry Council, Responsible Care at responsiblecare.americanchemistry.com
ATSDR Toxicological Profiles
    Agency for Toxic Substances and Disease Registry; Toxicological Profiles (readable short descriptions as well as compendia of information about chemicals)
    www.atsdr.cdc.gov/toxprofiles/index.asp
Carnegie Mellon Institute
    Carnegie Mellon Institute, Western Pennsylvania Brownfields Center main website: www.cmu.edu/steinbrenner/brownfields/index.html
Environmental Law Institute
    Environmental Law Institute main website
    www.eli.org/index.cfm (a source of environmental publications, programs and alerts)
EPA
    Superfund: Cleaning Up the Nation's Hazardous Waste Sites
    www.epa.gov/superfund

EPA

EPA, Water on Tap: What You Need to Know
water.epa.gov/drink/guide/index.cfm

EPA

EPA, Summaries and extensive information about various environmental laws and regulations
www.epa.gov/lawsregs

EPA

EPA Envirofacts with topical links for system data searches, including TRI
www.epa.gov/enviro

EPA

Superfund's 30th Anniversary
www.epa.gov/superfund/30years/index.htm

FDA

www.fda.gov

National Toxicology Program Report on Carcinogens

Congressionally mandated biennial report on cancer causing substances
ntp.niehs.nih.gov/?objectid=03C9B512-ACF8-C1F3-ADBA53CAE848F635

OSHA

www.osha.gov

Index